SUMMER LEARNING

Research, Policies, and Programs

SUMMER LEARNING

Research, Policies, and Programs

Edited by

Geoffrey D. Borman
University of Wisconsin—Madison

Matthew Boulay
Teachers College, Columbia University

LEA LAWRENCE ERLBAUM ASSOCIATES, PUBLISHERS
2004 Mahwah, New Jersey   London

Lawrence Erlbaum Associates, Inc., Publishers
10 Industrial Avenue
Mahwah, New Jersey 07430

Cover design by Kathryn Houghtaling Lacey

Library of Congress Cataloging-in-Publication Data

Summer learning : research, policies, and programs / edited by Geoffrey D. Borman,
  Matthew Boulay.
      p. cm.
    Includes bibliographical references and indexes.
    ISBN 0-8058-4223-3 (cloth : alk. paper)
    1. Summer schools—United States. I. Borman, Geoffrey D. II. Boulay, Matthew.
LC5751.S78 2004
371.2′32—dc22
                                                                    2003064153
                                                                    CIP

Books published by Lawrence Erlbaum Associates are printed on acid-free paper,
and their bindings are chosen for strength and durability.

Printed in the United States of America
10 9 8 7 6 5 4 3 2 1

Contents

Preface   ix

**PART I: SUMMER LEARNING, SCHOOLING,
AND THE ACHIEVEMENT GAP: SETTING THE CONTEXT**   **1**

1   Is the School Calendar Dated? Education, Economics,
and the Politics of Time   3
Harris Cooper

2   Schools, Achievement, and Inequality:
A Seasonal Perspective   25
Karl L. Alexander, Doris R. Entwisle, and Linda S. Olson

3   The American Summer Learning Gap From
an International Perspective   53
Alexander W. Wiseman and David P. Baker

**PART II: SUMMER SCHOOL
AND THE STANDARDS MOVEMENT**   **71**

4   Summer in the City: Achievement Gains
in Chicago's Summer Bridge Program   73
Melissa Roderick, Brian A. Jacob, and Anthony S. Bryk

5   Summer School 2000 and 2001: The Boston Public
     Schools Transition Services Program   103
     John Portz

6   Assessing the Effectiveness of Summer
     Reading Programs   121
     Scott G. Paris, P. David Pearson, Gina Cervetti,
     Robert Carpenter, Alison H. Paris, Jennifer DeGroot,
     Melissa Mercer, Kai Schnabel, Joseph Martineau,
     Elena Papanastasiou, Jonathan Flukes, Kathy Humphrey,
     and Tamara Bashore-Berg

PART III: THE IMPLEMENTATION AND EFFECTS
OF NATIONALLY REPLICATED SUMMER
SCHOOL PROGRAMS   **163**

7   Addressing the Summer Learning Loss: An Evaluation
     of the Voyager Summer Reading Intervention Program   165
     Greg Roberts and Jeri Nowakowski

8   Translating Results From Impact Studies Into Changes
     in Operating Programs: Improving Upward Bound
     Through Targeting More At-Risk Students   183
     Mary T. Moore and David E. Myers

9   Evaluation of the Summerbridge Intervention Program:
     Design and Preliminary Findings   199
     Jennifer A. Laird and S. Shirley Feldman

PART IV: COMBATING SUMMER LEARNING LOSS
HEAD ON: PROGRAMS AND PRACTICES   **231**

10   Can a Multiyear Summer Program Prevent
     the Accumulation of Summer Learning Losses?   233
     Geoffrey D. Borman, Laura T. Overman, Ron Fairchild,
     Matthew Boulay, and Jody Kaplan

11   How Families, Children, and Teachers Contribute
     to Summer Learning and Loss   255
     Meredith Phillips and Tiffani Chin

12   Why Wait for Summer? Quicker Intervention,
        Better Results   279
        Charles Ballinger

Author Index   287

Subject Index   293

Preface

Most Americans accept the standard 9-month school calendar without question. They consider summer to be a time for leisure. Students and their teachers enjoy an extended break from the demands of schooling, and principals and other school administrators have a chance to prepare for the upcoming school year. Parents take advantage of this time to plan their family vacations, which are critical for the various recreation and vacation industries that depend on revenues generated during the summer months. State and local legislators, meanwhile, balance their budgets knowing that scarce public funds need only support the schools for 9 months out of the year. The long summer break, therefore, is rooted in a complex web of mutually shared cultural traditions, business interests, and fiscal constraints.

One important issue is missing from the calculus, however. This account of the rationale underlying the standard 9-month school calendar ignores the obvious: the impact of long summer vacations on student learning. If schools are instituted to foster academic achievement, what happens to student learning when they are closed?

There is, in fact, a significant body of research evidence showing that students lose considerable ground academically over the summer break. Since 1906, researchers have documented summer learning losses, or the "summer slide," by noting that students' fall achievement test scores tend to be markedly lower than the scores they achieved a few months earlier during the spring. Based on a quantitative review, or meta-analysis, of this research, Harris Cooper and his colleagues estimated that the typical child loses a little more than 1 month's worth of skill or knowledge in math and reading and language arts combined during the summer break (Cooper, chap. 1, this volume; Cooper, Nye, Charlton, Lindsay, and Greathouse, 1996). The degree to which children experience summer loss varies by grade level, subject or skill area, and socioeconomic status (Cooper et al., 1996). In particular, this research has established that the summer break has an especially deleterious impact on poor children's achievement. The long-term consequences of these income-based summer learning differences appear to be the primary cause of the widening achievement gaps that separate poor minority and White middle class students in the United States (Alexander, Entwisle, & Olson, chap. 2, this volume; Alexander & Entwisle, 1996; Phillips, Crouse, & Ralph, 1998).

Despite the fact that most American students still enjoy a long summer break, there has been significant growth in recent years in the prevalence of both summer programs and alternative school calendars (e.g., year-round schooling and extended school years). A recent survey of the 100 largest school districts in the nation found that every district reported that it had some type of summer program in operation during the summer of 1999 (Borman, 2001). About 25 years ago, similar data reported by Barbara Heyns (1978) indicated that only half of the school systems in the United States offered summer school to their students. In view of these survey results, summer programs clearly seem to be growing in popularity—perhaps doubling in prevalence over the past 25 years.

Research by Cox Newspapers revealed that, nationwide, about 5 million students, or 10% of students attending elementary through high school, were enrolled in summer school (Mollison & Brett, 1999). Meanwhile, advocates for year-round schooling claim that it is one of the largest school reform efforts in the country, with more than 2 million students now attending such schools (Ballinger, this volume). Proponents for extended school years argue that the U.S. Calendar, which averages about 180 days, falls short when compared to most other industrialized nations (Cooper, this volume).

The purpose of this book is to provide scholars and policymakers with the most current, research-based evidence concerning summer learning and a range of summer school programs. Specifically, we discuss four aspects of the summer learning issue. In Part I we present evidence describing seasonal variations in learning and how these learning differences affect equality of educational opportunity and outcomes in the United States. In Part II we discuss the development, characteristics, and effects of the most recent wave of summer programs, which are designed to play key roles in the recent standards movement and related efforts to end social promotion. In Part III we examine the impact of three of the most widespread, replicable summer school programs serving students across the United States. Finally, in Part IV, we consider the characteristics and effects of alternative programs and practices, which are designed to combat the problem of summer learning loss head on.

Taken together, the various chapters present theory and evidence that explain both the phenomenon of summer loss and the potential for effective summer programs to mitigate loss and increase student achievement. We document that summer programs have had positive impacts on student achievement, but also find that more can and should be done. In so doing, we hope that the strong combination of research evidence and practical discussion presented in this volume will provide scholars, policymakers, and school administrators with important guidance as they extend research, craft policies, and implement or expand summer programs.

This volume brings together many of the articles that were delivered on the Johns Hopkins University campus during the July 2000 "Summer Learning and the Achievement Gap: First National Conference." That conference, which was attended by a national audience of researchers, educators, and policymakers, suggested that what happens during the summer months has tremendous implications for understanding student learning and equality of educational outcomes. Although the literature on summer learning has a history of nearly 100 years, the research exploring its nuances and implications is just beginning to flourish.

The evidence presented in this volume is clear proof of this. Two of the summer interventions discussed here, Teach Baltimore and Upward Bound, provide impact estimates from randomized experiments. Further evidence on summer learning loss and the effects of summer school is derived from the systematic accumulation of research evidence: meta-analysis. Still more evidence is provided from leading national and local efforts to transform summer into a season of learning. Although future research is necessary, this volume provides the most complete collection of evidence to date concerning the summer achievement slide and the established and emerging summer school programs designed to transform summer into a season of learning gains.

ACKNOWLEDGMENTS

The authors gratefully acknowledge funding from the Open Society Institute, the Office of Educational Research and Improvement, U.S. Department of Education (Grant No. OERI–R–117–D40005), and the Smith Richardson Foundation (Grant No. 2000–1003). Opinions expressed in this work, however, do not necessarily represent positions or policies of the funding organizations.

A number of individuals also made significant contributions to this book. First, we thank all of the contributors for making this volume a reality. We also thank Paige Baker for her unending patience and skill in editing the manuscript, proofreading the pages, and compiling the index. Finally, we are grateful to Naomi Silverman and Lori Hawver of Lawrence Erlbaum Associates, Inc. for all of their hard work and helpful advice throughout every phase of the production process.

REFERENCES

Alexander, K. L., & Entwisle, D. R. (1996). Schools and children at risk. In A. Booth & J. F. Dunn (Eds.), *Family-school links: How do they affect educational outcomes?* (pp. 67–89). Mahwah, NJ: Lawrence Erlbaum Associates.

Borman, G. D. (2001). Summers are for learning. *Principal, 80*(3), 26–29.

Cooper, H., Charlton, K., Valentine, J. C., & Muhlenbruck, L. (1999). Making the most of summer school. A meta-analytic and narrative review. *Monographs of the Society for Research in Child Development, 65*(1, Serial No. 260).

Cooper, H., Nye, B., Charlton, K., & Greathouse, S. (1996). The effects of summer vacation on achievement test scores: A narrative and meta-analytic review. *Review of Educational Research, 66,* 227–268.

Heyns, B. (1978). *Summer learning and the effects of schooling.* New York: Academic Press.

Mollison, A., & Brett, J. (1999, July 6). Now more than ever, school's it for summer. *The Atlanta Constitution,* pp. A1, A4.

Phillips, M., Crouse, J., & Ralph, J. J. (1998). Does the Black-White test score gap widen after children enter school? In C. Jencks & M. Phillips (Eds.), *The Black-White test score gap* (pp. 229–272). Washington, DC: Brookings Institute.

SUMMER LEARNING

Research, Policies, and Programs

I

SUMMER LEARNING, SCHOOLING, AND THE ACHIEVEMENT GAP: SETTING THE CONTEXT

The three chapters in Part I present evidence describing seasonal variations in learning and how these learning differences affect equality of educational opportunity and outcomes in the United States. The book begins with an overview of the research on summer learning loss and the effectiveness of summer school. Harris Cooper and his students at the University of Missouri-Columbia have played a crucial role in synthesizing the relevant research. By connecting critical findings across dozens of studies, Cooper's meta-analyses give form to a previously disparate set of studies and identify summer loss as a recognizable phenomenon defined by a coherent body of research.

Cooper covers a lot of ground in chapter 1. He begins by describing the average decline associated with an extended summer vacation, as well as the differential impact of grade level, subject area, and home socioeconomic status. He then considers the effectiveness of summer school as a potential remedy to learning loss and describes the specific characteristics of summer school that are related to program effectiveness. Finally, he describes the emerging research on the impact of extended school years and year-round schooling.

If researchers are correct in describing differential rates of summer learning by home socioeconomic status, then what are the long-term consequences for low-income and minority students who experience summer loss year after year? The widening of achievement gaps as students proceed through school gives the impression that schooling contributes to the gap, thereby lending support to the contentions of researchers such as Bowles and Gintis (1976) that schools magnify existing inequities by reinforcing outside sources of disadvantage. In chapter 2, Karl Alexander, Doris Entwisle, and Linda Olson offer another perspective by presenting data from their long-term Beginning School Study. By separating achievement gains during the school year from gains made during the summer months, Alexander and his colleagues show that the widening of the gap is not explained by differential school-year learning rates, but by summer learning differences.

In chapter 3, Wiseman and Baker use cross-national data from the Third International Mathematics and Science Study to examine the summer learning gap and its implications for nonschool instructional opportunities from an international perspective. Their comparison of school calendars confirms the widely held belief that students from the United States enjoy longer summer vacations than students in most other national school systems. This finding, combined with an extensive literature search of international social science and educational literatures, leads them to conclude that the summer learning gap is a "uniquely American" issue. A shorter school calendar does not mean, however, that American students have less in-class time to learn in comparison to students in other nations, at least with respect to middle school mathematics and science instruction than the international average. Although the data do not allow them to focus specifically on summer learning, they are able to document the worldwide growth of a broad array of nonschool formal learning activities sought out by individual students and their families. Despite wide participation in these out-of-school activities, Wiseman and Baker suggest that these opportunities probably lead to a widening of the achievement gaps between advantaged and disadvantaged students.

Given the evidence on summer loss, what do we know about specific strategies for preventing this troubling phenomenon and for enhancing summer learning? This is the question that we turn to in the remaining chapters. The interventions vary, from mandatory and remedial summer programs that seek to prevent summer loss among vulnerable students, to enrichment programs that target high-achieving students.

REFERENCES

Bowles, S., & Gintis, H. (1976). *Schooling in capitalist America*. New York: Basic Books.

1

Is the School Calendar Dated? Education, Economics, and the Politics of Time

Harris Cooper
Duke University

The relationship among school calendars, student achievement, and family life first crept into my awareness during the spring of 1993, in response to budget cuts proposed by the newly elected Congress. Two years earlier, I had won a seat on the school board in my hometown of Columbia, Missouri. I had run for office as part of a longtime commitment to civic involvement. I was also open to the possibility that immersing myself in the operation of the local school district might provide new insights into important issues for future study.

At a work session that spring, the school administration informed us that summer school for disadvantaged children was one of the programs that might be cut because of the congressional proposals. As we discussed our response—specifically, whether we could afford to fund these programs locally—I became motivated to learn more about our school calendar. Where did it come from? Why did it operate the way it did? Most importantly, did it operate in the best interests of children and families?

I should state at the outset that the most general and robust conclusion of my investigations is that both change and resistance to change in the school calendar has been dictated by local and national economic interests, not by the educational benefit to children. Suggesting that economics play a role in educational decisions is no great insight. Educators consider economics when they calculate the cost–benefit ratios of programs and pedagogical strategies. School funding mechanisms and levels of funding for schools are always front-burner issues. Still, changes in school calendars introduce some unique considerations. They can have an impact on money issues that extend beyond the schoolyard gate.

For example, local business cycles respond to when children are in and out of school. More importantly, certain businesses, and even national industries, may flourish or flounder depending on when families take vacations. Further, reactions of individual families to changes in the school year can be tied to family wealth. I reveal this conclusion at the outset because it is an important thread, beyond educational considerations, that ties together the issues and research I am about to describe.

HISTORICAL ROOTS OF THE CURRENT SCHOOL CALENDAR

I began with a search for information on the historical roots of the current calendar configuration. I found that 19th century school calendars were adopted independently by school districts. Calendars reflected the needs of the families and communities they served (Richmond, 1977). Children who lived in agricultural areas rarely attended school during the summer, or during planting and harvesting, so they could be free to help tend crops or livestock around the farm. If children lived in urban areas, however, it was not unusual for them to attend school for at least 2 of summer's 3 months.

By the turn of the century, family mobility and the growing integration of the national economy made it important to standardize school curricula. Families moving from one community to another needed to find that children of similar age were learning and were expected to know roughly the same things in their new community as in their old one. This need for standardization led to the current 9-month calendar compromise between town and country, and summer became a time without school for children, regardless of where they lived (Association of California School Administrators, 1988).

SUMMER LEARNING LOSS

Next, I wanted to know what impact the long summer break might have on students. To find out, my colleagues and I undertook a synthesis of the research on summer learning loss—specifically, on whether students' achievement test scores declined over the summer vacation (Cooper, Nye, Charlton, Lindsay, & Greathouse, 1996). We found 39 studies examining the effects of summer vacation, and 13 of those studies provided enough information for use in a statistical synthesis. Our meta-analysis of these results indicated that summer learning loss equaled at least 1 month of instruction. On average, children's grade-level equivalent achievement test scores were at least 1 month lower when they returned to school in the fall than when they left in the spring.

This meta-analysis also found dramatic differences in the effect of summer vacation on different skill areas. Summer loss was more pronounced for math facts and spelling than for other tested skill areas. We rested our explanation of this result on the observation that both math computation and spelling skills involve the acquisition of factual and procedural knowledge, whereas other skill areas (especially math concepts and problem solving, and reading comprehension) are more conceptually-based. Cognitive psychology suggests that, without practice, children are most susceptible to forgetting facts and procedural skills (e.g., Cooper & Sweller, 1987).

The meta-analysis also suggested that summer loss was more pronounced for math overall than for reading overall. We speculated that children's home environments might provide more opportunities to practice reading skills than to practice mathematics.

In addition to subject area, we examined other differences among students as potential influences on summer learning loss. Overall, the meta-analysis revealed little evidence to suggest that intelligence had an impact on the effect of summer break. Likewise, neither the student's gender nor ethnicity appeared to have a consistent influence on summer learning loss. Although educators expressed special concern about the impact of summer vacation on the language skills of students who do not speak English at home, we found little evidence to support this concern.

Finally, we examined family economics as an influence on what happens to children over summer. The meta-analysis revealed that all students, regardless of the resources in their home, lost roughly equal amounts of math skills over the summer. Substantial economic differences were found for reading, however. On some measures, middle-class children actually showed gains in reading achievement over the summer, but disadvantaged children showed losses. Reading comprehension scores for both income groups declined, but disadvantaged students' scores declined more. Again, we speculated that income differences could be related to differences in opportunities to practice and learn reading skills over the summer, with more books and reading opportunities available for middle-class children.

My colleagues and I proposed two approaches to combating summer learning loss. First, the summer loss implied it might be beneficial to continue summer remedial and enrichment programs. We suggested that a focus on mathematics instruction in the summer would seem to be most effective for all students. Alternatively, if one purpose of summer pro-

grams was to lessen inequities across income groups, then a focus on summer reading instruction for disadvantaged students would be most beneficial. Second, the existence of summer learning loss could be used to
argue for adopting changes in the school calendar (see Worsnop, 1996),
perhaps modifying it to do away with the long summer break.

We were quick to point out, however, that the existence of summer
learning loss could not, *ipso facto,* be taken to mean our proposed solutions
would be effective remedial interventions. The impact of both summer educational programs and modified calendars had to be evaluated on their
own merits. Summer school might not change the educational trajectory
of students who took part in such programs. Modified calendars might
merely substitute several periods of small losses for one large loss.

My interest in exploring alternatives to the current calendar led me to
seek and obtain a grant from the United States Department of Education. I
agreed to carry out three research syntheses—one on the effectiveness of
summer school, one on extended school years, and one on modified
school calendars that do away with the long summer break. To date, my
students and I have completed the work on summer school and are near-
ing completion of our work on modified school calendars. I first describe
our work on summer school.

SUMMER SCHOOL

History and Goals

As with the school calendar in general, my colleagues and I found that the
impetus for summer programs for school-aged youth first sprang from
economic considerations. As the 20th century took hold, the economy of
the country shifted from an agricultural base to an industrial one. Most
children were either immigrants from abroad who made their homes in
large urban areas, or they were part of the great migration of Americans
from the farm to the city. Many preadolescent children and adolescents
held jobs during the summer, but those who were idle were a cause of
concern for city dwellers (Dougherty, 1981). The passage of the first child
labor law in 1916, however, meant that school-aged children had little to
do during their vacation from school. Community leaders demanded that
organized recreational activities be made available for students when
school was out. Today, the purposes of summer programs stretch far beyond the prevention of delinquent behavior, but this certainly remains
among summer school's major functions.

By the 1950s, educators realized that summertime held opportunities to
remediate or prevent learning deficits (Austin, Rogers, & Walbesser,

1972). Because the wealthy were able to hire tutors for their children, the educational summer programs made available through schools largely served students from disadvantaged backgrounds.

Summer programs to remediate learning deficits can be grouped into four categories. First, some summer programs are meant to help students meet minimum competency requirements for graduation or grade promotion. For example, Chicago Public Schools has a policy that establishes district-wide standards of promotion for students completing third, sixth, and eighth grades. If students do not meet minimum grade-equivalent reading and math scores, report card grades, and attendance criteria, they are either retained or must attend the Summer Bridge Program (Chicago Public Schools, 1997). Similar programs of both mandatory and recommended summer remedial education are in operation in other large metropolitan areas. Second, high school students who fail a particular course during the regular academic year use summer school as an opportunity to retake the course.

A third type of remedial summer school occurs in response to the movement to ensure students with disabilities receive a free and appropriate education. In 1979, the United States District Court ruled that the Pennsylvania Department of Education had to provide a program beyond the regular school year for children with disabilities. The ruling was based on the premise that the long summer break would lead to regression of skills in students covered by the Individuals with Disabilities Education Act.

Finally, the Elementary and Secondary Education Act of 1965 and its successors recognized the special needs of students residing in areas with high concentrations of poverty. These programs were meant to break the cycle of poverty by providing supplemental educational services. To accomplish this goal, the law suggested that children have full access to effective, high-quality, regular school programs and receive supplemental help through extended-time activities. The latter injunction led to the establishment of educational summer programs for disadvantaged youth.

With the passage of time, the purposes of summer school have grown beyond the provision of remedial education. In 1959, Conant (1959) recommended that boards of education provide summer opportunities not only for students who were struggling in school, but also for those who needed more flexible course schedules or who sought enriched educational experiences. Conant suggested that students who were heavily involved in extracurricular activities, or who held work-study positions, could use summer school as a way to lighten their academic burden without delaying their graduation. Students who wished to graduate early could speed up their accumulation of credits. In the 1960s, school administrators, faced with the space crunch created by the baby boom, saw the use of summer school to speed graduation as a way to make room for the growing number of students.

Recently, summer vacation has also been embraced as an ideal time to provide specialized programs for students with academic gifts and other talents. Such programs often involve offering advanced instruction that goes beyond the typical course of study. At the high school level, the content of these courses might be based on college-level curricula. Many enrichment and acceleration summer programs operate out of colleges on a fee basis, and some offer scholarships.

Finally, summer school also provides opportunities for teachers. Summer schools allow teachers to make additional money and to develop professional competencies.

Effectiveness

Our meta-analysis of research on summer school summarized the results of 93 evaluations. We drew five principle conclusions from this research synthesis. First, we concluded that summer school programs focused on lessening or removing learning deficiencies have a positive impact on the knowledge and skills of participants. Overall, students completing remedial summer programs can be expected to score about one fifth of a standard deviation higher than the control group on outcome measures. We based this conclusion on the convergence of numerous estimates of summer school effects.

I should also make clear that the overall impact of summer school needs to be viewed as an average effect found across diverse programs evaluated with a wide variety of methods. As our search for effective programs revealed, these variations influence the effect-size estimate in significant ways. Put in practical terms, the overall estimate of effect could guide policy decisions at the broadest level, say by federal or state policymakers. However, a local official about to implement a specific summer program for a particular type of student may find effects quite different from the overall finding. In general, however, both our overall confidence intervals and those associated with specific categories of programs suggested the effect of most programs is likely to be greater than zero.

Our second conclusion was that summer school programs focusing on other goals, including acceleration of learning, also have a positive impact on participants, roughly equal to programs focusing on remediation. However, due to the smaller number of evaluations, we were reluctant to test for the robustness of these findings across methodological, student, program, and outcome variances.

The third conclusion from the meta-analysis was that summer school programs have more positive effects on the achievement of middle-class students than on achievement levels of students from disadvantaged backgrounds. The difference between the economic groups was significant, whether or not effects were adjusted for methodological confounds and regardless of the assumptions used to model error variance. We speculated that the availability of more resources for middle-class families supplements and supports the activities occurring in the classroom in ways that may augment the impact of the summer program. Alternatively, summer programs in middle-class school districts may have better resources available—leading, for example, to smaller classes. Heyns (1978) suggested that these economic differences in summer school outcomes might occur because "programs are less structured and depend on the motivation and interest of the child" (p. 139). Finally, the learning problems of disadvantaged youth may be simply more intransigent than the problems of middle-class students.

I should also emphasize two points. First, although the effect was larger for middle-class students, all estimates of summer school's impact on disadvantaged students were significantly different from zero. Second, if summer programs are targeted specifically at disadvantaged students, they can serve to close the gap in educational attainment.

The fourth conclusion of the meta-analysis was that remedial summer programs have larger positive effects when the program is run for a small number of schools or classes or in a small community, although even the largest programs showed positive average effects. We speculated that the size-related program characteristics may serve as proxies for associated differences in local control of programs. That is, small programs may give teachers and administrators greater flexibility to tailor class content and instruction to the specific needs of the students they serve and to their specific context. Small programs may also facilitate planning, and they may remove roadblocks to the efficient use of resources. Teachers and parents cited the last-minute nature of decision making and the untimely arrival of necessary materials as some of the reasons for the failure of summer programs. These problems may be more prevalent when programs are large.

As a caution to this interpretation, I should point out that the size-related program variables might also be related to the economic background of the community being served, with larger programs serving poorer communities. If this is the case, then economics, rather than local control, might be the underlying causal factor for lower gains in achievement in larger programs.

Finally, the meta-analysis revealed that summer programs providing small-group or individual instruction produced the largest impact on student outcomes. Further, teachers who commented on the positive aspects of summer school on evaluation forms often suggested that small-group and individual instruction were among their program's strengths. We see no reason why the more general educational literature showing a relation between class size and achievement ought not apply to summer programs as well (Mosteller, 1995).

In addition to these principal conclusions, there are five other inferences we think can be drawn from the research synthesis, although with less confidence. First, summer programs that require some form of parent involvement produce larger effects than programs without this component. Second, remedial summer programs may have a larger effect on math achievement than on reading. It is possible to interpret this finding in relation to summer learning loss. Recall that our synthesis of summer loss research (Cooper et al., 1996) revealed that students' achievement scores in math showed more of a drop during summer than reading achievement scores. If this is the case, then control group students in summer school studies are likely to have had less practice in math than in reading. Thus, the difference in the experiences of control students may explain the difference in summer school effects.

By highlighting the finding that summer school may be more efficacious for math outcomes than for reading, I do not want to leave the impression that promoting literacy ought to be a secondary goal of summer programs. Summer school has positive effects on reading as well as math. Further, illiteracy is a strong predictor of negative social behavior in both children and adults (Adams, 1991).

Our third tentative conclusion is that the achievement advantage gained by students who attend summer school may diminish over time. We must caution, however, against concluding that this finding indicates summer school effects are themselves not long-lasting. We uncovered multiple, subtle processes that might serve to obscure lasting effects—the most obvious of which is that students who do not attend summer programs may receive similar programs during the school year that are not needed by summer attendees (e.g., additional pull-out instruction in reading). Also, summer school may have positive effects on developmental trajectories that go unnoticed if students in a study are not carefully matched.

Fourth, remedial summer school programs had positive effects for students at all grade levels, although the effects may be more pronounced for students in early primary grades and secondary school. We speculated that three largely independent approaches to summer instruction (associated with different grade levels) may contribute to this, and we based this speculation on Albuquerque Public Schools' (1985) interviews of teachers following a summer program for all students. The interviews revealed that elementary school teachers felt summer school gave them the opportunity to be more creative and to individualize instruction. Middle school teachers said they emphasized study and organizational skills more during the summer session, whereas high school teachers, because of the credit structure, adhered most closely to regular session content.

If these differences in approaches to summer school hold generally, we might expect the greatest achievement gains in the earliest and latest grades because it is here that teachers place the greatest emphasis on instruction in subject matter. Summer school in the middle years may place more emphasis on the teaching of subject-related study skills that eventually, but not immediately, have an impact on achievement outcome measures.

Finally, summer programs that undergo careful scrutiny for treatment fidelity, including monitoring to ensure that instruction is being delivered as prescribed, monitoring of attendance, and removing students with many absences from the evaluation, may produce larger effects than unmonitored programs.

There were two findings of the meta-analysis that deserve mention because we did not find consistent or significant results. First, there was inconsistent evidence on whether or how the achievement label given to students was associated with the amount of benefit they derived from remedial summer programs. As I noted earlier, one impetus for summer school is the federal requirement that children with disabilities have access to extended-year services. Our results showed clear and reliable benefits of summer school for these children, but these benefits appeared no greater in magnitude than the benefits for other students.

Second, we had speculated that volunteering to attend summer school would serve as an indicator of motivation and engagement and would positively influence the impact of the summer program—but compulsory, remedial summer programs appeared no less effective than voluntary programs. It may be that compulsory attendance requirements are associated with students whose performance levels are most likely to benefit from summer school activities.

Implications for Summer School Policies and Practices

We used our statistical results to offer some guidelines to policymakers and program implementers who are concerned with the funding, development, and operation of summer schools. Although our proposals were in no way inconsistent with the results of our research synthesis—and most were based on them—on occasion, our proposals went beyond recommendations that have identifiable research underpinnings. When we did this, we were inspired by reading district summer school materials and research reports, as well as by conversations with educators and others interested in summer school.

Most obviously, we suggested that federal, state, and local policymakers should continue to fund summer school programs. The research demonstrates that summer programs are effective at improving the academic skills of students who take advantage of them. Further, summer school is likely to have positive effects well beyond those that have been measured in past research, including the possibility that summer programs may inhibit delinquency among idle youth. In other words, there is considerable evidence that the congressional proposal to cut funding for summer school programs was a bad idea.

To ensure that summer programs are most effective and are accepted by the general public, policymakers should require that a significant portion of funds for summer school be spent on instruction in mathematics and reading. Because of the deeply engrained American mythos surrounding summers, there is a tendency to accept summer school primarily for child care and guided recreation. Indeed, for single-parent families, and for families in which both parents work outside the home, summer school will serve a child care function. For children who live in high-crime and high-poverty areas, summer programs will provide safe and stimulating environments clearly preferable to the alternatives. Summer programs are also proven vehicles to remediate, reinforce, and accelerate learning, however, and this opportunity should not be missed.

We suggest that policymakers set aside funds for the specific purpose of fostering participation in summer programs, especially participation by disadvantaged students. Summer programs often face serious problems in attracting students and maintaining their attendance. They compete for youthful attention with alternative activities that are often more attractive, but less beneficial. Even the most well-conceived program will fail if students choose not to enroll or attend. We think policymakers should earmark funds for transportation to and from summer programs and for food service at the program site. Visionary policymakers might even make provisions for siblings to attend summer programs, so that parents will not keep older brothers and sisters home to provide child care for younger family members.

Policymakers should offset the mandate for reading and math instruction by providing for significant local control concerning program delivery. The research suggests that flexible delivery systems may lead to important contextual variations that significantly improve the outcomes of summer programs. Therefore, policymakers ought to resist the temptation to micromanage programs and give local schools and teachers leeway in how to structure and deliver programs.

We recommend that policymakers require rigorous formative and summative evaluation of program outcomes. Credible evaluations provide the accountability that is necessary to justify expenditure of public funds. Policymakers can make a substantial contribution to future data-driven decision making by requiring systematic, ongoing program evaluation and providing funds to support it.

Our research synthesis suggests numerous ways to implement successful summer programs. Teacher surveys often point to a lack of planning
time and program materials that arrive late as two of the most severe im-
pediments to the success of a summer program. Thus, just as policymakers need to provide stable and continuing sources of funds for summer schools, program implementers need to plan early. We suspect that
the pragmatics of program operation will take on a higher priority as summer schools are seen less as "add-ons" and more as integral parts of the array of services provided by schools.

We pulled together many of our implementation proposals in a package we called the "Running Start" summer program. The guiding principle behind this proposal is that summer school can be profitably viewed
as an extension of regular-session instruction. A Running Start summer
program would begin close to the start of the new school year rather than
follow immediately on the heels of the old year. It would also require the
participation of regular classroom teachers, although they need not be
full-time summer instructors. In such a program, a regular teacher might
function as the resource teacher who pulls students out from their ongoing summer classes. A key feature of a Running Start program would be
that teachers meet with, get to know, assess the strengths and weaknesses
of, and begin instructing, students who will be in their class when the regular session begins. This strategy would seem most beneficial for students
who are struggling in school, need special attention, or have the potential
to present behavior problems when school begins.

Teachers should find that a running start with certain students more
than compensates for their time, although they should receive additional
pay as well. A Running Start program will smooth the transition to the
new school year by reducing the time needed to review material when
classes begin and, hopefully, by diminishing disruptions caused by struggling students. These outcomes should benefit all class members, not just
the program participants. Participation by teachers could also be incorporated into staff development opportunities to make the early return to
school more attractive. Running Start students would benefit from extended instruction presented individually, or in small groups, and from
the added sense of familiarity they achieve with their new teachers.

EXTENDED SCHOOL YEAR

When we completed our review of summer school, our research team next
turned its attention to the issue of extending the school year. After a brief
foray into this literature, we set it aside and decided to tackle the research
on modified calendars first. We reached this decision partly because the

arguments for and against extended school years are already well documented in the literature, and partly because research assessing the effects of extended school years is relatively scarce. The modified calendar literature, on the other hand, is largely fugitive in nature, so we felt a systematic review could make more of a contribution to sound decision making. For the sake of completeness, however, a few comments on extended school years are in order.

We found that most of the arguments offered in support of extended school years invoke international comparisons showing that the number of days American students spend in school lags behind most other industrialized nations. For example, the National Education Commission on Time and Learning (1993) reported that most students in the United States spend between 175 and 180 days in school each year, whereas students in Japan spend 240 days in school. Implicit in this argument is the notion that as time on task increases, so should knowledge acquisition.

Arguments against extending the school year generally take no issue with the theory of time on task but do question whether more time in school truly translates into more time on task. For example, the National Educational Association (1987) questioned whether additional time in school might simply lead to additional fatigue for students. Others have suggested that, if only a few days are added to the school calendar, no change will result in the amount of material taught to students. Unless additional time is accompanied by changes in teaching strategy and curricula, the added time may be frittered away (Karweit, 1985).

Related to this argument is the notion that adding, for example, five or six days to a school year represents only a 3% increase in school time. Hazelton, Blakely, and Denton (1992), based on work by Karweit (1984), suggested that 35 extra days would be needed to produce a noticeable change in student achievement. Thus, given other options for spending education dollars, opponents of extending the school year ask whether money might not be spent more effectively on improving the quality of instruction or reducing class size.

As I noted earlier, summer school can be viewed as a type of extended school year. It sends some children to school for additional amounts of time that do make a difference in achievement. Unlike the general proposals for extending the school year, however, summer school is an extension of the school year that is often prescribed for only a portion of students— most often children who are doing poorly in school. It is voluntary for other students, most often children who are doing well and who also have the motivation and resources to do better.

Based on my cursory examination of this literature, I would caution against simply adding a few extra days to the mandatory school calendar and expecting this to result in impressive changes in student achievement.

More likely, changes that are generalizable and robust would require the addition of a substantial number of days and would need to be accompanied by corresponding changes in curricular materials.

MODIFIED SCHOOL CALENDARS

Turning to our last calendar variation, we found that some proponents of calendar change call for arrangements in which children may or may not attend school for more days each year, but the long summer vacation disappears. Instead of the traditional calendar, children might go to school for 9 weeks and then have 3 weeks off, or go 12 weeks and then have 4 weeks of vacation. These schedules are often referred to as "year-round schooling," but, because the term is a source of much confusion, I call these proposals "modified school calendars."

My research into modified calendars included not only gathering and reading documents but also involved visiting numerous school districts that operate during the summer. In addition, I have attended several national and regional meetings of associations for year-round education, where educators freely share their experiences in implementing and evaluating modified calendars, and I have held telephone discussions with opponents of doing away with the long summer break.

Multitracking

Modified calendars have been especially popular in school districts where there is a great need for space. By using a modified calendar, children can be placed in alternate vacation sequences. In this way, some students can be on vacation at any given time, while the building is in use year-round. This increases the number of students a particular school facility can accommodate. The strategy is called "multitracking," and it is done frequently in states such as Florida, California, and Colorado, where population growth has been rapid, but increased funding for schools has not kept pace with enrollments.

Opponents of multitracking claim that the money saved is often not as much as might be suspected at first. When schools are open 12 months a year, maintenance workers, office workers, administrators, and some teaching specialists have to be paid for 12 months, rather than the usual nine. The number of classroom teachers—the largest expense in any school district's budget—remains the same. The wear and tear on buildings is greater, so maintenance costs are higher, and the usable life of buildings may decrease as a result.

Proponents of multitracking acknowledge these costs, but counter that dealing with growing student populations by building new schools (or adding modular classrooms to existing buildings) also requires hiring additional staff. For proponents of multitracking, more schools mean more inefficiency. They cite cost analyses indicating that multitracking becomes more cost-effective than other alternatives when a school's population has grown to over 116% of its building capacity (Coleman & Freehorn, 1993).

Opponents counter that there are hidden costs to multitracking that are difficult to put into economic terms. I have observed these costs after visiting numerous districts that use multitracking (see also, Orellana & Thorne, 1998). Some parents complain that having students on different tracks can cause disruptions in family and friendship patterns if siblings or friends in the same neighborhood are not on the same track. Employees who have 12-month contracts often suffer burnout, especially principals, who find it difficult to take vacation knowing that their school is in session but they are not there. Teachers often have to keep their teaching materials in movable storage closets and must change rooms when they return from vacations. And, perhaps most seriously, some recent evidence suggests that multitracked schools end up with pernicious forms of de facto segregation (Mitchell & Mitchell, 1999). Particular tracks can come to overrepresent students from different ethnic groups or ability levels. When the better teachers follow the better students into certain tracks, issues of educational equity can be raised within a single school building.

I found very few parents, teachers, or administrators whose attitude toward multitracking was better than neutral, beyond suggesting that it saved tax dollars. The most positive remark I heard came from a mother who told me that having her two children on different tracks allowed her to spend time one-on-one with each child, and this improved the quality of their time together.

In general, however, most districts that adopt multitracked calendars seem to do so grudgingly. In fact, we might say that having to adopt multitracking provides impetus to pass the bond issues voters initially rejected that led to adopting multitracking in the first place. Still, multitracking may be a viable option for districts that face severe space shortages, given that the alternatives, (e.g., split shifts or modular classrooms attached to the school building with no additional gyms, lunchrooms, or restrooms) also have considerable drawbacks. As an interesting side note, many school districts that adopt multitracking for economic reasons retain a modified single-track calendar after multitracking is dismantled.

Arguments For and Against Modified Calendars

Many educators believe that modified calendars will be most beneficial for students who are struggling in school, be they slow learners, students with disabilities, or students with limited English skills. Teachers who now work on modified calendars say that seeing students struggling through the traditional calendar was often frustrating, because of their limited ability to intervene until summer. These teachers describe themselves as forced to watch some children fall further and further behind as the year progressed. Now that breaks occur after 9 or 12 weeks, the breaks provide an opportunity for more timely remedial activities. Advocates hold up as positive examples schools that make remedial, enrichment, and acceleration classes available to students during the multiple breaks.

However, opposition always forms when communities consider modifying the school calendar. Teachers are not the most adamant opponents, although they do voice initial skepticism. They worry that without the long summer break, they will be more susceptible to burnout. Advocates of calendar change point to teachers working in schools with modified calendars, who report that the more frequent but shorter breaks actually prevent burnout rather than cause it.

Several interest groups question the value of the modified calendar, however. Some parents who might be called "social conservatives" oppose calendar change because they say that summer vacation provides an opportunity to spend a long period of time with their children without the influence of schools. Proponents of change counter that the modified calendars do not shift the balance of influence between schools and families. Modifying the calendar does not necessarily increase the amount of actual time that children spend in school.

Parents of secondary-school children who are active in extracurricular activities also express concern. They worry that sports teams, bands, and other clubs that compete or travel to schools on the traditional calendar will be adversely affected because some team members could be on vacation when the big game or competition occurs. Proponents counter that experience suggests students participate even when they are on vacation. They point to the Tempe, Arizona, high school that adopted an alternative calendar and recently won the state football championship.

What about students who work during the summer? Advocates of change say that employers in communities with alternative school calendars can adopt job-sharing arrangements. For example, four high school students might move in and out of the same grocery-bagging job as they go from school to break and back. Indeed, advocates say, this strategy can reduce drop-out rates because adolescents do not settle into a job routine. They know the job will be there for them the next time school lets out. Advocates do admit, however, that the vast majority of modified calendar schools are at the elementary level, partly because of concerns about the calendar's impact on adolescents' after-school activities.

Family economics also play a role in reactions to modified calendars. I found considerable skepticism about modified calendars among middle-class and upper-middle-class parents, especially among mothers who did not work outside the home. These families have both the time and economic resources needed to piece together high-quality educational and recreational experiences for their children over the summer. They pick and choose activities that are focused on the strengths or weaknesses of their children and pay the required school tuition or camp fees. Parents want to control these options for their children, rather than turn control over to school districts.

Proponents of change counter that equivalent individualized opportunities will arise during the intersessions of modified school years, so these options will not disappear. Proponents also point out that having four seasonal breaks from school can help well-to-do families take advantage of new vacation opportunities, by reducing the expense and crowds often associated with summer travel.

Related to this last point, the most organized and well-funded opposition to modified calendars comes from business interests that are threatened by the loss of the long summer break. Time to Learn, an organization that lobbies against school calendar reform, is partially funded by the International Association of Amusement Parks and Attractions. The American Camping Association and the day-care industry also keep a close eye on calendar reform.

Effectiveness

The kind of evidence we have on modified calendars leaves much to be desired. When it comes to school schedules, it is virtually impossible to do studies where students are randomly assigned to different calendars, or where other careful controls rule out all the alternative explanations for why a result might favor one calendar over another. Therefore, it is not possible to make strong inferences about the effectiveness of modified calendars based on existing research.

Complicating matters even further, our preliminary evidence revealed ambiguous results even within a weak inferential framework. We examined the data on modified calendars in three different ways. First, we found 16 school districts that attempted some statistical or matching control of preexisting student differences and then compared student achievement in modified and traditional calendar schools. There was no difference in achievement between calendar types. The effect size was near zero, whether or not studies were weighted by sample size. The length of time a school had been on a modified calendar made a difference in the comparisons, however. Traditional calendar schools were favored when compared with schools that had spent just 1 year on a modified calendar. However, schools that had been on modified calendars for more than 1 year were favored over schools with traditional calendars.

Second, we looked at district-level comparisons that employed no controls for preexisting differences among students. Overall, about two thirds of 59 such comparisons revealed students on modified calendars did better on achievement measures than other samples in their districts. These data are certainly less trustworthy than experimental or statistically controlled comparisons, but the bias could go either way, favoring traditional calendars or modified calendars. I say this because we noticed a tendency for modified calendars to be adopted more often by schools that served poorer neighborhoods, where pre-implementation achievement scores were likely to be lower than in other schools in their district. Our preliminary estimate from these comparisons suggested that, in any given year, the positive effect of the modified calendar was small—approximately .08 standard deviation units. When we looked at the modified calendar effect in poor school districts, however, it was twice this size and significantly more positive than the effect for districts with higher socioeconomic status.

Finally, we found over 50 school districts that surveyed teachers, parents, students, administrators, and staff members about their reactions to living with a modified school calendar (Barnett, Charlton, Cooper, & Valentine, 2000). These surveys overwhelmingly described the experience as positive, with average responses about 1 standard deviation above the scale midpoint. Put differently, over 80% of responses were on the positive side of the scale. Post-implementation responses were more positive than pre-implementation ones, and much of the pre-implementation negativity disappeared if preplanning included making available intersession activities for students out of school. Respondents also perceived that the modified calendar had a positive effect on student achievement.

In sum then, my working conclusion is that, although some forms of evidence stand in contradiction, the effect of modified calendars on achievement is generally positive, but small, compared to many other educational interventions—and may be negligible in some instances. As many educators have suggested, the positive effect may be more substantial and reliable for poorer children. Also, we do not know if this effect accumulates over time. The few studies that permitted cross-sectional comparisons of students on modified calendars for 1 year versus more than 1 year suggest this is an important consideration. If the effect does accumulate over the course of a student's school career, then the positive impact of the modified calendar could be substantial. I must emphasize again, however, that well-conducted future research is critical to appraising the impact of calendar variations. These studies need to employ longitudinal designs, include variations in program characteristics (especially the availability of instruction during intersessions), and evaluate the impact of modified calendars on different types of students. (For a more recent description of this analysis, see Cooper, Valentine, Charlton, & Barnett, 2003).

CONCLUSION

What do we know, then, about alternatives to the traditional school calendar, and what does the future hold? First, it is clear that students on the traditional calendar do forget mathematics material over the summer, and poor children lose reading skills as well. Second, summer programs are an effective intervention for purposes of academic remediation, enrichment, or acceleration, and we have accumulated a knowledge base that can help make the most of summer school. Third, extending the school year by a few days is a questionable intervention, but we should not rule out the possibility that substantial increases in the length of the school year—coupled with corresponding curricular reform—could have a general and robust positive impact on student learning. Fourth, modified school calendars may have a positive impact on student achievement, but the existing research contains some contradictory evidence and suffers from design flaws that render this conclusion tentative at best. What is clearer is that those who live and work with the modified calendar are satisfied with the experience and think the innovation has positive effects on achievement.

As for the future, I believe that change in the school calendar is inevitable. The present calendar became dominant when 85% of Americans were involved in agriculture. Currently, only about 3% of Americans have livelihoods that are tied to the farming cycle (Association of California School Administrators, 1988). Today, American families are characterized by enormous variation in how they live and work. The most common American family is one in which both parents work outside the home, and about one in five families is headed by a woman without a spouse (Farley, 1996). For these parents, summer may be hazy but it is not lazy, and finding appropriate activities for children when school is out is a real problem. Eventually, the shift in business and family economics evident in the late 20th and early 21st century will overcome the resistance to change, but the process may be long and potentially painful.

Because change will be slow, use of summer programs as adjuncts to the traditional calendar is likely to expand to meet the needs of parents and children. Advocates for poor families, who lack the resources to provide quality educational and recreational activities over the summer, will lead the call for government-sponsored programming when school is out. Families who do have adequate resources are likely to request these services as well. The growing number of middle-class families in which no adult is home during the day suggests that these families may increase their reliance on organized summer programs, be they free or tuition-based.

Modified school calendars which offer educational activities during intersessions are also likely to grow in popularity, albeit slowly, given the greater resistance this innovation will face from both affected businesses and traditional and well-to-do families. Surprisingly, however, the calendar reform movement today affects over 2 million students (National Association for Year-Round Education, 2000)—many more students than the charter school movement, although you might not know this because the latter receives so much more attention from policymakers and the national media.

Our research synthesis and my conversations with employees, parents, and students in districts with modified school calendars suggest that communities interested in adopting this form of innovation are best served by a "go-slow" approach. School boards and administrators might begin with pilot schools that not only break the mold of the school calendar but also introduce flexibility into the daily school schedule. Such experimental schools would have educational intersession programs that are available on a tuition basis for families who can afford it and also for those who use federal funds for disadvantaged students. They would also have exemplary optional before- and after-school programs, similarly funded, that run from early in the morning until dinner time.

The object of these innovations—be they summer programs meant to extend the traditional calendar, or rearrangements of the year to do away with the long summer break—should focus on using time to optimize student learning, while also serving the needs of various modern American family configurations. The history of school calendars in the United States suggests that the only potentially successful innovations will be those that consider the education of children in the context of local and national economics and the politics of family time.

ACKNOWLEDGMENTS

This article was presented at the conference, "Summer Learning and the Achievement Gap: First National Conference" held at the Johns Hopkins University Center for Social Organization of Schools, Baltimore, July 18, 2000. Portions of this research were supported by a grant from the U.S. Department of Education, National Institute on the Education of At-Risk Students (R306F60041–97). The opinions expressed herein are those of the author and not necessarily the funding agency. Thanks are extended to

Kelly Charlton, Jeff Valentine, and April Barnett for their assistance in conducting the reported research and preparing the manuscript. Harris Cooper can be contacted by email at cooperh@duke.edu

REFERENCES

Adams, M. J. (1991). *Beginning to read: Thinking and learning about print.* Cambridge, MA: MIT Press.

Albuquerque Public Schools. (1985). *What I did instead of summer vacation: A study of the APS summer school program.* Albuquerque, NM: Author. (ERIC Document Reproduction Service No. ED281932)

Association of California School Administrators. (1988). *A primer on year-round education.* Sacramento, CA: Author.

Austin, G. R., Rogers, B. G., & Walbesser, H. H. (1972). The effectiveness of summer compensatory education: A review of the research. *Review of Educational Research, 42,* 171–181.

Barnett, A., Charlton, K., Cooper, H., & Valentine, J. (2000, May). *Public impressions of alternative school calendars: A narrative and meta-analytic review.* Paper presented at the meeting of the Midwestern Psychological Association, Chicago.

Chicago Public Schools. (1997). *Guidelines for promotion in the Chicago public schools.* Chicago: Author.

Coleman, R. W., & Freehorn, C. L. (1993, February). *A comparative study of multi-track year-round education and the use of relocatables.* Paper presented at the meeting of the National Association for Year-Round Education, San Diego, CA.

Conant, J. B. (1959). *The American high school.* New York: McGraw-Hill.

Cooper, G., & Sweller, J. (1987). Effects of schema acquisition and rule automation on mathematical problem-solving transfer. *Journal of Educational Psychology, 79,* 347–362.

Cooper, H., Nye, B., Charlton, K., Lindsay, J., & Greathouse, S. (1996). The effects of summer vacation on achievement test scores: A narrative and meta-analytic review. *Review of Educational Research, 66,* 227–268.

Cooper, H., Valentine, J. C., Charlton, K., & Barnett, A. (2003). The effects of modified school calendars on student achievement and school community attitudes: A research synthesis. *Review of Educational Research, 73,* 1–52.

Dougherty, J. W. (1981). *Summer school: A new look.* Bloomington, IN: Phi Delta Kappa.

Farley, R. (1996). *The new American reality: Who we are, how we got here, where we are going.* New York: Russell Sage Foundation.

Heyns, B. (1978). *Summer learning and the effects of schooling.* New York: Academic.

Hazelton, J. E., Blakely, C., & Denton, J. (1992). *Cost effectiveness of alternative year schooling.* Austin: University of Texas, Educational Economic Policy Center.

Karweit, N. (1984). Time-on-task reconsidered: Synthesis of research on time and learning. *Educational Leadership, 41*(8), 32–35.

Karweit, N. (1985). Should we lengthen the school term? *Educational Researcher, 14*(6), 9–15.

Mitchell, R. E., & Mitchell, D. E. (1999). *Student segregation and achievement tracking in year-round schools.* Manuscript submitted for publication.

Mosteller, F. (1995). The Tennessee study of class size in early grades. *Future of Children, 5,* 113–127.

National Association for Year-Round Education. (2000). *Twenty-sixth reference directory of year-round education programs for the 1999–2000 school year.* San Diego, CA: Author.

National Education Association. (1987). *What research says about: Extending the school day/year: Proposals and results.* Washington, DC: Author.

National Education Commission on Time and Learning. (1993). *Research findings.* Washington, DC: Author. (ERIC Document Reproduction Service No. ED372491)

Orellana, M. F., & Thorne, B. (1998). Year-round schools and the politics of time. *Anthropology & Education Quarterly, 29*(4), 446–472.

Richmond, M. J. (1977). *Issues in year-round education.* Hanover, MA: Christopher Publishing House.

Worsnop, R. L. (1996). Year-round schools: Do they improve academic performance? *CQ Researcher, 6,* 433–456.

2

Schools, Achievement, and Inequality: A Seasonal Perspective

Karl L. Alexander
Doris R. Entwisle
Linda S. Olson
Johns Hopkins University

"Pupils Lose Ground in City Schools: The Longer Children Stay in the System, [the] More They Fall Behind." This headline ran in the *Baltimore Sun* (Bowie, 1997),[1] but it could apply equally to Chicago, Philadelphia, the District of Columbia, or any of the nation's other large-city, high-poverty school systems. When they are evaluated against national achievement norms, these school systems almost always fare badly: their pupils lag behind in the early grades and fall farther back over time (e.g., Quality Counts, 1998). Such comparisons signal a problem of immense proportions, but whether these comparisons also show that the school systems in those communities are failing our neediest children, as the aforementioned headline seems to imply, is much less certain.

When test results for places like Baltimore are compared against national norms, it can hardly be said that like is being compared with like. Baltimore's public school enrollment in 1999 was 86% African American (Maryland State Department of Education, 1999a), and 68% of its students qualified for free or reduced-price meals, indicating low family income relative to family size (Maryland State Department of Education, 1999b). Indeed, in over half of Baltimore's elementary schools, participation in the

---

[1]The accompanying article reviews citywide test results in reading and math, comparing them to national norms over grades 1 through 5.

subsidized school meal program topped 80% (*The Ultimate Guide to Baltimore Schools,* 1999)—hardly the national profile.[2]

Recognizing that "place" is a proxy for economic standing and other dimensions of social advantage or disadvantage puts such comparisons in broader perspective. The out-of-school context explains why test scores of low-income and minority youth already lag behind when they begin school—a lag documented recently at the national level in the Early Childhood Longitudinal Study (West, Denton, & Germino–Hausken, 2000). The same pattern of early educational disadvantage is evident, too, when Baltimore's school children are evaluated against national norms, as in the *Baltimore Sun* headline with which we began. Moreover, comparisons within the Baltimore City system show much the same pattern: lower socioeconomic status (SES) children in our Baltimore research already test below higher SES children in the fall of first grade (e.g., Entwisle, Alexander, & Olson, 1997).

The very same life circumstances that undercut school readiness over the preschool years are always present in children's lives. The drag of poverty and of family stress does not suddenly end when children turn 6 and the school's influence begins to weigh in. Because of this, we would expect the achievement gap across social lines to widen over time for reasons having nothing at all to do with the schools.[3] This is especially true for the primary grades, where foundational verbal and math skills dominate the curriculum. These kinds of skills are rehearsed at home—albeit more so in some kinds of households than others (e.g., Hess & Holloway, 1984; Scott–Jones, 1984; Slaughter & Epps, 1987)—and are infused in daily experience outside the household as well—although, again, not in equal measure across social lines.

Simple time trends like those at issue in the *Baltimore Sun* headline confound effects of home, school, and community, so it is not easy to clarify exactly how schools figure into the equation. Do schools exacerbate unequal school performance across social lines, or do they mitigate such inequality? Here is where the seasonal perspective we allude to in our title can prove useful. During the school year, all the social contexts that support children's academic development contribute to achievement gains—the home, the community, and the school. During the summer months, however, learning is situated exclusively in the out-of-school environment. This partitioning of the calendar approximates a schooled versus unschooled natural experiment that can be used to isolate the schools'

---

[2]For the 1993 to 1994 school year, participation nationwide at the elementary level was 38.8%, but it was 52.1% in central city schools and 65.5% in schools with 50% or more minority student enrollment (U.S. Department of Education, 2001, p. 424).

[3]Likewise, the Black–White gap in achievement seems to increase from the elementary grades through high school. For an overview and analysis, see Phillips, Crouse, and Ralph (1998).

contribution to learning (for an overview, see Cooper, Nye, Charlton, Lindsay, & Greathouse, 1996; Heyns, 1978, 1987).

We use information from our project, the Beginning School Study (BSS), to illustrate how a seasonal perspective on achievement brings into relief patterns that are obscured in the more typical approach to monitoring trends, which relies on year-end, or spring, testing data. An ongoing panel study, the BSS consists of a representative random sample of children ($N = 790$) from 20 of Baltimore's public schools who began first grade in the fall of 1982. We evaluated the first 5 years of the study group's schooling. This time frame covers all of elementary school for children promoted regularly each year (about 60% of the total) and aligns with the time frame of the *Baltimore Sun* newspaper article (Bowie, 1997).

The achievement data extend from fall 1982 to spring 1987, which predates recent increases in summer remediation programs for children in the primary grades (e.g., Cooper, Charlton, Valentine, & Muhlenbruck, 2000). Accordingly, few members of the study group attended summer school during the years at issue. In this respect, the analysis is a relatively clean implementation of the schooled–unschooled logic that directs attention to seasonal differences in learning. It would be much harder to achieve such clarity in current data because of the proliferation of summer programs.

Testing was done in the fall and spring each year, which means we were able to assess achievement trends over 5 school years and 4 summers. We report two kinds of "assessments." The first is descriptive. It plots achievement annually and on a seasonal basis over these 5 school years. The objective of these descriptive comparisons is to see how comparisons track across social lines, and especially to note the insights afforded by taking a seasonal approach. The second assessment is analytic. We estimate within-person growth curve trajectories for the 5 years in a way that allows for summer "deflections" and for socioeconomic differences in the magnitude of those deflections. The descriptive comparisons seem to implicate out-of-school learning differences as driving the increasing achievement gap across social lines. The growth curve analysis provides a rigorous test of this proposition.

METHODS

The BSS Research Design

We used a two-stage process to select children for participation in the BSS study. First, we chose 20 schools at random from within strata defined by racial mix (six were predominantly African American, six were predominantly White, and eight were integrated) and by SES (14 were inner-city or working class, 6 were middle class). Then we took a random sample of

students from first-grade classrooms; that sample was based on kindergarten rosters from the previous school year, supplemented by class rosters after school began in the fall. We were able to recruit into the project
97% of children and families selected in this way.

The Baltimore context is low income and urban. This was reflected in
the makeup of the study group. The Baltimore City Public School (BCPS)
enrollment in the early 1980s was about 77% African American, so to sustain comparisons by race, the BSS deliberately oversampled Whites. The
final sample of 790 first-time (nonrepeating) first-graders was 55% African American and 45% White. Mother's education averaged just over 11
years, and almost 40% lacked high school degrees. According to school
records, 67% of BSS families received free or reduced-price school meals—
about the same percentage as in the school system at the time. In addition,
at the beginning of first grade, 44% of the youngsters in the study were living in single-parent households (30% of Whites, 56% of African Americans). These are the kinds of children for whom a good start at school is especially important and especially problematic.

The analysis used achievement data from school records, demographic
information (race or ethnicity and sex) from school records, and data on
family socioeconomic standing obtained from parent interviews and
school records.

Data Sources

California Achievement Test (CAT) Scores.   When the BSS began in fall
1982, the BCPS system was administering the CAT battery twice annually
(fall and spring). With data available on this schedule, calculating school-
year gains separately from summer gains was a simple matter. Figure 2.1
illustrates how it is done.

School-year gains were obtained by subtracting fall scores for a given
school year from spring scores for the same year; summer gains were obtained by subtracting spring scores from fall scores across adjacent school
years. We tracked CAT gains, season by season, over 5 years, from first
grade through the end of elementary school.

We used two subtests from the CAT battery: Reading Comprehension
(CAT–V: 20 items in the fall of first grade), and Math Concepts and Applications (CAT–M: 36 items in the fall of first grade). Several considerations
directed us to these particular domains of performance—first and foremost, the importance of the skill areas themselves. In addition, ceiling
constraints were a problem for other components of the CAT battery. In
the spring of first grade, for example, 16.6% of the cohort received the
highest score possible on the Math Computation subtest, compared with

Winter Gains:

    First Winter: [Spring Year 1 - Fall Year 1]
    Second Winter: [Spring Year 2 - Fall Year 2]

Summer Gains:

    First Summer: [Fall Year 2 - Spring Year 1]
    Second Summer: [Fall Year 3 - Spring Year 2]

FIG. 2.1. Illustrative time-line for seasonal comparisons of cognitive growth.

3.5% on the Math Concepts and Applications subtest. The corresponding figures for Vocabulary (not used) and Reading Comprehension (used) were 17.3% and 3.7%, respectively. Also, modules to assess competence in these two areas were included in all versions of the CAT battery from first grade through high school. This means we were able to monitor development in the same cognitive domains throughout. Trends are reported using CAT scale scores. These were vertically calibrated across versions of the CAT battery designed for administration at different grade levels, meaning that children could be ranked along a single continuum of performance at all points of comparison.

Demographic Data. Race (White = 0; African American = 1) and sex (male = 0; female = 1) designations came from school records, supplemented by self-reports.

Family SES was measured as a composite, using information on mother's and father's educational levels, a ranking of mother's and father's occupational status (Featherman & Stevens, 1982), and receipt of reduced-price school meals, indicating low family income relative to family size. The first four indicators were self-reported by parents; the last came from school records. The composite was constructed as the average of available measures, after conversion to z scores. Scale scores were available for 787 of the 790 students in the group, with just under 70% calculated on four or five indicators and 5.4% on a single indicator. Alpha reliability for the 386 youngsters covered by all five items was .86.

For descriptive comparisons, we used a three-category version of the SES composite. Mother's education averaged 10.0 years for the lower SES group, 12.0 years for the middle group, and 14.6 years for the upper group. In the lower SES group, 95.1% of study participants took part in the meal-subsidy program for low income families; the percentages in the middle and upper group were 53.4% and 13.1%, respectively. There were few genuinely wealthy households in the BSS, and it should be understood that these descriptors (i.e., "lower" and "higher or upper") were relative to the makeup of the sample. In fact, half the cohort was located in the lower SES category, a reflection of the study group's low socioeconomic standing overall.

A Note on Sample Attrition

Coverage on the background measures was good. Sex and race or ethnicity were known for everyone, and only three cases lacked scores on the scale that ranks family socioeconomic standing. The CAT data, however, came from 10 test administrations over 5 years, and missing data are a concern. Coverage was best for children who remained in Baltimore's schools all through the primary grades (about 75% of the total), but transfers, absences, lost records, and the like took a toll. There were just 368 children (of the original 790) with all 10 scores on the CAT-V, and 371 children with all 10 scores on the CAT–M. These gaps in the testing record obliged us to consider the consequences of sample attrition carefully. The first and third columns of Table 2.1 show how youngsters with complete testing data compared with the original sample on various indicators from first grade. The comparisons were reassuring: despite a high degree of sample loss, attrition was not selective along academic lines and was only moderately selective along social lines.

Accordingly, we used all the available data in the analysis. The only cases we screened out were those for whom growth trajectories could not reasonably be estimated: those with fewer than three overtime data points per achievement domain (three being the minimum number required to estimate a growth trajectory, allowing for curvature), and those lacking "anchoring" baseline scores from the fall of first grade. These restrictions yielded a (maximum) case base of 665 for the CAT–V analysis and a base of 678 for the CAT–M analysis.[4] These "restricted coverage" samples were compared against the original sample and the complete data panel in Table 2.2. Again, little attrition bias was evident.

---

[4]For these groups, data coverage is good. In both domains, over half have complete California Achievement Test data and just under three fourths (73.5% on the CAT reading comprehension subtest; 73.6% on the CAT math concepts and applications subtest) have at least 8 of the 10 scores.

TABLE 2.1

Seasonal Attrition Checks: Background and Other Characteristics
from First Grade for Cross-Sectional, Restricted, and
Listwise Samples (Ns in parentheses; SDs in brackets)

	Cross-Sectional Coverage[a]	Restricted Coverage[b]	Full Panel Coverage[c]
Family SES level	−.04/(787)	−.05/(665)	−.13/(368)
Pooled SD	[.80]		
Mother's years of education	11.67/(750)	11.72/(635)	11.60/(353)
Pooled SD	[2.55]		
Proportion low income	.67/(701)	.67/(627)	.68/(366)
Pooled SD	[.47]		
Proportion two-parent household	.56/(754)	.56/(637)	.54/(355)
Pooled SD	[.50]		
Proportion African American	.55/(790)	.57/(665)	.62/(368)
Pooled SD	[.50]		
Proportion female	.51/(790)	.51/(665)	.53/(368)
Pooled SD	[.50]		
CAT–V, fall first grade	280.62/(691)	280.71/(665)	280.74/(368)
Pooled SD	[40.81]		
CAT–M, fall first grade	292.49/(708)	293.50/(653)	294.38/(362)
Pooled SD	[31.94]		
Academic self-image, spring first grade	4.17/(717)	4.17(627)	4.20/(355)
Pooled SD	[.60]		
Marks, fall first grade	2.06/(704)	2.07/(623)	2.12/(354)
Pooled SD	[.71]		
Absences, first grade	13.28/(702)	13.23/(622)	13.15/(355)
Pooled SD	[11.64]		
Work habit ratings, fall first grade	10.03/(702)	10.08/(620)	10.25/(352)
Pooled SD	[2.12]		

Note. SES = socioeconomic status; CAT = California Achievement Test; CAT–V = CAT reading comprehension subtest; CAT–M = CAT math concepts and applications subtest.

[a]All possible cases.

[b]Sample coverage is cross-sectional but screened on CAT availability for fall of Grade 1 and scores for at least two other time points. Samples are drawn separately for verbal and quantitative domains. Results reported here are for the verbal sample.

[c]The full panel sample screens on complete CAT coverage (five winters and four summers), separately by verbal and quantitative domains. Results reported here are for the verbal sample.

RESULTS

Annual Versus Seasonal Achievement Gains

So, what does the achievement pattern look like when assessed on an annual basis? As already mentioned, lower SES youth in the BSS enter first grade already behind. Table 2.2 provides the relevant details. In the fall of

TABLE 2.2
California Achievement Test (CAT) Performance Over
5 Years, Differences by Socioeconomic Status (SES)
Level (restricted samples, N = 665, 678)

	Fall 1982	Spring 1983	Spring 1984	Spring 1985	Spring 1986	Spring 1987
CAT–V Mean						
Low SES	273.12	329.15	375.95	397.92	433.58	461.17
(N)	(345)	(329)	(308)	(282)	(274)	(292)
Medium SES	278.48	348.68	388.43	423.93	467.52	495.51
(N)	(168)	(161)	(144)	(120)	(118)	(129)
High SES	300.40	361.01	418.09	460.81	506.20	534.60
(N)	(152)	(150)	(137)	(109)	(99)	(93)
High–low difference	27.28	31.86	42.14	62.88	72.62	73.43
Difference/pooled SD	.67	.70	.87	1.09	1.04	.99
CAT–M Mean						
Low SES	282.27	331.27	371.87	397.80	427.63	457.76
(N)	(356)	(339)	(315)	(289)	(281)	(295)
Medium SES	295.98	350.45	387.08	418.88	457.76	491.66
(N)	(171)	(162)	(146)	(122)	(122)	(134)
High SES	313.80	357.39	407.30	448.09	487.02	514.62
(N)	(151)	(147)	(135)	(110)	(98)	(91)
High–low difference	31.53	26.12	35.42	50.29	59.39	56.85
Difference/pooled SD	.99	.72	.92	1.04	1.09	.93

Note. CAT–V = CAT reading comprehension subtest; CAT–M = CAT math concepts and applications subtest.

the year, they trail their higher SES counterparts by .67 *SD*s in the verbal domain, and by .99 *SD*s in the quantitative. After first grade, they fall farther back, mirroring the local–national comparisons with which we began. This holds both for raw score differences (i.e., number of CAT points) and when raw score differences are expressed relative to the variability in performance observed at the time of the comparisons.[5]

Lower SES youngsters in the BSS thus are not keeping up, which is the typical pattern when achievement is assessed at year's end—the *Baltimore Sun* article with which we began could easily have been written around the experience of children in the BSS. Some details in Table 2.2 hint at a more complicated story line, however. We elected to start the trend comparison at the fall of first grade because problems at that point most likely can be traced to out-of-school influences. Had we chosen to use the spring

[5]Such a relative perspective is important, as a given achievement gap—say 20 points—will seem more impressive if scores range over a narrow band (e.g., from 0–100) than if they range over a broad band (e.g., 0–1000). In our data, as with testing data generally, variability in performance increases with children's age. That being the case, a constant gap in points implies a smaller relative difference.

TABLE 2.3
California Achievement Test (CAT) Gains by Season
and Socioeconomic Level: Five Winters, Four Summers
(restricted samples, N = 665, verbal; N = 678, quantitative)

	CAT–V			CAT–M		
	Low SES[b]	Mid SES[b]	High SES[b]	Low SES[b]	Mid SES[b]	High SES[b]
Winter gains						
1st	55.94	69.86	60.09	48.84	53.79	43.71
2nd	46.00	43.19	39.82	42.35	44.06	42.92
3rd	30.46	34.34	34.68	35.50	35.68	35.96
4th	33.57	41.29	28.52	32.94	32.88	34.71
5th	25.28	27.86	23.58	24.35	30.90	26.35
Total gain	191.25	216.54	186.69	183.98	197.31	183.65
Mean gain per month[a]	4.78	5.41	4.67	4.60	4.93	4.59
Summer gains						
1st	–3.67	–3.11	15.38	–4.89	–8.22	7.18
2nd	–1.70	4.18	9.22	–5.18	–.50	3.14
3rd	2.74	3.68	14.51	–1.25	6.15	2.28
4th	2.89	2.34	13.38	5.50	4.31	6.30
Total gain	.26	7.09	52.49	–5.82	1.74	18.90
Mean gain per month[a]	.02	.44	3.28	–.36	.11	1.18

Note. CAT–V = CAT reading comprehension subtest; CAT–M = CAT math concepts and applications subtest; SES = socioeconomic status.

[a]Based on 8 months of winter (October–May) and 4 months of summer (June–September).

[b]Sample size ranges for seasonal gains: low SES N = 264 to 339; mid SES N = 113 to 162; high SES N = 85 to 150.

of first grade as baseline (i.e., the second entries in Table 2.2), however—a strictly annual accounting—the growth over time in quantitative CAT score inequality would have been much greater. This is because the high SES–low SES differential is smaller at the end of first grade than at the beginning: .72 SDs versus .99 SDs. The gap across SES lines in math achievement scores thus narrowed during the school year, and such shrinkage is not limited to first grade. This is documented in Table 2.3, which presents school-year gains (along with SES differentials therein) and summer gains (along with SES differentials therein) period-by-period and cumulatively over the first 5 years of these youngsters' schooling.[6]

Table 2.3 informs a whole host of issues having to do with schools and achievement. First, CAT gains posted while children are in school (top half of Table 2.3) exceed gains over the summer months (lower half of Ta-

---

[6]Variations of Table 2.3 have been reported previously (Alexander & Entwisle, 1996a, 1996b; Entwisle, Alexander, & Olson, 1997). This version incorporates recent data enhancements—one being the inclusion of achievement data for some children who transferred to schools outside the Baltimore City Public School system.

ble 2.3), with the margin of advantage large whether calculated as raw score gains or gains per month.[7] Children, it is reassuring to see, learn more and learn more efficiently when they are in school. Second, verbal gains over the summer generally exceed quantitative gains, suggesting that, at least in the early grades, quantitative learning is more school dependent than verbal learning. This too seems reasonable. Third, consistent with the idea that early schooling is foundational, school-year gains generally are larger the first 2 years than later.

These insights alone would be ample reason to look at learning on a seasonal basis. Our present interest centers, however, on a fourth issue informed by Table 2.3: how CAT gains differ by season according to children's family background. School-year gains year by year are not very different across SES levels (upper panel). Indeed, in the early years, the comparisons sometimes favor lower and middle SES children over upper. The summer pattern is strikingly different, however, especially across the SES extremes. Then lower SES youth essentially tread water, sometimes gaining a few points, sometimes losing a few, with losses most pronounced over the first two summers. This means lower SES children start the new school year about where they had been the previous spring. Not so for upper SES children, whose scores continue to improve over the summer months (lower panel). And these differences across social lines are large: looked at cumulatively, the summer achievement differential that favors children from upper SES households can account for almost all the growth in inequality that emerges over the first 5 years of the panel's schooling.[8] Schooling thus appears to help disadvantaged children keep up academically, whereas the out-of-school contexts of their development do not.

Figure 2.2 affords additional perspective on this pattern by projecting these summer and winter patterns year-round. In the first instance, the average verbal gain per summer month is applied over the entire 5-year period, adding onto the fall of first grade baseline averages for lower and higher SES children. With these extrapolations, a large initial difference increases to truly gigantic proportions over the 5 elementary years. Upper SES children forge ahead, whereas lower SES children stagnate. This is "summer slide" made vivid. On the other hand, when the school-year rate

---

[7]Gains per month are only approximate. Testing was done in October and May, but exact dates are unknown. The 8-month and 4-month intervals used thus lack precision, but the consequences of this probably are conservative. First, some school-year gain is "credited" to the summer, so errors when estimating raw summer gains and gains per month will tend to be on the high side. Second, when the actual interval between spring and fall testing is more than 4 months, dividing through by 4 will overstate monthly summer gains.

[8]And much the same is observed when the exercise is repeated on a full panel (i.e., listwise data present) basis.

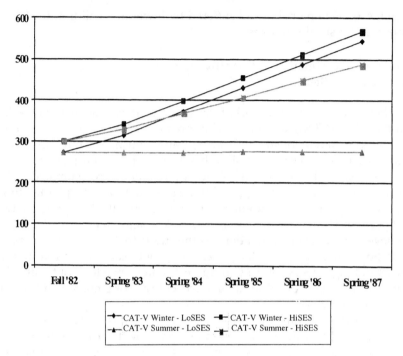

FIG. 2.2.   CAT–V averages over 5 years, by SES level, projecting summer and winter gains year-round.

of gain is applied year-round in Fig. 2.2, the lines pretty much remain parallel (and they terminate at a higher level of performance than is implied by the summer gains). The initial gap between upper SES and lower SES children does not widen over time because the two groups progress at about the same rate during the school year. With out-of-school influences strongly favoring children of privilege, to see such parity during the school year seems to us impressive indeed.

These extrapolations, we caution, are to highlight properties of the time-trend in Table 2.3 and should not be taken literally. In particular, we are not saying that year-round schooling or high-quality summer programs would maintain achievement parity across social lines. In fact, such a proposition seems to us highly dubious, as the conditions outside school that favor upper SES children very likely are too powerful for any such corrective to be wholly effective. That said, these descriptive comparisons certainly seem to implicate the long summer break in lower SES children's achievement shortfall during the primary grades, and that in itself is important.

Note that we have just said "seem to," and that also is important. Impressions, we know, can be misleading, and for that reason the issues also need to be addressed in a more analytic mode—one that allows us to test whether the summer shortfall suffered by lower SES children relative to upper is statistically reliable.

Modeling the Timeline of Cognitive Growth on a Seasonal Basis

Analysis Plan.   For this part of the assessment, we use hierarchical linear modeling (HLM) to estimate within-person achievement growth models (Bryk & Raudenbush, 1992; Bryk, Raudenbush, & Congdon, 1996).[9] Our particular application of HLM has two levels: within-person and between-person.[10] Person-specific growth parameters are estimated at the within-person, or level-1, stage. With these results, we can plot the timeline of CAT gains across the entire sample—essentially the average or typical pattern. The between-person, or level-2, stage evaluates variability in the level-1 parameters in relation to other traits that also vary across persons. So, for example, does the pattern of school-year CAT gains differ for lower and higher SES youth? Our interest centers on effects of family SES, but to guard against confounding, effects of race or ethnicity and sex are controlled at level-2.

How summer gains differ from school-year gains is examined in two ways. Both specifications of within-person growth fit three growth parameters: a baseline intercept term, a linear growth term, and a quadratic term to allow for curvature in the growth trajectory (the rate of gain is expected to decline over time, e.g., Schneider, 1980; Stephens, 1956). Both specifications also assess variability in the three growth parameters in relation to family SES, race, and sex.

The two specifications also estimate summer adjustments to the school-year pattern of achievement gains—our main substantive concern—but they differ in how this is done. The first approach implements a single summer adjustment to gauge how summer gains differ from winter gains on average. However, we also want to evaluate whether the summer gain differential by family SES level varies across years, as seems to be the case in the descriptive comparisons presented in Table 2.3 and elsewhere (Alexander & Entwisle, 1996a, 1996b; Entwisle & Alexander, 1992, 1994; Entwisle et al., 1997). The difference appears largest over the first two

---

[9]The only other strictly comparable analysis of which we are aware is didactic: Bryk and Raudenbush (1992) modeled seasonal effects on achievement growth to illustrate within-person applications of hierarchical linear modeling. An unpublished article by Karweit, Ricciuti, and Thompson (1994) reported growth curve results over one summer and two winters using a repeated measures analysis of variance approach that is similar in intent.

[10]The software we use can accommodate three levels: children nested within classrooms nested within schools, for example.

summers—a pattern that, if reliable, would implicate the early period of schooling as being especially critical in a foundational sense (e.g., Entwisle & Alexander, 1988, 1992).

To examine this matter, we estimate a second specification of the growth model that includes a separate summer adjustment term for each of the four summers subsumed under the 5-year time frame. The data requirements for estimating this second specification of summer deflections are severe, however. The level-1 estimates represent person-specific growth trajectories. With separate codings for each summer, these models fit seven parameters (intercept, growth, growth-squared, and four summer adjustment variables) against a maximum of 10 data points (fall and spring CAT scores over 5 years). This more refined specification thus approaches the limits of the information available, and HLM screens out many cases owing to strategic gaps in the testing record (Ns range from 448 to 458 when four separate summer adjustment parameters are estimated, compared to Ns of 646 to 656 when an average summer adjustment is estimated). Notwithstanding such technical concerns, attrition bias owing to missing CAT data is minor (e.g., Table 2.2) and all models converged.[11]

Maximum likelihood estimates are reported. The level-1 and level-2 equations for the four summer adjustment model are as follows:[12]

Level-1 Model: Within-Person Growth Trajectories

$$Y_{ti} = \beta_{0i} + \beta_{1i}S1_{ti} + \beta_{2i}S2_{ti} + \beta_{3i}S3_{t1} + \beta_{4i}S4_{ti} + \beta_{5i}T_{ti} + \beta_{6i}T^2_{ti} + \varepsilon_{ti} \quad (1)$$

where

Y_{ti} is CAT level at time t for student i;

$S1_{ti}$ to $S4_{ti}$ are summer adjustment dummy variables (each "switches" to "1" beginning in the fall of its referent summer period);

T_{ti} is time, coded at zero for fall 1982 and incrementing by unit steps thereafter for each testing occasion (spring and fall);

T^2_{ti} is time-squared, to allow for curvature in the growth trajectory;

β_{0i} is the expected baseline CAT value for child i;

---

[11]This is a technical concern: In every instance, our statistical software was able to solve the equations, which is not guaranteed when information is incomplete for some of the cases in the statistical analysis.

[12]The specifications for the single summer adjustment model is the same, except there is only one summer adjustment parameter estimated at level-1. Accordingly, at level-2, between-person effects are estimated for four, rather than seven, level-1 parameters.

β_{1i} to β_{4i} are summer adjustments to the school-year learning rate for student i;

β_{5i} and β_{6i} map the learning rate during the school year; and

ε_{ti} is an estimate of person-level disturbance.

Level-2 Model: Between-Person Background Contingencies[13]

$$\beta_{0i} = \pi_{00} + \pi_{01}SES_i + \pi_{02}RACE_i + \pi_{03}SEX_i + v_{0i} \qquad (2)$$

$$\beta_{1i} \text{ to } \beta_{4i} = \pi_{10} \text{ to } \pi_{40} + \pi_{11} \text{ to } \pi_{41}SES_i + \pi_{12}$$
$$\text{to } \pi_{42}RACE_i + \pi_{13} \text{ to } \pi_{43}SEX_i + v_{1i} \text{ to } _{4i} \qquad (3)$$

$$\beta_{5i} = \pi_{50} + \pi_{51}SES_i + \pi_{52}RACE_i + \pi_{53}SEX_i + v_{5i} \qquad (4)$$

$$\beta_{6i} = \pi_{60} + v_{6i} \qquad (5)$$

where

β_{0i}, β_{1i} to β_{4i}, β_{5i}, β_{6i} are person-level parameter estimates from the level-1 model; and

πs are level-2 coefficient estimates (intercept and slopes), and v_{0i} to v_{6i} are level-2 random effects.

Growth Models With a Single Summer Adjustment. Table 2.4 reports estimates for growth-curve models that include a single, average, summer-adjustment term. Results for CAT–V are reported on the left side of the table; results for CAT–M are on the right side.[14] The first level-1 equation (Column I) fits linear and quadratic growth terms, with time set at baseline zero for fall 1982 (fall of first grade) and increasing one unit per subsequent testing occasion.

Children's CAT averages at the start of first grade are in the vicinity of 300 scale points in both domains. Both baseline means are significantly different from zero, as are all four growth terms, with negatively signed coefficient estimates for the quadratic terms (–.96 for CAT–V; –.47 for CAT–M). This indicates that the rate of growth slows over time, as ex-

---

[13]In the level-2 specification, all level-1 parameters (save that representing curvature or nonlinearity in the rate of achievement gains, that is, β_{6i}, are allowed to vary in relation to student socioeconomic status, race, and sex.

[14]A baseline model that fits just the grand mean is used to partition the variance in test scores into between-person and within-person components. For the California Achievement Test (CAT) reading comprehension subtest, 25.4% of the variance is between-person; for the CAT math concepts and applications subtest, 22.6% of the variance is between-person.

TABLE 2.4

Growth Curve Analysis Estimated With a Single Average Summer Adjustment (N = 646-678)[a]

Model	CAT-V				CAT-M			
	I	II	III	IV	I	II	III	IV
Intercept	293.63**	292.11**	286.84**	285.70**	302.40**	307.23**	295.82**	300.28**
SES		16.25**		17.56**		15.89**		16.64**
Race		-1.26		-1.34		-4.83*		-4.33*
Sex		6.05*		5.57*		-2.09		-1.82
Linear growth term	29.56**	29.90**	48.17**	47.34**	23.36**	23.74**	41.56**	42.61**
SES		3.11**		-.34		1.87**		-.13
Race		-1.98**		-1.44		-1.62**		-2.64*
Sex		1.72**		2.91+		1.28**		.69
Quadratic growth term (squared) h	-.96**	-.94**	-.93**	-.91**	-.47**	-.46**	-.44**	-.43**
Summer adjustment			-38.93**	-36.38**			-38.03**	-39.35**
SES				7.11**				4.08**
Race				-1.25				2.05
Sex				-2.44				1.14

Note. CAT-V = CAT reading comprehension subtest; CAT-M = CAT math concepts and applications subtest; SES = socioeconomic status.
[a]Within-person, level-1, growth-curve estimates are italicized. Coefficients for SES, race, and sex are between-person, level-2 effects. For the CAT-V analyses, Ns range from 646 to 665; for the CAT-M analysis, Ns range from 656 to 678.
+ significant at the .10 level. *significant at the .05 level. **significant at the .01 level.

pected. These details of the general timeline of achievement growth are all unexceptional. The specification in Column I does not adjust for summer differences, however, which means the parameter estimates describe the growth path period-by-period ($N = 10$) without regard to possible differences by season.

The second column of results evaluates between-person variability in these growth parameters in relation to family SES (here measured using the full scale metric), sex (with girls coded "1"), and race or ethnicity (with African Americans coded "1"). Because of the way level-1 and level-2 parameter estimates are linked in the HLM framework, the level-1 coefficients in Column II are analogous to intercept estimates in ordinary least squares (OLS) regression. They represent the expected value of the dependent variable for the group defined by the intersection of level-2 predictors at score zero. In the present instance, that corresponds to White males with average family SES scores—recall that the SES distribution has a mean of (approximately) zero by construction. Thus, the intercept estimate of 292.11 in Column II of the CAT–V results is the expected score of such youngsters at baseline (fall of first grade). The associated level-2 coefficients are increments or decrements to the baseline level of test performance at school entry associated with different values of SES, race or ethnicity, and sex. For CAT–V, effects of family SES and sex are significant. With SES scaled in standard deviation units, its associated coefficient in Table 2.4 indicates a 16.25 point CAT–V difference at the start of first grade for children who are a standard deviation apart in family SES. The standard deviation of the CAT–V distribution at baseline is 40.8 points, so 16.25 points corresponds to approximately .40 SDs.[15] And the difference, not surprisingly, favors children in upper SES households. The CAT–V results also show girls scoring a bit above boys at baseline.

The level-2 SES difference is much the same for CAT–M performance as for CAT–V, but on the CAT–M there is also a small, but significant, race effect, indicating that African American children start school a little behind their White counterparts in the quantitative domain. The 4.8 point difference, net of SES and sex, corresponds to about .15 CAT–M SDs, or about the same magnitude as the boy–girl difference in the verbal domain.

These level-2 effects on baseline cognitive scores tell us that, first, lower SES youth start school already behind in both skill areas, and, second, that initial disparities associated with family socioeconomic level exceed initial race and sex differences. The growth terms show what happens from that point forward. Because the trend is nonlinear, the two terms that describe

---

[15]A one SD difference in family socioeconomic status corresponds, roughly, to the difference between having parents who are high school dropouts and having parents with some time spent attending college.

the growth path have to be evaluated jointly. However, because preliminary analyses revealed little in the way of level-2 effects on the deceleration parameters, in Table 2.4 (and later, in Table 2.5) only the "main effect" terms are specified as contingent on level-2 influences. Under that framework, lower SES youths' gains over the elementary years lag behind upper SES youths' in both domains; African American youths' gains lag behind White youths' in both domains; and, boys' gains lag behind girls', all significant at the .01 level.

In these results, then, lower SES youth fall farther back over time, much as we saw previously when plotting simple averages (Table 2.2). These es-

TABLE 2.5
Growth Curve Analysis With Four Separate Summer Adjustments[a]

	CAT–V		CAT–M	
Model	I	II	I	II
Intercept	283.23**	282.63**	293.10**	297.42**
SES		16.58**		16.86**
Race		−.82		−4.26*
Sex		3.77		−1.62
Linear Growth Term	57.22**	56.03**	49.24**	49.85**
SES		−.62		−.51
Race		−.87		−2.04+
Sex		3.16*		.97
Quadratic Growth Term	−2.01**	−2.01**	−1.35**	−1.35**
1st Summer	−48.80**	−47.79**	−47.70**	−47.12**
SES		11.04**		4.48*
Race		−3.32		−.01
Sex		2.90		−.33
2nd Summer	−47.96**	−38.89**	−43.74**	−43.40**
SES		5.90*		6.94**
Race		−7.72+		1.55
Sex		−7.70+		−.85
3rd Summer	−31.79**	−33.10**	−33.55**	−33.32**
SES		7.95**		3.60+
Race		2.94		−.42
Sex		0.00		.93
4th Summer	−20.14**	−15.66**	−22.30**	−25.63**
SES		5.90*		3.04
Race		−1.19		2.83
Sex		−5.98		4.19

Note. CAT–V = CAT reading comprehension subtest; CAT–M = CAT math concepts and applications subtest; SES = socioeconomic status.

[a]Within-person, level-1, growth-curve estimates are italicized. Coefficients for SES, race, and sex are between-person, level-2 effects. For the CAT–V analysis, $N = 448$; for the CAT–M analysis, $N = 458$.

+ significant at the .10 level. *significant at the .05 level. **significant at the .01 level.

timates do not allow for seasonal differences in growth trajectories, however. Whether in fact there are such differences, and how they affect growth patterns across social lines, is assessed in the last two columns of Table 2.4.

Column III adds a single summer adjustment term to the general time trend. In essence, the adjustment it implements represents an average effect across the four summers encompassed by the model's 5-year time frame. Both summer adjustment coefficients are negatively signed and highly significant, but smaller than their corresponding linear growth coefficients. The descriptive pattern in Table 2.3 suggested that growth slows during the summer relative to school-year growth, and the results here are consistent with this pattern. The summer deflection coefficients in Table 2.4 do not represent summer drop-off or gain per se, however, and to compare winter and summer gains precisely requires some further calculations. This is because the summer coefficients are adjustments to the per-period growth that would otherwise be expected over the interval at issue.

"Time," as construed in this exercise, increases one "unit" each season, fall to spring, and spring to fall. To see the model's implications in terms of actual summer growth (or loss), we first need to derive the growth implied at time "t" by the general growth specification (i.e., linear and quadratic terms), and then correct that estimate for the summer–winter differential. The first part of the calculation is accomplished by taking the first derivative of the equation implied by Column III at time "t." Evaluating the CAT–V equation at $t = 2$, for example, yields an estimate of (instantaneous) growth of 44.45 CAT–V points at fall of Year 2. Adjusted for the average summer deflection (–38.93, from Table 2.4), the average expected gain over the first summer is 5.52 CAT–V points.[16] Similar calculations could be done throughout, but, in general, the model indicates a lower rate of cognitive gain over the summer months compared with the school-year rate of gain.

Column IV of Table 2.4 adds level-2 predictors to the model to test whether the within-person level-1 intercept estimates, growth term parameters, and summer adjustment coefficients just reviewed vary significantly in relation to SES, race or ethnicity, and sex. Adding these terms addresses our main substantive concern: the level-2 effects in Column II establish that the SES gap widens over time, but does this happen to the same degree summer and winter?

When comparing level-2 effects across Columns II and IV, several changes are evident. For example, the race coefficient in the CAT–V

---

[16]By way of comparison, the observed first summer drop-off is 1.12 points sample-wide. The estimated effect is much larger, but the estimate derives from an average summer adjustment across all summers. In fact, the summer adjustment is larger the first two summers, so this averaging sacrifices precision.

growth term results drops to nonsignificance, as does the sex coefficient in the CAT–M results. However, consequences for the family SES effect particularly stand out: whereas previously the SES effect on growth was large in both domains, SES effects in Column IV are nonsignificant and trivially small. The frame of reference in the two instances is different, however, and this is fundamental to the interpretation. The growth parameters in Column II describe the pattern of growth across all periods; in Column IV, with the summer adjustment term included in the model, the growth terms pertain to school-year growth specifically. SES thus apparently has no bearing on achievement gains during the school year. Not so for summer gains, as the level-2 SES effect on the summer adjustment coefficient is highly significant in both the CAT–V and the CAT–M results (see Column IV). And both coefficients are positively signed, which means the negative summer adjustment is attenuated for upper SES children relative to lower SES children.

The implications of this adjustment are easiest to see when exact summer gains are calculated. As an example, for children scoring one standard deviation below the sample-wide SES mean, the predicted CAT–V change over the first summer is +.21 points; for children at the SES mean, the predicted first summer gain is +7.32 points; and for children one standard deviation above the SES mean, the predicted gain is +14.43 CAT–V points.[17]

As mentioned, race and gender differences involving (school-year) growth also attenuate when the summer adjustment is implemented, although African Americans' school-year gains still lag behind Whites' school-year gains on the CAT–M, and there is a significant difference favoring girls on the CAT–V. But the seasonal adjustment has its greatest effect on the size and patterning of SES differences, and achievement disparities are larger altogether across socioeconomic lines than across racial or ethnic and gender lines. On this last point, the metric coefficients reported in Table 2.4 (and, later, in Table 2.5) make it hard to compare effect sizes across level-2 predictors, but, as an example, when effects are standardized on overall verbal growth, the coefficients in Column II become as follows: SES, .32; race, .23; sex, .17. Because significant SES differences emerge only during the summer, however, they must be traced to sources outside school.

Growth Models With Separate Summer Adjustments. In Table 2.3, differences in summer learning between higher and lower SES youth seem more pronounced in the early years, so we also evaluate a specification of the growth model that implements summer adjustments for each summer

---

[17]Recall, however, that the summer adjustment in the model from which these estimates are derived is constrained to be the same all four summers. That constraint is relaxed in Table 2.5.

separately. These results are reported in Table 2.5. Despite the reduced sample size due to missing data when summers are indexed individually, school-year CAT gains still do not respond to family SES in either domain (see Column II entries for both CAT–V and CAT–M). Other results that can be compared across Tables 2.4 and 2.5 are also similar.

And what of the more detailed specification of the summer adjustment coefficients? All eight summer adjustment effects are significant, and for seven of the eight, the level-2 effect of family SES is also significant (one borderline, at the .10 level). These summer adjustments all favor upper SES children, but the evidence that summer gains are conditional on SES is more compelling for the first two summers than for the last two, at least for quantitative achievement. These results thus give limited support for the idea that the first couple of years of elementary school are foundational, and much stronger support for the idea that differential summer learning over the primary grades is the scaffolding that supports disparities in school achievement—a conclusion that holds especially for achievement differentials across socioeconomic lines (i.e., there is not a single, fully significant level-2 effect on these many summer adjustment coefficients for sex or race or ethnicity).

Figure 2.3 puts all the pieces together in a way that makes the general trends, if not the fine details, a bit easier to follow. The two plots are derived from the HLM CAT–V results in Column II of Table 2.5 (the specification which allows for variable summer deflections across years). The plots represent the expected growth trajectories for upper SES youth (top line) and for lower SES youth (bottom line), with the two groups selected at about one standard deviation above and one standard deviation below the sample-wide SES average (race and sex are held constant at their respective means, again sample-wide).

The two timelines mirror the descriptive picture pretty well. Upper SES youth start school already ahead, and, after 5 years, the gap across social lines has increased substantially. The line segments representing school year increases are essentially parallel, however, whereas the gains registered by lower SES youth lag behind in most summers. These summer lags, we now know, are statistically significant. We also know that the newspaper headline with which we began this chapter, although right on the facts, needs a different "spin." Perhaps it should have read as follows: "The Pernicious Effects of Social Disadvantage Haunt Children All Along the Way."

DISCUSSION

When our study group of Baltimore children started school, their pre-reading and premath skills reflected their uneven family situations, and these initial differences were magnified across the primary grades. The

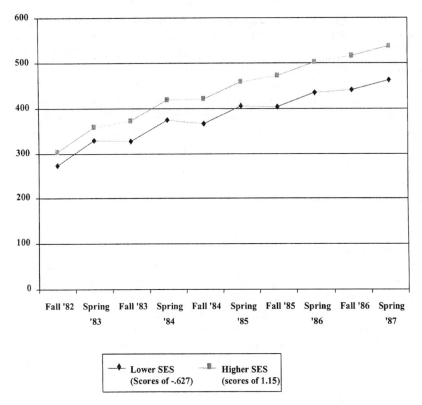

FIG. 2.3. The trajectory of CAT–V gains over time, with summer deflections: The pattern for lower and upper SES youth.

picture on the surface appears straightforward, but a bit of probing reveals a complex dynamic at play. Poor children lag behind at the end of elementary school because they started at a lower point than better-off children did, and because they registered virtually no achievement gains
during the summers, whereas better-off children continued to advance.
During the school year, on the other hand, 9 months out of 12, lower SES
children pretty well kept pace.

A seasonal perspective on learning thus brings into sharp focus how
the powerful forces of family and community affect children's academic
development, presumably year-round. However, it also brings into focus
the powerful force of schooling by highlighting the gains registered by all
children during the school year. Such school-year progress establishes
that poor children can keep up, but they start out behind and fall farther
back when out of school—so for them to achieve at the level of their
nonpoor peers will require extra help, and even then the challenge will be
a formidable one.

If "the problem" can be traced to summer stagnation and disadvantaged children's out-of-school resource shortfall, then year-round schooling (Gándara & Fish, 1994), high-quality summer programs (Cooper et al., 2000), and home–school partnerships that continue when school is closed (Epstein, 1991, 1992), would all seem to be promising solutions—but no single program or intervention is likely to prove sufficient. Therefore, we conclude by sketching our thoughts on what a more comprehensive agenda might entail. Our ideas are hardly novel, but all are supported by solid research (BSS and non-BSS) and, for that reason, deserve serious consideration.

Some Programmatic Implications

Where do we start? Before first grade is the obvious answer. Prevention, as a rule, is easier than remediation. For poor children to "catch up" after starting behind requires them to make greater-than-average strides, but keeping pace is challenge enough for them. So, the goal should be to minimize the achievement gap at the point of school entry.

That will not be easy, because, at present, disadvantaged children are the ones least likely to attend preschool (Hofferth, Shauman, Henke, & West, 1998). Yet we know that good preschools can improve their early school success. This is firmly established in projects like Abecedarian in North Carolina (e.g., Ramey, Campbell, & Blair, 1998) and Perry Preschool in Michigan (e.g., Schweinhart & Weikart, 1998).[18]

Disadvantaged children also need to attend high-quality, full-day kindergarten programs. Because kindergarten is not compulsory in all states, a surprisingly large number of children do not attend at all, and many more do not attend full-day kindergarten. And we are sure that it will come as no surprise to learn that poor children are the ones who most often skip kindergarten. Ten percent of the first-graders in our study group did not attend kindergarten, for example, and more of those from the poorest families attended half-day programs.

Does this matter? Our evidence certainly suggests it does. The benefits of full-day as compared to half-day kindergartens for our study children are striking. Allowing for family background and many other variables, first-graders who attended full-day kindergarten were absent fewer days in first grade, were retained less often, and earned higher marks and test scores than the half-day attendees (Entwisle, Alexander, Cadigan, & Pallas, 1987).

Preschool and kindergarten can reduce the achievement gap when children start first grade, but, to keep up later, those children will also need

---

[18]For a general overview, see Barnett, 1995.

extra resources of the sort that middle-class parents routinely provide for their children. This leads us to support summer school or extended year programs for poor children during the early grades.

The Chicago Longitudinal Study shows that intense supplementation of learning resources in the early grades helps poor children maintain the academic edge they get from attending a good preschool, and that these benefits then continue into the upper grades (Reynolds, 1994; Reynolds & Temple, 1998; Temple, Reynolds, & Miedel, 1998). The Chicago study makes the important point that it is the combination of the two that makes the difference—preschool alone or school-year supplementation alone is not sufficient. The Chicago intervention is not a summer program, but, in light of the summer shortfall, it seems reasonable to us that summer enrichment programs before and after first grade would confer similar, if not greater, benefits.

Of what should these summer programs consist? Here are some principles we have culled from various sources. The first, of course, is a strong curriculum, probably focusing on reading, because reading is the foundation for all that follows. Low-income children involved in Atlanta, Georgia's, summer schools back in the 1980s read more on their own than did students who did not attend (Heyns, 1978). Likewise, BSS first- and second-graders who went to the library more often in summer and who took out books did better the following year than did other children.

However, summer schools should not be limited to traditional academics. Better-off children in the BSS also did things in summer that were different from what they did during the school year. They attended day camps, took swimming lessons, went on trips, visited local parks and zoos, and played organized sports, to name a few. Poor children need these kinds of experiences as well. Building on such leads, summer programs for disadvantaged children should probably supplement academics with a heavy dose of physical activity and enrichment experiences. On the "activity" front, games like soccer, field hockey, and softball have complicated rule systems and require children to take multiple roles—qualities that have positive cognitive "spillover."[19]

Such an expanded agenda is important for another reason: the need to make summer school fun. Children need to be brought on board as enthusiastic partners in the enterprise. Learning works best that way, and to realize their potential, summer programs should be engaging and nonpunitive. Planners need to take this seriously. For many children, "school" is synonymous with "failure." For them, school is punishing, not fun, and summer school will not work well if all it offers is more of the same. This

---

[19]For a discussion of the link between organized sports and academic progress, see Entwisle, Alexander, and Olson (1994).

may be a particular problem with mandatory programs for children who fall short of promotion guidelines. Putting a positive spin on compulsory summer school attendance will not be easy, but it could well be the key to success.

Our comments to this point focus on "programs," but much also can be accomplished by attacking attitudes. Media coverage of American education leans toward "the lurid, the scandalous and the negative" (Kaplan, 1992, p. 48). This emphasis on the system's failures, especially its failures vis-à-vis the most disadvantaged students, undercuts popular support for public education (e.g., Loveless, 1997) and fosters negative stereotypes regarding the academic potential of poor and minority children. One especially perverse effect of the latter is that poor parents may also come to doubt their children's potential.

Parents and the public need to be disabused of these ideas, and a good way to begin would be to balance concern over how far children have yet to go with praise for how far they have come. For example, despite having gained as much as other children in first grade, poor children's performance was rated much more harshly by teachers in the BSS. Their progress on standardized tests was comparable, but their report card marks were much lower.

Report cards are more public than are achievement test scores, and the "signals" they send about children's competence are influential for that reason. Parents and children understand their meaning and pay attention to them. It is quite telling, therefore, that despite comparable achievement gains over first grade, at year's end, lower SES children's marks fell almost a full marking unit below the marks received by upper SES children in math and reading—and this on a rating scale that recognizes just four levels of performance: excellent, good, satisfactory, and unsatisfactory. This kind of feedback will shadow children for years to come. It colors how their second-grade teachers will view their potential, signals problems to their parents, and eventually filters through to children's own emerging sense of self in the student role.

This mismatch between children's actual progress and how that progress is rated is both inequitable and counterproductive. Middle-class parents provide more tangibles for their children (i.e., books, trips, computers, etc.), but they also provide more of the kind of emotional support that boosts school performance. An upbeat attitude, realistically grounded, is an important form of psychological capital. It certainly will not help the cause if poor parents believe their children are not progressing as fast or as well as they really are progressing. This undercuts support for learning at home, including learning over the summer months. A further step, then, would be to recognize and reward academic progress, not just children's level of performance.

Finally, a comment on today's reality. In places like Baltimore, the public schools are doing more to help needy children develop their academic skills than is generally appreciated. Absent some countervailing force—and extrapolating the summer pattern year-round—the achievement gap across socioeconomic lines would be expected to widen appreciably from September through May. Yet, in our research, the gap widens hardly at all. This is strong testimony to the equalizing power of schools. Schools do matter, and they matter the most when support for academic learning outside school is weak. School-based public resources do not offset completely the many and varied advantages that accrue based on private family resources, but, in a meritocracy based on family, it hardly seems realistic to think that they would—or could (e.g., Coleman, 1990). Yet, this is the standard, albeit implicit, to which our public schools are held when Baltimore's test results are compared against national norms and results are found wanting when compared against national norms.

Our intent in saying this is not to paper over disappointing test results and other serious problems that beset high-poverty school systems. With central city dropout rates reaching 40% and higher in many localities (e.g., Alexander, Entwisle, & Horsey, 1997; Alexander, Entwisle, & Kabbani, 2001; Bomster, 1992; Council of the Great City Schools, 1994), and with many high school graduates reading at a fifth-grade level (Quality Counts, 1998), clearly there are big problems to be tackled. If finding solutions to these problems is construed as a public trust, then we will turn to our schools for answers, of course—as well we should, and as we have in the past.

However, our expectations ought to be framed by a realistic sense of what is being asked of these school systems. We look to the public schools in high-poverty cities to fix problems not of their making—asking them to do more, often with less. These schools need the tools and support required to do their good work, and their victories will be hard-won even then. But that there are victories, if only partial ones, is easily overlooked. In our view, the compensatory effect of schooling is one such victory.

REFERENCES

Alexander, K. L., & Entwisle, D. R. (1996a). Early schooling and educational inequality: Socioeconomic disparities in children's learning. In J. Clark (Vol. Ed.), *James S. Coleman: Falmer sociology of education series 1* (pp. 63–79). Hampton, England: Falmer.

Alexander, K. L., & Entwisle, D. R. (1996b). Schools and children at risk. In A. Booth & J. Dunn (Eds.), *Family-school links: How do they affect educational outcomes?* (pp. 67–88). Mahwah, NJ: Lawrence Erlbaum Associates.

Alexander, K. L., Entwisle, D. R., & Horsey, C. (1997). From first grade forward: Early foundations of high school dropout. *Sociology of Education, 70,* 87–107.

Alexander, K. L., Entwisle, D. R., & Kabbani, N. (2001). The dropout process in life course perspective: Early risk factors at home and school. *Teachers College Record, 103,* 760–822.

Barnett, W. S. (1995). Long-term effects of early childhood care and education on disadvantaged children's cognitive development and school success. *The Future of Children, 5*(3), 25–50.

Bomster, M. (1992, September 18). City's dropout rate ranked 9th worst in nation in 1990. *The Baltimore Sun,* pp. C1, C4.

Bowie, L. (1997, November 12). Pupils lose ground in city schools. *The Baltimore Sun,* pp. A1, A12.

Bryk, A. S., & Raudenbush, S. W. (1992). *Hierarchical linear models: Applications and data analysis methods.* Newbury Park, CA: Sage.

Bryk, A. S., Raudenbush, S. W., & Congdon, R. T., Jr. (1996). *HLM: Hierarchical linear and nonlinear modeling with the HLM/2L and HLM/3L programs.* Chicago: Scientific Software International.

Coleman, J. S. (1990). Inequality, sociology, and moral philosophy. In J. S. Coleman (Ed.), *Equality and achievement in education* (pp. 31–54). Boulder, CO: Westview.

Cooper, H., Charlton, K., Valentine, J. C., & Muhlenbruck, L. (2000). Making the most of summer school: A meta-analytic and narrative review. *Monographs of the Society for Research in Child Development, 65*(1, Serial No. 260).

Cooper, H., Nye, B., Charlton, K., Lindsay, J., & Greathouse, S. (1996). The effects of summer vacation on achievement test scores: A narrative and meta-analytic review. *Review of Educational Research, 66,* 227–268.

Council of the Great City Schools. (1994). *National urban education goals: 1992–93 indicators report.* Washington, DC: Author.

Entwisle, D. R., & Alexander, K. L. (1988). Factors affecting achievement test scores and marks received by Black and White first graders. *The Elementary School Journal, 88,* 449–471.

Entwisle, D. R., & Alexander, K. L. (1992). Summer setback: Race, poverty, school composition, and mathematics achievement in the first two years of school. *American Sociological Review, 57,* 72–84.

Entwisle, D. R., & Alexander, K. L. (1994). Winter setback: School racial composition and learning to read. *American Sociological Review, 59,* 446–460.

Entwisle, D. R., Alexander, K. L., Cadigan, D., & Pallas, A. M. (1987). Kindergarten experience: Cognitive effects or socialization? *American Educational Research Journal, 24,* 337–364.

Entwisle, D. R., Alexander, K. L., & Olson, L. S. (1994). The gender gap in math: Its possible origins in neighborhood effects. *American Sociological Review, 59,* 822–838.

Entwisle, D. R., Alexander, K. L., & Olson, L. S. (1997). *Children, schools, and inequality.* Boulder, CO: Westview.

Epstein, J. L. (1991). Effects on student achievement of teachers' practices of parent involvement. In S. Silvern (Ed.), *Literacy through family, community, and school interaction: Vol. 5. Advances in reading/language research: A research annual* (pp. 261–276). Greenwich, CT: JAI.

Epstein, J. L. (1992). School and family partnerships. In M. Alkin (Ed.), *Encyclopedia of educational research* (6th ed., pp. 1139–1151). New York: Macmillan.

Featherman, D. L., & Stevens, G. (1982). A revised socioeconomic index of occupational status: Application in analysis of sex differences in attainment. In R. M. Hauser, D. Mechanic, A. O. Haller, & T. S. Hauser (Eds.), *Social structure and behavior: Essays in honor of William Hamilton Sewell* (pp. 141–182). New York: Academic.

Gándara, P., & Fish, J. (1994). Year-round schooling as an avenue to major structural reform. *Educational Evaluation and Policy Analysis, 16,* 67–85.

Hess, R. D., & Holloway, S. D. (1984). Family and school as educational institutions. In R. D. Parke (Ed.), *Review of child development research: Vol. 7. The family* (pp. 179–222). Chicago: University of Chicago Press.

Heyns, B. (1978). *Summer learning and the effects of schooling.* New York: Academic.

Heyns, B. (1987). Schooling and cognitive development: Is there a season for learning? *Child Development, 58,* 1151–1160.

Hofferth, S. L., Shauman, K. A., Henke, R. R., & West, J. (1998). *Characteristics of children's early care and education programs: Data from the 1995 National Household Education Survey* (NCES Publication No. 98–128). Washington, DC: U.S. Department of Education, National Center for Education Statistics.

Kaplan, G. R. (1992). *Images of education: The mass media's version of America's schools.* Washington, DC: Institute for Educational Leadership.

Karweit, N., Ricciuti, A., & Thompson, B. (1994). *Summer learning revisited: Achievement profiles of Prospects' first grade cohort.* Washington, DC: Abt Associates.

Loveless, T. (1997). The structure of public confidence in education. *American Journal of Education, 105,* 127–159.

Maryland State Department of Education. (1999a). *Maryland public school enrollment by race/ethnicity and gender and number of schools.* Baltimore: Author.

Maryland State Department of Education. (1999b). *Maryland school performance report, 1999: State, systems and schools.* Baltimore: Author.

Phillips, M., Crouse, J., & Ralph, J. (1998). Does the Black–White test score gap widen after children enter school? In C. Jencks & M. Phillips (Eds.), *The Black–White test score gap* (pp. 229–272). Washington, DC: Brookings Institute.

Quality Counts, '98: An *Education Week*–Pew Charitable Trust report on education in the 50 states. (1998). [Special issue]. *Education Week, 17*(17).

Ramey, C. T., Campbell, F. A., & Blair, C. (1998). Enhancing the life course for high-risk children: Results from the Abecedarian Project. In J. Crane (Ed.), *Social programs that work* (pp. 163–183). New York: Russell Sage Foundation.

Reynolds, A. J. (1994). Effects of a preschool plus follow-on intervention for children at risk. *Developmental Psychology, 30,* 787–804.

Reynolds, A. J., & Temple, J. A. (1998). Extended early childhood intervention and school achievement: Age thirteen findings from the Chicago Longitudinal Study. *Child Development, 69,* 231–246.

Schneider, B. L. (1980, April). *Production analysis of gains in achievement.* Paper presented at the meeting of the American Educational Research Association, Boston.

Schweinhart, L. J., & Weikart, D. P. (1998). High/Scope Perry Preschool program effects at age twenty-seven. In J. Crane (Ed.), *Social programs that work* (pp. 148–83). New York: Russell Sage Foundation.

Scott–Jones, D. (1984). Family influences on cognitive development and school achievements. In E. W. Gordon (Ed.), *Review of research in education* (pp. 259–304). Washington, DC: American Educational Research Association.

Slaughter, D. T., & Epps, E. G. (1987). The home environment and academic achievement of Black American children and youth: An overview. *Journal of Negro Education, 56,* 3–20.

Stephens, J. M. (1956). *Educational psychology.* New York: Holt, Rinehart & Winston.

Temple, J. A., Reynolds, A. J., & Miedel, W. T. (1998). *Can early intervention prevent high school dropout? Evidence from the Chicago child–parent centers* (Discussion Paper No. 1180–1198). Madison: University of Wisconsin, Institute for Research on Poverty.

The Ultimate Guide to Baltimore Schools. (1999). Baltimore: *The Baltimore Sun.*

U.S. Department Of Education. (2001). *Digest of education statistics, 2000.* (NCES Publication No. 2001–2034). Washington, DC: Author.

West, J., Denton, K., & Germino–Hausken, E. (2000). *America's kindergartners: Findings from the Early Childhood Longitudinal Study, Kindergarten Class of 1998–99, fall 1998* (NCES Publication No. 2000–2070). Washington, DC: U.S. Department of Education, National Center for Education Statistics.

3

The American Summer Learning Gap From an International Perspective

Alexander W. Wiseman
University of Tulsa

David P. Baker
Pennsylvania State University

The policy debate following Barbara Heyns's (1978) groundbreaking analysis of summer learning focused on two issues: (a) the loss of knowledge and skills during extended breaks in schooling, such as summer vacation; and (b) how this loss contributes to an educational gap between the haves and have-nots in American society (e.g., Poe & Cohen, 1998). As the other chapters in this volume show, this topic addresses more than just the summer learning gap, and it raises the issue of how much time in school is useful and how the school year should be organized to be most effective (Huyvaert, 1998; Shields & Oberg, 2000).

At the same time, this topic raises the even broader issue of how much schools and school communities of the future will impact and shape children's time while they are not in school. We examine these issues from an international perspective by asking and answering three questions. First, is the summer learning gap issue unique to American education? Second, how do American students compare with their international peers when it comes to measuring instructional time in the classroom? Third, how do the demands of schooling shape the use of time outside of school for students around the world?

Heyns's (1978) analysis suggests that American students' learning opportunities are stratified—both during formal schooling and during school breaks. In particular, several aspects of schooling contribute to this stratifying process and make it a uniquely American issue: (a) agrarian or seasonal school calendars (Stover, 1989), (b) informal boundaries between school activities and outside-school learning or educational opportunities (Sirotnik & Oakes, 1986), and (c) the uniquely American blend of comprehensive schooling alongside stark educational inequality (Gamoran & Weinstein, 1998). Yet, in part because of these U.S.-specific elements, researchers and policymakers have rarely discussed the summer learning phenomenon in the context of other nations' schooling and characteristics of educational stratification. Using international data, some cross-national comparisons of instructional time and content have been made (e.g., Pill, 1972; Schmidt, McKnight, Cogan, Jakwerth, & Houang, 1999; Schmidt, McKnight, & Raizen, 1997; Veenman, Lem, & Winkelmolen, 1985), but they have not specifically addressed the summer learning phenomenon. Thus, U.S.-specific concerns related to the stratification of learning processes both inside and outside formal schooling have overlapped with analyses of education in other nations without any empirical evidence for this association. Our analysis, however, takes a systematic approach to cross-national comparisons of instructional time and content both inside and outside of school.

By looking at instructional time and content as the primary factors influencing student achievement, we suggest that two approaches are fundamental to the summer learning dilemma from an international perspective. First, we suggest that inside-school instructional time and content provide important information about opportunities to learn. Second, outside-school learning is an important and increasingly structured and legitimate supplement or replacement for formal inside-school opportunities to learn. Using these inside-school and outside-school aspects of opportunity to learn, we produce an international comparison which demonstrates that the summer learning phenomenon is minimal, due to the expanding institutionalization of formal instruction, both in the classroom and after the regular school day has ended.

THE SUMMER LEARNING GAP
AS A UNIQUELY AMERICAN ISSUE

Schools everywhere take extended breaks for holidays and for a demarcation between grade progressions. Frequently, marked curricular and instructional changes follow these breaks. Therefore, how much students retain of what they have learned, or enhance it, during these breaks is an interesting empirical question. Analyses of American students showing that learning retention and enhancement is far more likely among students from advantaged homes raise a number of policy issues about whether the organization of the school calendar creates educational inequalities (Baker, Akiba, LeTendre, & Wiseman, 2001). Although the reproduction of social inequality is a frequent topic of international discussions about education, this empirical issue is not part of research policy debate in most other nations. The summer learning gap appears to be a uniquely American issue.

To determine whether this is, in fact, the case, we undertook an extensive literature search of non-American sources on the issue of learning and school breaks. We conducted this search in English and several other major languages. Employing a number of social science and educational literature indexes, we used approximately 50 key words and phrases in computer-aided searches. In addition, we searched the names of authors from the American literature on summer learning, as well as research citations in the American studies.

All of our efforts yielded no evidence of research on summer learning, or school-break learning, in nations other than the United States. Although our search was extensive, it is possible that we missed a stray research report on this topic in another nation. It is also important to note that government documents from other nations are not usually included in standard indexes of social science and education research. Nevertheless, at the very least, our lack of findings indicates that this topic is not a significant research undertaking—or issue—outside of the United States.[1]

There are several obvious reasons why this is the case: first and foremost is the unique (some would say "anachronistic") American school calendar, which was based on agrarian families' need for seasonal child labor (Stover, 1989). The custom of basing the school calendar on the needs of farm families stemmed from a rapidly expanding, mass school system in rural areas of the United States during the 19th century, and the practice has been imbedded in the modern American school schedule (Baker, 1999; Meyer, Tyack, Nagel, & Gordon, 1979). This means that American schools have a longer continuous break during the summer than most other national school systems, which often spread breaks out in smaller amounts over the school year (the ramifications of in-class time are considered later). Given the more localized and multilayered governance structure in the United States, it would be difficult to change these traditions for the entire nation. Consequently, American researchers who study summer learning have chosen a question that is particularly salient in the American schooling process: namely, what happens to students' ability to retain learned material over a relatively long break from school? We could also ask this question about students in nations with shorter

---

[1]We did find one exception to this trend. Due to extremes in daylight and traditional agrarian rhythms, the Icelandic school year contains an extensive summer break that is even longer than the average U.S. break. This has generated some research and policy discussion in this country about a summer learning gap (I. Sigfusdottir, personal communication, May 15, 2001).

breaks, but it is unlikely that one would see the types of dramatic losses found in the United States.

The second reason that summer learning loss is a uniquely American issue is that the institutional arrangement of schooling focuses American politics and research on educational inequalities. Historically, educational inequalities have been a significant issue in American political debates on a number of major social questions (Riordan, 1997). From racial integration to social welfare policy, the way in which American schools bring different levels of resources to bear on educating different groups of children has been a central research area (Baker, 1994). Heyns's (1978) original analysis of summer learning was very much within this historical tradition, and the salience to the public of findings that socioeconomic status and race are related to gaps in learning retention and enhancement over the summer are evidence of this broader issue of inequality in American education. In fact, compared to other nations, the uniquely American blend of comprehensive schooling and multilayered local governance has yielded stark educational inequality (Gamoran & Weinstein, 1998), and this paves the way for research on many topics that shed light on the creation of learning gaps.

Finally, one should not underestimate the impact of the world's largest national collection of education researchers all searching for relevant research topics. At last count, there was approximately one American PhD doing education research for every 2,000 students in kindergarten through 12th grade (Baker, 1994). There are a number of reasons for this that we do not describe here, but the fact is that this number represents, by a significant margin, the largest pool of analysts in any one nation. Given this, any and all salient features of the American education system will be studied—often by a number of researchers. The literature on the summer learning gap has that quality to it. In other words, the issue exists and hence it should be studied. Furthermore, when reading this literature, one is struck by the general lack of theoretical perspectives brought to bear on the issue. The questions tend to be purely empirical and technocratic— what does this feature do to learning and what does this mean for policy?

DOES THE AMERICAN SUMMER BREAK
LOWER IN-CLASS TIME TO LEARN?

Research making the distinction between instructional time and instructional content is a perennial favorite among scholars and policymakers who engage in cross-national comparisons (McKnight et al., 1987; Purvis & Levine, 1975; Schmidt et al., 1998; Smith, 2000; Stevenson & Stigler, 1992). Although in reality these are inseparable, researchers often examine the amount of time devoted to instruction in schools as a separate and central resource in the schooling process. The growing literature on opportunities to learn in schools frequently analyzes the amount of time devoted to academic instruction, and instructional time is a common point in comparisons of cross-national studies of educational resources (Borg, 1980; Huyvaert, 1998; National Education Commission on Time and Learning, 1994; Nelson, 1990; Slattery, 1995; Smith, 2000; Walberg, 1988; Wayne & Walberg, 1980). There are often thresholds of both low and high levels of resources that seem to constrain some of the effects of instructional time (Tedesco, Finn, Krallman, Salmon, & Davis, 1979). However, time devoted to instruction and learning, especially subject-specific instruction, seems to be positively related to student achievement, in general, and in the corresponding subject area, in particular (Holsinger, 1982; Larsen, 1989; Office of Educational Research & Improvement, 1986; Smith, 2000; Stevenson, 1983; Tedesco et al., 1979). In addition, although instructional time is interwoven with the quality, timing, and content of instruction, it is nevertheless a central component of school resources (Fisher & Berliner, 1985; Lee, Smith, & Croniger, 1997; Ralph, 1994; Yair, 2000b).

Across the roughly 15,000 local American school districts, the average school calendar is notable for its long, formal summer break, especially when compared to school calendars in many other nations (Stover, 1989). Most other nations have systems with shorter, more equally spaced breaks, and some nations (e.g., Japan) have formal school mechanisms built into the system to help students retain what they have learned over breaks. What does the American school calendar mean for in-class instructional time compared to other nations?

An answer to this question, at least for the academic subjects of mathematics and science, is provided by the data of the Third International Mathematics and Science Study (TIMSS). TIMSS was a large international study of 4th-, 8th-, and 12th-graders and was conducted during the 1994 to 1995 academic year (Beaton, Martin, Mullis, Gonzalez, Smith, & Kelly, 1996; Beaton, Mullis, Martin, Gonzalez, Kelly, & Smith, 1996). The data included a wide variety of information about the schooling process in a number of nations; information came from nationally representative samples of students and their teachers and schools. For our analysis, we use the available data on instructional time from approximately 41 nations, and focus solely on the eighth grade.[2]

---

[2]Nation data available from the Third International Mathematics and Science Study include the following: Australia, Austria, Belgium (French and Flemish independently), Bulgaria, Canada, Colombia, Cyprus, the Czech Republic, Denmark, England, France, Germany, Greece, Hong Kong, Hungary, Iceland, the Islamic Republic of Iran, Ireland, Israel, Italy, Japan, the Republic of Korea, Kuwait, Latvia, Lithuania, Mexico, the Netherlands, New Zealand, Norway, the Philippines, Portugal, Romania, the Russian Federation, Scotland, Singapore, the Slovak Republic, Slovenia, South Africa, Spain, Sweden, Switzerland, Thailand, and the United States.

We measure several elements related to in-class instructional time, as well as how school time relates to course offerings in mathematics and science. First, in-class time simply represents the amount of time in hours, days, and weeks per year that schools devote to academic instruction. Second, instructional time and its effects on students' opportunity to learn represents the hours per year devoted to either math or science instruction.

Across these nations, eighth-grade students are in school for a yearly average of 38.5 weeks (*SD* = 4.5). During the school year, they receive an average of 1,124 hours (*SD* = 249) of academic instruction in all subjects. The average school calendar in the United States yields about 3 fewer weeks of schooling than the average among all of the nations in our sample. However, school calendars in other nations like Hong Kong, Iceland, and New Zealand yield even fewer weeks in school. The United States is also below the international average in total instructional time, with a national average of 1,101 hours, but there is a wide range of variation in hours of instruction across these nations—many yield considerably fewer hours of instruction than the United States. For example, although school calendars in Sweden, Iceland, Germany, and Singapore have relatively similar numbers of weeks in school, the organization of the school day in the these nations yields fewer total instructional hours than one would find in the average American school. These trends are illustrated for the United States and selected other industrial nations in Fig. 3.1.

The picture becomes even more interesting when we compare only hours of instruction in mathematics and science across these nations. Although the average American school calendar produces fewer weeks in school, and slightly fewer total hours of instruction than the international average, American schools actually provide higher-than-average hours of mathematics and science instruction. The international average is 125 and 131 hours per year in mathematics and science instruction, respectively, whereas the U.S. average is 145 and 140 hours, respectively. As Fig. 3.2 shows, time devoted to mathematics and science instruction in the average American school is greater than the international average and is on par with most other industrial nations that participated in the TIMSS.

Despite its relatively long summer break, the American school calendar does not appear to render lower amounts of instructional time for the core academic subjects of mathematics and science. Indeed, the average school in the United States tends to devote more time to these subjects during the school year than schools in many other nations. Given the relatively short school year in the United States, this is most likely due to the emphasis placed on these subjects in both popular and policy discussions of education.

Recently, educational reforms in the United States have been driven in large part by concerns over student performance in international compari-

Instructional hours per year

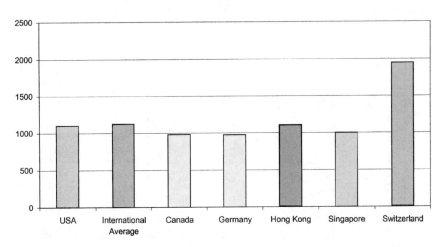

Instructional weeks per year

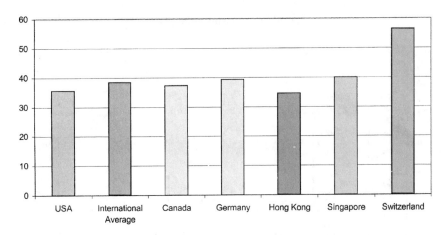

FIG. 3.1.   Instructional time per year for eighth grade.

sons of mathematics and science education. Starting with responses to the "Nation at Risk" report (Commission on Excellence in Education, 1983), American schools have been encouraged to reorganize mathematics and science curricula, and it is likely that the result has been more instructional time devoted to these subjects. Unfortunately, the TIMSS data cannot tell us about how language arts, music, visual arts, and other subjects fare in international comparisons of in-school instructional time.

Math hours per year

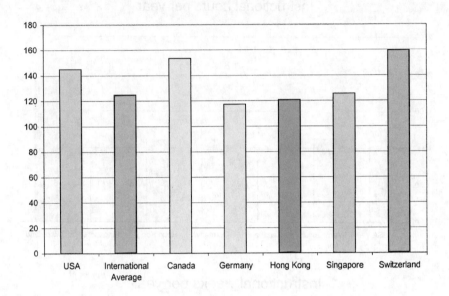

Science hours per year

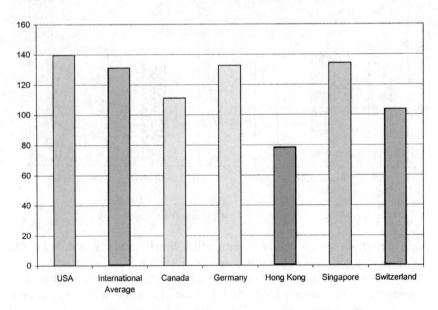

FIG. 3.2. Instructional time by content area for eighth grade.

THE IMPACT OF SCHOOLING ON OUT-OF-SCHOOL
TIME: THE RISE OF SHADOW EDUCATION

A major theme across the chapters in this book is that what happens outside of formal schooling matters to what happens during school. The skills, home resources, and attitudes that students bring with them to school have often been shown to make large differences in how much material students actually learn during the hours of school. But, increasingly, what happens outside of school is done explicitly by families to enhance their children's learning in school. Another way to think about this is to turn the issue around and ask what has been the ever-growing impact of schooling on the lives of children and families in terms of their use of time outside of school. One distinct trend in the United States and elsewhere is that more and more families are using formally organized attempts to help their children master academic material during time outside school. There is a rise in the number of families purchasing extra instruction for their children in the form of tutoring, so-called "cram" schools, correspondence courses, and other formal outside-school venues to help their children master school curricula. Researchers studying the dynamic relation between school and family influences on achievement have come to refer to the host of structured outside-school achievement activities as "shadow education" (Stevenson & Baker, 1992).

The term *shadow education* conveys the image of students using outside-school learning activities that parallel features of their formal schooling to increase their own educational opportunities (Bray, 1999; George, 1992; LeTendre, 1994; Tsukada, 1991). These activities go well beyond routinely assigned homework: instead, they are organized, structured learning opportunities that adopt the processes used by regular schools. The after-hours cram schools found in some Asian countries (e.g., *juku* in Japan) are the most extreme in mimicking in-school forms. However, there is a wide variety of activities that share a similar logic, such as correspondence courses, one-on-one private tutoring, examination prep courses, and full-scale preparatory examination schools (e.g., Japanese *yobiko*; Rohlen, 1980). For example, systems of tutoring are extensive in Hong Kong, Singapore, Taiwan, Korea, Greece, and Turkey. Observers of education systems throughout the world have commented on the growth in shadow educational activities (Bray, 1999; de Silva, 1994; Foondun, 1998; Hussein, 1987; Kwan–Terry, 1991; Stevenson & Baker, 1992).

Figure 3.1 illustrates both the prevalence of shadow education worldwide and some interesting variation across nations. In these nations, 4 out of 10 seventh and eighth graders (39.6%) participate weekly in outside-school tutoring sessions, cram schools, and other forms of shadow education. Approximately one third of students worldwide, on average, are

buying significant amounts of shadow education. Although in some nations these proportions are much lower (e.g., Denmark and England), in
other nations (e.g., Colombia, Latvia, and the Slovak Republic), the proportion of families using shadow education is well over 75%. American
students typically use these outside-school learning opportunities at a rate
of 35% to 40%. Other analyses of the cross-national pattern of use of
shadow education found that nations with lower per-pupil public funding for schooling and less-well-developed access to public education were
more likely to have very high rates of shadow education use (Baker et al.,
2001). It is also of interest that the presence of high-stakes examinations in
nations did not drive the use of shadow education.

This leads to the last point of interest about the spread of outside
schooling through many nations, as shown in Fig. 3.3. Why do most students use outside-school instruction? For participants in the TIMSS sample, it turns out that remediation is by far the most common reason to use
shadow education. That is, in most nations, the families who bought these
activities for their children did so because their children were having
problems mastering mathematics in school.

Figure 3.4 illustrates the dominant trend of remedial outside-school instruction in most nations. There are very few nations in which families use
shadow education to enhance the skills of students who are already good
at math and prepare them for advanced educational opportunities. Even
the much-acclaimed Japanese system of shadow education for enhancement of students' chances on high-stakes entrance examinations for secondary school and university is not completely an enhancement model.
As in other nations, Japan has a significant proportion of students using
these activities just to keep up with basic mathematics. In all nations, there
are students who use shadow education for enhancement, but, for most,
the larger component is remedial.

These findings about shadow education have several implications for
thinking about how schools shape nonschool time. Clearly, the importance of academic achievement for children's future opportunities has
been at the heart of a spreading use of outside-school instruction. The
role of school in everyday life takes on greater intensity and import for
families and students as schooling becomes the primary formal institution by which social status is channeled across generations within families; a major socializing agent to an increasingly complex, adult world;
and the main generator of a society's technical knowledge (Meyer,
Ramirez, & Soysal, 1992). Organizing outside-of-school learning as a
part of everyday family life (through either shadow education or direct
teaching by parents) is one clear outcome of this process that will only
intensify in the future.

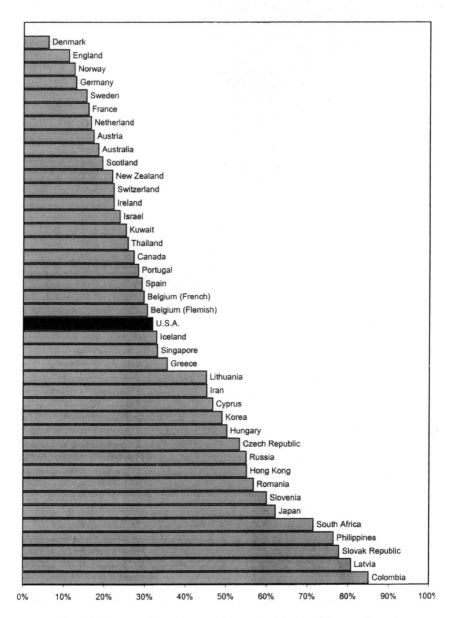

FIG. 3.3. Percent of weekly extra lesson participation by seventh and eighth grade math students.

63

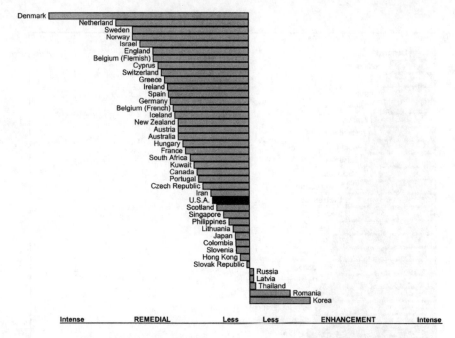

FIG. 3.4.   Intensity of remedial versus enhancement strategy for use of shadow education in nations.

A second implication points to the creation of achievement gaps between students who have access to better formal schooling, the ability to purchase shadow education, and enriched family environments to help them learn academic material—and those who do not. There is a significant body of literature which suggests that, although the structure of schooling is comprehensive and massified, the resources for and content of instruction remain highly stratified, and that it is this aspect of schooling which influences or correlates with students' retention or reinforcement of academic content outside of schooling. Yair (2000a) argued that minority students are particularly susceptible to educational inequality regarding access to formal schooling both inside and outside of schools. So, the instructional time argument is intricately woven into the argument over stratification of content of instruction because disengaging content leads to decreased instructional time overall, especially for minority students.

Like all educational resources, shadow education presents yet another avenue to deepen already significant gaps in educational opportunity and performance based on social class (Stevenson & Baker, 1992). This presents an array of challenging problems for policymakers as they attempt to address education inequalities. The issues now go well beyond what happens in schools to include what happens informally at home.

CONCLUSIONS

Looking at the American summer learning gap from an international point of view and in comparison with other nations brings a new perspective to this important issue. We have suggested that the summer learning gap is a uniquely American issue because of the characteristics of the U.S. school calendar and the American system of educational policymaking. We also suggest that the American summer break, although lengthy, does not significantly lower in-class time to learn in comparison to other nations. And, in fact, we find evidence that American schools provide more hours of instruction in math and science than the international average. Finally, we suggest that there is a great deal of afterschool instruction or out-of-school instructional time (i.e., shadow education) in many nations, including the United States. We present evidence that not only is there formal instruction and structure to this shadow education, but also that, in most nations, it is used for remedial rather than enhancement purposes. So, although shadow education presents an opportunity to amplify social gaps in educational opportunity and performance in a way not often discussed in previous analyses of the summer learning gap, simply participating in shadow education does not necessarily constitute an academic advantage for either the individual participating or the individual students' nation as a whole.

So, what policy lessons can we take from this comparative analysis? First, the summer learning gap is not a pressing issue in other nations, as it is in the United States. Indeed, such a gap certainly exists in the United States, but, because of the rise of formal out-of-school instruction, the benefits and privileges of social class may no longer be as academically advantageous for students as they once were because access to shadow education is no longer privileged. We are not suggesting that the summer learning gap has disappeared. In fact, there is still much evidence to the contrary. Instead, we suggest that formal instruction is becoming increasingly incorporated into students' lives, both in and out of school—meaning that the opportunity to learn is no longer simply a function of in-school instructional time.

Consequently, our second policy point is that increased in-school instructional time is not necessarily the solution to an American summer learning gap. Although examples from other nations have often focused on the extended school hours in typically high-achieving nations like Japan, American policymakers can take heart that U.S. students receive as much or more in-school instructional time as students in other nations. Our international analyses also show that, as institutions and organizations outside of the formal school organization itself begin to incorporate schooling processes into their activities, families in less funded and less enrolled systems increasingly use out-of-school instruction. So, shadow education is a viable option even in systems or districts that are economically or otherwise disadvantaged. This contradicts many assumptions of previous discussions of the summer learning gap, especially the assumption that only families in advantaged communities or situations would have access to, or take advantage of, out-of-school learning. In other words, shadow education makes the debate over summer learning much more complex.

Third, the growth of formal out-of-school instruction is not a clear-cut solution to gaps in learning during school breaks, but the phenomenon certainly warrants further investigation and attention from both researchers and policymakers. Because even year-round school schedules provide extended, albeit shorter, breaks for students, the real question is not whether or how much learning takes place during these extended breaks, but instead, how formal out-of-school instruction throughout the whole year influences students' opportunities to learn. Therefore, policymakers should be looking at opportunity and access issues to formal out-of-school instruction.

An international perspective on the American summer learning gap suggests that gaps in learning during extended breaks in school may no longer be the most pressing concern. Both advantaged and disadvantaged families are increasingly taking the opportunity to give their children formal out-of-school instruction. This gives rise to another question for future research: Is more opportunity for formal instruction, both inside and outside of schools, always the best solution to achievement or learning disadvantages? The evidence, and our analysis of the summer learning gap, suggest not, but until educational researchers and policymakers embrace the investigation of shadow education in the United States and in other nations, we will not know with any certainty.

REFERENCES

Baker, D. P. (1994). In comparative isolation: Why comparative research has so little influence on American sociology of education. *Research in Sociology of Education and Socialization, 10*, 53–70.

Baker, D. P. (1999). Schooling all the masses: Reconsidering the origins of American schooling in the postbellum era. *Sociology of Education, 72*, 197–215.

Baker, D. P., Akiba, M., LeTendre, G. K., & Wiseman, A. W. (2001). Worldwide shadow education: Outside-school learning, institutional quality of schooling, and cross-national mathematics achievement. *Educational Evaluation and Policy Analysis, 23*, 1–18.

Beaton, A. E., Martin, M. O., Mullis, I. V. S., Gonzalez, E. J., Smith, T. A., & Kelly, D. L. (1996). *Science achievement in the middle school years: IEA's Third International Mathematics and Sci-*

ence Study (TIMSS). Chestnut Hill, MA: Boston College, Center for the Study of Testing, Evaluation, and Educational Policy.

Beaton, A. E., Mullis, I. V. S., Martin, M. O., Gonzalez, E. J., Kelly, D. L., & Smith, T. A. (1996). *Mathematics achievement in the middle school years: IEA's Third International Mathematics and Science Study (TIMSS)*. Chestnut Hill, MA: Boston College, Center for the Study of Testing, Evaluation, and Educational Policy.

Borg, W. R. (1980). Time and school learning. In C. Denham & A. Lieberman (Eds.), *Time to learn* (pp. 33–72). Washington, DC: National Institute of Education.

Bray, M. (1999). *The shadow education system: Private tutoring and its implications for planners*. Paris: UNESCO International Institute for Educational Planning.

Commission on Excellence in Education. (1983). *A Nation at Risk*. Washington, DC: Government Printing Office.

de Silva, W. A. (1994). *Extra-school tutoring in the Asian context with special reference to Sri Lanka*. Maharagama, Sri Lanka: Department of Educational Research, National Institute of Education.

Fisher, C. W., & Berliner, D. C. (Eds.). (1985). *Perspectives on instructional time*. New York: Longman.

Foondun, A. R. (1998). *Private tuition: A comparison of tutoring practice in Mauritius and some Southeast Asian countries*. Bangkok, Thailand: UNICEF East Asia & Pacific Regional Office.

Gamoran, A., & Weinstein, M. (1998). Differentiation and opportunity in restructured schools. *American Journal of Education, 106*, 385–415.

George, C. (1992, April 4). Time to come out of the shadows. [Singapore] *Straits Times*, p. A1.

Heyns, B. L. (1978). *Summer learning and the effects of schooling*. New York: Academic.

Holsinger, D. B. (1982, September). *Time, content and expectations as predictors of school achievement in the USA and other developed countries: A review of IEA evidence*. Paper presented at the meeting of the National Commission on Excellence in Education, New York.

Hussein, M. G. A. (1987). Private tutoring: A hidden educational problem. *Educational Studies in Mathematics, 18*, 91–96.

Huyvaert, S. H. (1998). *Time is of the essence: Learning in schools*. Needham Heights, MA: Allyn & Bacon.

Kwan–Terry, A. (1991). The economics of language in Singapore: Students' use of extracurricular language lessons. *Journal of Asian Pacific Communication, 2*, 69–89.

Larsen, R. W. (1989). Beeping children and adolescents: A method for studying time use and daily experiences. *Journal of Youth and Adolescence, 18*(6), 511–530.

Lee, V. E., Smith, J. B., & Croninger, R. G. (1997). How high school organization influences the equitable distribution of learning in mathematics and science. *Sociology of Education, 70*, 128–150.

LeTendre, G. K. (1994). Distribution tables and private tests: The failure of middle school reform in Japan. *International Journal of Educational Reform, 3*, 126–136.

McKnight, C. C., Crosswhite, F. J., Dossey, J. A., Kifer, E., Swafford, J. O., Travers, K. J., et al. (1987). *The underachieving curriculum: Assessing U.S. school mathematics from an international perspective*. Champaign, IL: Stipes.

Meyer, J. W., Ramirez, F. O., & Soysal, Y. N. (1992). World expansion of mass education, 1870–1980. *Sociology of Education, 65*, 128–149.

Meyer, J. W., Tyack, D., Nagel, J., & Gordon, A. (1979). Public education as nation-building in America: Enrollments and bureaucratization in the American states, 1870–1930. *American Journal of Sociology, 85*, 591–613.

National Education Commission on Time and Learning. (1994). *Prisoners of time*. Washington, DC: U.S. Department of Education. (ERIC Document Reproduction Service No. ED 366 115)

Nelson, S. (1990). *Instructional time as a factor in increasing student achievement.* Portland, OR: Northwest Regional Educational Laboratory.

Office of Educational Research and Improvement. (1986). *Time spent on mathematics instruction and homework by Japanese and U.S. 13-year-old students* (OERI Bulletin). Washington, DC: U.S. Department of Education, National Center for Education Statistics.

Pill, G. (1972). U.S. schedule and British timetable: A comparison of concepts. *Journal of General Education, 24,* 37–50.

Poe, J., & Cohen, J. S. (1998, June 19). School's out but not for long. *Chicago Tribune,* p. A1.

Purvis, A., & Levine, D. (Eds.). (1975). *Educational policy and international assessment: Implications of the IEA Survey of Achievement.* Berkeley, CA: McCutchan.

Ralph, J. (1994). Understanding the performance of U.S. students on international assessments. *Education policy issues: Statistical perspectives.* Washington, DC: National Center for Educational Statistics.

Riordan, C. H. (1997). *Equality and achievement: An introduction to the sociology of education.* New York: Longman.

Rohlen, T. (1980). The *Juku* phenomenon: An exploratory essay. *Journal of Japanese Studies, 6,* 207–242.

Schmidt, W. H., McKnight, C. C., Cogan, L. S., Jakwerth, P. M., & Houang, R. T. (1999). *Facing the consequences: Using TIMSS for a closer look at U.S. mathematics and science education.* Boston: Kluwer.

Schmidt, W. H., McKnight, C. C., Jakwerth, P. M., Cogan, L. S., Raizen, S. A., Houang, R. T., et al. (1998). *Facing the consequences: Using TIMSS for a closer look at United States mathematics and science education.* Boston: Kluwer Academic.

Schmidt, W. H., McKnight, C. C., & Raizen, S. A. (1997). *A splintered vision: An investigation of U.S. science and mathematics education.* Boston: Kluwer Academic.

Shields, C. M., & Oberg, S. L. (2000). *Year-round schooling: Promises and pitfalls.* Lanham, MD: Scarecrow Press.

Sirotnik, K. A., & Oakes, J., (Eds.). (1986). *Critical perspectives on the organization and improvement of schooling.* Boston: Kluwer.

Slattery, P. (1995). A postmodern vision of time and learning: A response to the National Education Commission Report "Prisoners of Time." *Harvard Educational Review, 65,* 612–633.

Smith, B. (2000). Quantity matters: Annual instructional time in an urban school system. *Educational Administration Quarterly, 36*(5), 652–682.

Stevenson, D. L., & Baker, D. P. (1992). Shadow education and allocation in formal schooling: Transition to university in Japan. *American Journal of Sociology, 97,* 1639–1657.

Stevenson, H. W. (1983). *Making the grade: School achievement in Japan, Taiwan, and the United States. Annual report of the Center for Advanced Study in the Behavioral Sciences* (Tech Report No. ClQ12675). Stanford, CA: Stanford University, Center for Advanced Study in the Behavioral Sciences.

Stevenson, H. W., & Stigler, J. W. (1992). *The learning gap: Why our schools are failing and what we can learn from Japanese and Chinese education.* New York: Simon & Schuster.

Stover, D. (1989). Should schools plow under the old agrarian calendar? *American School Board Journal, 176*(10), 37.

Tedesco, L. A., Finn, J. D., Krallman, D. A., Salmon, M. J., & Davis, E. L. (1979, April). *School and classroom processes: A secondary analysis.* Paper presented at the annual meeting of the American Educational Research Association, San Francisco.

Tsukada, M. (1991). *Yobiko life: A study of the legitimation process of social stratification in Japan.* Berkeley: University of California Press.

Veenman, S., Lem, P., & Winkelmolen, B. (1985). Active learning time in mixed age classes. *Educational Studies, 11,* 171–180.

Walberg, H. J. (1988). Synthesis of research on time and learning. *Educational Leadership, 45*(6), 76–85.
Wayne, F. C., & Walberg, H. J. (1980). Learning as a function of time. *The Journal of Educational Research, 20,* 183–194.
Yair, G. (2000a). Not just about time: Instructional practices and productive time in school. *Educational Administration Quarterly, 36*(4), 485–512.
Yair, G. (2000b). Reforming motivation: How the structure of instruction affects students' learning experiences. *British Educational Research Journal, 26,* 191–210.

II

SUMMER SCHOOL AND THE STANDARDS MOVEMENT

The Chicago Summer Bridge program, discussed in chapter 4, and the Boston Transition Services program, discussed in chapter 5, are examples of the recent wave of summer programs designed to play key roles in the educational standards movement and related efforts to end social promotion. Although many schools have long offered some type of summer school programming, these efforts were generally relegated to the periphery of school reform and improvement.

The introduction in 1996 of Chicago's Summer Bridge program marked the first time in recent history that summer school was designed to be a core element of school reform. The centerpiece of the Chicago effort is a set of promotion standards for key grades with specific-cutoff scores on standardized tests. Students who do not meet the cutoff score face retention in grade or may attend summer school and attempt the test again at the end of the summer.

In chapter 4, Roderick, Jacob, and Bryk use achievement test data from the first 3 years of implementation to examine the impact of Chicago's approach on students at different skill levels. Roderick and her colleagues also meet significant methodological challenges by developing estimates of program impacts that adjust for the fact that students are placed in the Summer Bridge program because of low test scores. These methods, which may inform other efforts to measure the impacts of targeted interventions, provide far more reasonable estimates of the value-added effects of the program than simple pretest and posttest gain scores.

As part of a broader effort to end social promotion and raise performance on statewide tests, Boston's Transition Services program provides a
similar mandatory summer school for low-performing students. Boston's
program differs from Chicago's Summer Bridge, however, in some important ways. In contrast to the centrally designed and administered Summer
Bridge program, Boston's summer curriculum is designed primarily by
individual schools and teachers. In chapter 5, John Portz uses enrollment
data, end-of-summer test scores, and final promotion–retention decisions
to highlight some of the design and implementation issues that seem to be
unique to summer school programs. For instance, should the summer curriculum be an extension of the curriculum used during the regular year or
should summer school provide an alternative approach? Portz also takes a
close look at the rates of student enrollment and daily attendance. Given
Boston's mandatory attendance policy and the threat of retention, the
rates of noncompliance appear to be higher than one might expect. Portz's
data allow him to examine the rate of promotion among both compliant
and noncompliant students.

Michigan's summer programs, described by Scott Paris and his colleagues in chapter 6, provide an interesting contrast to the summer programs in Chicago and Boston. Whereas the preceding chapters each focused on the summer school programs of a single district, Paris and his
colleagues looked at 19 reading programs for grades kindergarten
through third across the state of Michigan. Beyond standardized test
scores, Paris and his colleagues examine data from authentic reading assessments, extensive surveys of parents and teachers, teacher logs that describe daily classroom practices, and observations of summer classrooms
by the research team. Among other things, this rich data set provides
classroom-level information which allows the research team to identify
the characteristics of the most successful programs. Paris and his colleagues show that summer reading programs can provide significant advantages to young children who are at risk for low achievement, and that
those gains are sustained during the following school year. The greatest
gains appeared for the youngest and most struggling readers.

4

Summer in the City: Achievement Gains in Chicago's Summer Bridge Program

Melissa Roderick
University of Chicago

Brian A. Jacob
Harvard University

Anthony S. Bryk
University of Chicago

Until recently, the summer offerings of most major school systems were an array of small and diverse programs, such as remedial or accelerated summer school classes or programs for special populations. Although such efforts provided supplemental opportunities, they were not viewed as core elements of school systems' instructional programs or reform initiatives. In 1996, the Chicago Public Schools (CPS) began a national trend by including a required summer program, Summer Bridge, as a central component in the system's efforts to end social promotion. Over the past several years, mandatory summer programs have expanded rapidly as school administrators struggle with how to provide extra support for students to meet the demands of high-stakes testing. In 1999, New York, Detroit, Boston, and Washington, DC, as well as many states, ran large mandatory summer programs (Johnston, 2000; Mathews, 2000).

This chapter presents an analysis of the gains in achievement test scores in the CPS Summer Bridge program during the first 3 years of implementation. We address three broad questions. First, does Summer Bridge increase student achievement scores? Second, do some students benefit more than others? Third, to what extent does the effect of the program vary across schools?

The first section of this chapter presents a methodology for estimating presummer and postsummer achievement test gains that adjusts for the fact that students get into this program because of a low test score. Using the adjusted summer gains, we compare the achievement gains in Summer Bridge to the effects of other summer school programs and to gains during the academic year. The second section of this chapter examines variation in summer gains across students and schools. Using a two-level Hierarchical Linear Model, we estimate the effect of student and school demographics and prior achievement levels on adjusted achievement test-score gains in Summer Bridge.

CHICAGO'S EFFORTS TO END SOCIAL PROMOTION

In 1996, CPS began an ambitious new initiative aimed at ending social promotion and raising student achievement. Chicago's efforts were heralded by President Clinton in the 1999 State of the Union address and have spurred a wave of similar reforms in major school systems throughout the country. The centerpiece of this initiative is a set of promotional test-score cutoffs for third, sixth, and eighth graders. Students in these grades must now achieve a minimum score on the Iowa Test of Basic Skills (ITBS) in reading and mathematics to be promoted to the next grade.[1] Students who do not meet the criteria in the spring are required to participate in the Summer Bridge program and are retested at the end of the summer. Those who again do not meet the criteria are retained or, if they are 15, are sent to alternative schools called Transition Centers. In the first several years, more than one third of third, sixth, and eighth graders failed to meet the promotional test-score cutoffs by the end of the school year. Of these, more than 22,000 students have attended Summer Bridge each year. Over the past 3 years, CPS retained almost 20% of eligible third graders and approximately 10% of sixth- and eighth-grade students.

From the start, the Summer Bridge program was seen as the innovation that set Chicago's effort apart from previous unsuccessful efforts to end social promotion based on test scores (House, 1998; Roderick, Bryk, Jacob, Easton, & Allensworth, 1999). Summer Bridge is intended to provide students with the extra help they need to remediate poor skills. The program provides third and sixth graders with 6 weeks of instruction for 3 hours per day. Eighth graders attend 4 hours a day for 7 weeks. Summer Bridge

---

[1]The Iowa Test of Basic Skills (ITBS) reports scores in grade equivalents on national norms. A student who is at grade level when the test is given receives a score of that grade plus 8 months. Thus, a third grader who is reading at grade level on national norms would receive a score of 3.8. The promotional test cutoff was set at 2.8 for third graders, 1 year below grade level. Sixth graders needed a 5.3, which equates to 1.5 years below grade level. In 1997, the ITBS cutoff for eighth graders was 7.0. The eighth-grade promotional cutoff was raised to 7.2 in 1998, and to 7.4 in 1999.

is distinguished by its small class sizes, highly prescribed and centrally developed curriculum, and its mandatory high-stakes approach. First, the average class size in the program in 1999 was 16. This is substantially below the average class size in CPS schools of 22. Second, the program is highly monitored and prescribed. There is a centrally developed curriculum that is aligned to the content of the ITBS. Teachers are provided with day-to-day lesson plans and all instructional materials. Teachers are expected to keep up with the pace of the lesson plans, and monitors visit classrooms to check if teachers are on pace. Finally, the mandatory nature of the program, with participation followed by retesting, is intended to increase student motivation, attendance, and work effort.

EVIDENCE ON THE EFFECT OF SUMMER PROGRAMS AND SUMMER BRIDGE IN CHICAGO

In a recent meta-analysis of 93 summer programs, Cooper, Charlton, Valentine, and Muhlenbruck (2000) concluded that remedial summer school programs have a significant positive impact on student achievement. This analysis found that achievement effects of summer programs were larger in mathematics than in reading, and were larger among students in the early primary grades than in the middle grades. Their findings on the components of successful programs would suggest that, among summer programs, Chicago's approach might be particularly effective. Achievement gains in summer school were larger when the program had small class sizes and provided individualized instruction, which Summer Bridge did. Although initially positing that mandatory programs would be less effective because students might be less motivated, Cooper et al. (2000) found that mandatory programs did not provide fewer benefits to students than voluntary ones. In addition, programs where there is a high degree of monitoring of instruction and attendance, and where there is a prescribed program of instruction, produce greater benefits. On the other hand, smaller programs and programs in smaller districts tended to produce greater effects than large-scale programs, possibly due to less administrative complexity.

Early evidence on the effect of Summer Bridge was promising. In a report on the progress of the first group of students who faced the promotional standards, we found that Summer Bridge, and the second chance opportunity it affords, was effective across all three grades in raising the proportion of students who met the test-score criterion for promotion (Roderick et al., 1999; Roderick, Nagaoka, Bacon, & Easton, 2000). In the context of the larger body of research on summer school, these early results suggest that summer programs may be a particularly effective means of helping students to raise their skills under high-stakes testing.

METHOD

Research Questions

This chapter focuses on estimating the extent to which students' experienced test-score gains in the Summer Bridge program. Once we have calculated average program effects, we examine how these gains vary across students and schools. A central question in evaluating the effect of summer programs under high-stakes testing is whether summer intervention is more effective for students who have very low skills, as opposed to students who face more moderate deficits. Although all students in Summer Bridge are selected for the program because their ITBS scores are below the promotional cutoff, some students may be very close to the cutoff standard, whereas others face significant learning gaps. Students with the lowest skills may benefit most from extended instructional time in more homogenous environments, where teachers have the opportunity to spend more class time on basic concepts. On the other hand, students who have very low skills may simply be too far behind to show major gains in short periods of time such as the summer. This problem is exacerbated because of the use of a standardized curriculum in Summer Bridge that is fast-paced, intended to be on "grade level," and focused primarily on the set of skills tested on the ITBS. Students with very low skills may need both more time and different levels of intervention.

In addition, a central component of Summer Bridge is its mandatory approach that uses the threat of retention and a second-chance opportunity to pass the test to motivate students to work hard. Research on motivation finds that students are more motivated to achieve a goal if they believe that goal is attainable and if they feel efficacious in shaping that goal (MacIver, Reuman, & Main, 1995; Stipek, 1996). Students who are closer to the test-score cutoff may show greater motivation in the summer because they are more likely to believe that the goal is within their reach with high levels of work effort. Students who have very low skills, however, may feel less efficacious in their ability to meet the test-score cutoff and may perceive summer programs more as a punishment than as a support, further exacerbating disengagement.

The importance of motivation in shaping Summer Bridge outcomes may also mean that Summer Bridge effects will differ by race and ethnicity. Research on achievement motivation suggests that African American and second-generation students see limited payoffs to education, tend to exert less effort in school as a result, and often form peer groups that disparage achievement and working hard in school (Fordham & Ogbu, 1986; Mickelson, 1990; Suarez–Orozco & Suarez–Orozco, 1995). Steele and Aronson (1998) argued that because of racial stigma, African American students often feel less competent when they believe their ability and intelligence is being judged, leading to underperformance on standardized tests. This work suggests that African American students may be less likely to perceive high performance on a standardized test as something they value, or as a goal that they can obtain, and may be less likely to have peer groups that support a high work-effort response to high-stakes testing. At the same time, the threat of retention and the high-stakes environment of Summer Bridge may promote increased motivation. The consequence of not moving on to the next grade—particularly to high school—creates an incentive that is as much about a student's sense of social status and connection with peers as it is about achievement, which might have a strong motivational effect among minority students. The goal of advancing to the next grade, combined with the more focused attention provided to students in Summer Bridge, may have the potential to transform peer groups from seeing work effort and collaboration with teachers as "selling out" to seeing such effort as holding high personal and peer-group importance. MacIver et al. (1995) found that classrooms where teachers and students are working under the pressure of external assessments have lower levels of antiacademic peer norms and increased peer support for achievement when compared to control classrooms.

A third important source of variation in program effect is whether differences in school quality during the school year will translate into differences in program quality over the summer. The highly prescribed and centralized nature of Chicago's program may work to reduce school effects. School effects, however, could shape the effects of summer programs through two quite different mechanisms. On the one hand, schools that have better-than-average school-year performance may simply be more able to mount successful summer programs because of superior organization and instructional programs, principal leadership, or more highly qualified staff. This would suggest that students who attend Summer Bridge in schools in which students perform better during the school year will obtain better-than-average increases in test scores.

On the other hand, the incentive effects created by Summer Bridge may be greater in schools that are lower performing. To the extent that Summer Bridge effects depend on the motivation of students and of teachers, we might expect students in lower-achieving schools to do better. Schools in which a high proportion of students fail the promotion policy may be more motivated to place a strong emphasis on Summer Bridge. The individual motivational and incentive effects associated with the policy may

be larger in low-achieving schools where the entire community has mobi-
lized to respond to the policy. Students in low-performing schools may receive greater peer and teacher support to increase their test scores and
may feel less stigma associated with summer school than students in
higher performing schools. In addition, at the same time that Chicago
ended social promotion and began Summer Bridge, the school system also
instituted a high-stakes accountability program aimed at the lowest-
achieving elementary schools (Hess, 1999; Roderick, Jacob, & Bryk, 2002).
Thus, low-achieving schools in Chicago that are on, or face the threat of,
school-wide sanction are under more general pressure to raise test scores
across all grades and may see Summer Bridge as meeting the needs of
both individual students and school-wide goals. Most of this effect should
occur in predominantly African American schools, which make up the
majority of schools on probation in Chicago. Roughly 48% of CPS schools
are predominantly African American, but nearly 83% of the lowest-
achieving schools placed on probation were predominantly African American (Roderick, Jacob, & Bryk, 2001). In this chapter, then, we investigate
variation in test-score gains in Summer Bridge by both the achievement
level and racial and ethnic composition of the school.

Data

Data for this chapter are drawn from student test files and other administrative records provided by the CPS. All first-time third-, sixth-, and
eighth-grade students who attended summer school and have nonmiss-
ing test scores for May and August are included in the descriptive analysis. A smaller sample that included only students with complete demographic information and valid test scores in the prepromotional gate year
was used in the cross-school analysis. Approximately 3% of cases were
dropped due to missing data. The analytic sample is not significantly different than the full sample on any observable characteristics, including
race, gender, or prior achievement level.

Estimating Summer Achievement Gains

If Summer Bridge were effective, one would expect the test scores of students to improve from May to August. This suggests that one might simply examine the change in test scores from May to August as an indicator
of learning in summer school. The problem with a simple comparison of
means is that students are selected for Summer Bridge on the basis of scoring below a specific cutoff. On any standardized test, there is considerable
variation in student scores based on factors that are not related to a student's "true" ability. For example, one student may be sick on a testing

day or may accidentally miscode the answer key. Another may have a particularly good testing day or guess right on one question. This means that, given two students with the same true ability, the one who has a "bad" day will be more likely to attend summer school. When this student is retested at the end of the summer, his or her score will likely increase (simply due to chance) even if the program had no impact. This "regression to the mean" artificially inflates learning gains for summer school.

A similar problem occurs when trying to compare summer gains to school-year gains. The simplest method would be to compare learning gains in summer to the gain that students made during the prior school year (e.g., a student's May–August gain to the September–May gain). This is problematic for two reasons. First, if summer school students are those who, by definition, score particularly low in May of the prior year (given their "true" ability), we would artificially deflate the school-year gains. Second, if the new promotional policy encourages students and teachers to work harder during the academic year, achievement gains during the gate year will likely be larger than gains in previous years. To avoid these pitfalls, we use the predicted annual learning gain in years prior to the promotional gate to measure typical school-year gains in the absence of the policy.

In this chapter, we obtain a predicted end-of-year (pre-Bridge) test score and a predicted test-score gain (or prior rate of growth) by estimating a student growth model estimated through Hierarchical Linear Modeling (HLM). The model uses data on a student's entire testing history and on the learning trends of students in both prepolicy (1992–1996) and postpolicy (1997–1999) cohorts. The model is estimated separately for each grade (third, sixth, and eighth) and for each subject (mathematics and reading). The outcome variable is the student's test score in each year in that subject on the ITBS, measured in the grade equivalent (GE) metric. For the purposes of illustration, we describe the sixth-grade model later.

Level 1 is a measurement model in which Y_{ijk} is the achievement at grade i, for student j in school k as shown following:[2]

$$Y_{ijk} = \pi_{ojk} + \pi_{1jk} \text{ (Grade)}_{ijk} + \pi_{2jk} \text{ (Sixth)}_{ijk} + \pi_{3jk} \text{ (Repeat)}_{ijk} + e_{ijk} \quad (1)$$

The "Grade" variable is centered so that it takes on the value of zero in the fifth grade. "Sixth" is a dummy variable that equals 1 in the promotional gate grade and zero otherwise. The coefficient on this variable measures the extent to which the student's sixth-grade test score deviated

---

[2]This model uses a linear model to estimate growth curves. For the purpose of obtaining an adequate prediction of a May test score, this model is adequate and provides results consistent with nonlinear specifications.

from the score that would have been expected based on the student's initial status and learning trajectory up to that point. "Repeat" is a dummy variable that equals 1 when a pregate grade is repeated. This controls for any prior retention experience in estimating each individual's growth trajectory.

Level 2 models the coefficients from the individual growth trajectories as a function of student characteristics.

$$\pi_{0jk} = \beta_{00k} + \beta_{o1k} (Year94)_{jk} + \ldots + \beta_{5k} (Year99)_{jk} + r_{ojk}$$
$$\pi_{1jk} = \beta_{10k} + \beta_{11k} (Year94)_{jk} + \ldots + \beta_{5k} (Year99)_{jk} + r_{1jk}$$
$$\pi_{2jk} = \beta_{20k} + \beta_{21k} (Year94)_{jk} + \ldots + \beta_{5k} (Year99)_{jk} + r_{2jk}$$
$$\pi_{3jk} = \beta_{30k} \text{ (assumed fixed for simplicity)} \tag{2}$$

Because the random effects—r_{0jk}, r_{1jk}, and r_{2jk}—allow the initial status, learning rate, and sixth-grade deviation to vary across students, we have a separate learning curve for each student. The "Year" variables are dummy variables for each cohort in the sample. "Year93" is omitted so the coefficients on the other year indicators represent the extent to which initial status and linear learning rate varied from 1993. Thus, this model estimates a growth curve for each student across time, taking into account that cohort ability levels and achievement growth within grades may be changing over time because of more general changes in the school system (i.e., the effect of other reforms or general improvement in the school system in test scores, including differences in cohort characteristics, such as more affluent students entering the public school system or the expansion of kindergarten or prekindergarten programs). In this model, the 3rd or school level is left unconditional and simply serves to estimate the standard errors correctly.

Using the estimates from this model, we can calculate each student's predicted sixth-grade May test score as follows:

$$\hat{Y}_{6jk} = (\hat{\pi}_{ojk} + r^*_{ojk}) + (\hat{\pi}_{1jk} + r^*_{1jk}), \tag{3}$$

where $\hat{\pi}_{ojk}$ and $\hat{\pi}_{1jk}$ are the predicted fifth-grade score and average annual learning gain, respectively, based on the previously displayed model for students in a particular cohort and school, and r^*_{ojk} and r^*_{1jk} are estimated Bayes residuals for each student. For students who participated in Summer Bridge, the adjusted or "true" summer gain ($\Delta \tilde{Y}_{6jk}$) in the sixth grade is then calculated by subtracting their observed August test score ($Y_{6BRIDGEjk}$) from their predicted May test score($\hat{Y}_{6jk}$). We call this the adjusted summer gain.

$$\Delta \tilde{Y}_{6jk} = Y_{6\,bridgejk} - \hat{Y}_{6jk} \tag{4}$$

We then estimate a slight variation of the previously displayed model to gain an estimated school-year gain for students who attended summer school. In this second model, rather then estimating cohort effects, we estimate a differential effect for students who attended summer school in each year. Thus, at the student level (level 2), we replace equation 2 with the following:

$$\pi_{0jk} = \beta_{00k} + \beta_{01k} \, (Summer97)_{jk} + \pi_{02k} = (Summer98)_{jk} + \pi_{03k} = (Summer99)_{jk} + r_{ojk}$$
$$\pi_{1jk} = \beta_{10k} + \beta_{11k} \, (Summer97)_{jk} + \pi_{12k} = (Summer98)_{jk} + \pi_{13k} = (Summer99)_{jk} + r_{1jk}$$
$$\pi_{2jk} = \beta_{20k} + \beta_{21k} \, (Summer97)_{jk} + \pi_{22k} = (Summer98)_{jk} + \pi_{23k} = (Summer99)_{jk} + r_{2jk}$$
$$\pi_{3jk} = \beta_{30k} \ \text{(assumed fixed for simplicity)} \tag{5}$$

The average school-year gain prior to the gate grade for students who attended summer school in 1997 is then $\pi_{10k} + \beta_{11k}$.

Estimating Variation Across Students and Schools in Summer Bridge Gains: Methodology

This chapter restricts analysis of variation of learning gains to students who were first-time summer school enrollees (e.g., who had not been retained in the previous year) in 1999. We use a two-level HLM in which students i are nested within summer schools j:

$$\Delta \tilde{Y}_{ij} = \pi_{0j} + \pi_{1j}X_{ij} + \pi_{2j}Z_{ij} + e_{ij} \qquad \text{Student Model} \tag{6}$$

$$\pi_{0j} = \beta_{00} + \beta_{01}\overline{X}_j + \overline{Z}_j + r_{0j}$$
$$\pi_{2j} = \beta_{10} \qquad\qquad\qquad \text{School Model}$$
$$\pi_{2j} = \beta_{20} \tag{7}$$

This specification posits that a student's adjusted summer gain $(\Delta \tilde{Y}_{jk})$ varies as a function of his or her demographic characteristics X and his or her prior achievement level Z. Demographic characteristics include age, gender, race, a block measure of poverty rate, and whether the student was stable (e.g., did not change schools during the prior school year). Age is defined as a student's age as of May 1st of that year and is included to examine whether students who are overage for grade encounter greater difficulty in summer school. Race and gender variables include dummy variables for "Black," "Hispanic," and "Boys," as well as interaction terms for Black males and Hispanic males. As a proxy of a student's socioeconomic background, we include a neighborhood poverty measure that is based on 1990 Census data for the block group in which the student lives. The measure combines information on the percentage of men over the age of 18 who are employed and the percentage of families in poverty. To examine how adjusted summer test-score gains varied by students' prior achievement, we include three dummy variables indicating a student's risk of retention. As discussed earlier, because students are selected on the basis of a single test score, evaluating a student's achievement gap on the basis of the test used for placement into the program would introduce significant measurement error. Students may have very low test scores on the May exam either because of persistently low achievement or because of an abnormally poor testing day. Using the test score on which participation in the program is based would most likely result in students with the lowest pre-Summer Bridge test scores gaining the most because of regression to the mean, not because of difference in program impacts among groups. To address this problem, we estimated a student's adjusted test-score gains in Summer Bridge based on an evaluation of the test-score gap, or risk, a student faced on entrance into the promotional gate grade. Risk is defined by the size of the learning gain a student would have had to make in 1 year to meet the test-score cutoff. We evaluated risk based on the student's latent prior-year achievement obtained using the model described earlier (e.g., predicted fifth-grade score in the case of the sixth-grade model). A student was defined as *high risk* for retention if his or her latent prior-year achievement was 1.5 GEs or more below the cutoff at entry into that grade. Because the average sixth grader gains approximately 1.0 GEs on the ITBS, a student who is 1.5 years behind the cutoff at entry into a grade would have to have substantially greater-than-average learning gains to be promoted. Students whose prior achievement was between .5 and 1.5 GEs below the cutoff were considered at moderate risk. Students whose prior achievement scores were within .5 GEs above or below the cutoff were considered at low risk. Students whose prior predicted test scores were .5 GEs above the cutoff were considered at no risk.[3]

We included two additional variables at the student level. "Same school as summer" indicates whether the student attended the same school in the academic year and the summer. The variable "Did not fail in May" indicates whether the student had already met the promotional criteria in that subject. Summer school students were required to attend classes and take exams in both subjects, regardless of which subject(s) they failed in May. For example, a student who met the promotional stan-

---

[3]Risk levels were slightly different for third graders because the metric is quite compressed at the bottom of the scale. In the third grade, *high risk* is defined as one grade equivalent (GE) below test-score cutoff in the second grade. *Moderate risk* is defined as between 1 and .5 GEs below cutoff. *Low risk* is defined as at-cutoff to .5 GEs below, and *no risk* is defined as .5 GEs above cutoff.

dard in mathematics but failed to do so in reading would have attended summer classes in mathematics and taken the mathematics exam in August—although that score would not count for that student in his or her promotional decision.

Level 2 examines the extent to which the average summer gains in school j, π_{0j}, vary according to the demographic ($\overline{X}$) and achievement ($\overline{Z}$) characteristics of the school. Demographic characteristics include the following: the racial composition of the student body (predominantly Black, predominantly Hispanic, predominantly minority, racially mixed),[4] the school average of the school concentration of poverty (a mean of the student level concentration of poverty measure), and the percentage of students in the school that are Limited English Proficient (LEP) as reported by the State Board of Education. *School Mean Prior Achievement* is defined as the average of the student-level prior-achievement scores (i.e., the latent test score in the pregate grade). We also include the percentage of the student body in that grade that had met the test-score cutoff in May (percentage passed in May) and whether the school was on probation during that school year.

Achievement Gains in Summer Bridge: Results

Adjusted Versus Observed Summer Gains. Table 4.1 compares the observed to the adjusted test-score gains of students in Summer Bridge in 1997, 1998, and 1999.[5] A comparison of the observed to adjusted gains reported in Table 4.1 confirms that a simple comparison of pretest and posttest scores leads to substantial overestimates of test-score gains in summer programs. In many cases, adjusted gains are over 50% lower than gains calculated by simply subtracting the August from May test score. At the same time, adjusted gains, particularly in the sixth and eighth grades, remain quite large and are relatively consistent across years. Using the adjusted gains, the average sixth grader who participated in Summer Bridge increased his or her test score by almost 4 months in reading and mathe-

---

[4]A school was defined as the following: predominantly Black if at least 85% of the students were Black, predominantly Hispanic if at least 85% of the students were Hispanic, predominantly minority if at least 85% of the students were Black or Hispanic, and racially mixed if between 70% and 85% of the students were Black or Hispanic. The omitted category included schools with less than 70% of students who were Black or Hispanic.

[5]In this section, we restrict the analysis to those students who need to pass the test to be promoted. Most students who attended Summer Bridge did so because they had low scores in reading or in both reading and mathematics. In 1999, for example, 47% of students in Summer Bridge in all three grades passed the test-score cutoff in mathematics in the spring but failed to reach the cutoff in reading. An additional 35% failed in both subjects, and 18% passed in reading but were required to attend Summer Bridge for mathematics. In the next section, we estimate the effect of needing to pass the exam on test-score gains.

TABLE 4.1
Chicago Summer Bridge Iowa Test of Basic Skills Achievement Gains.
Observed Versus Adjusted Summer Learning Gains
in Reading and Mathematics (Grade Equivalents)

		Reading				Math		
	N	Observed Gain	Adjusted Gain	Effect Size[1]	N	Observed Gain	Adjusted Gain	Effect Size[1]
Third grade								
1997	8,585	.45	.25	.30	6,037	.69	.48	.61
1998	7,547	.32	.11	.13	3,734	.44	.18	.23
1999	6,824	.42	.20	.23	3,857	.51	.26	.34
Sixth grade								
1997	6,548	.69	.38	.37	3,757	.61	.37	.36
1998	4,671	.71	.32	.30	3,426	.68	.44	.44
1999	4,549	.79	.43	.42	2,861	.55	.31	.31
Eighth grade								
1997	4,006	.99	.64	.48	2,522	.73	.47	.51
1998	4,309	1.05	.67	.49	3,690	.78	.58	.64
1999	5,410	.99	.67	.50	2,817	.71	.49	.53

Note. In all cases, gains are statistically significantly greater than zero at the .001 level.
[1]The effect size converts the adjusted gain to a standard deviation increase. It is calculated by dividing the adjusted gain by the standard deviation of test scores in that subject in August. Traditionally, effect sizes would be calculated on the basis of the standard deviation of all students on that test (e.g., the standard deviation of the entire sixth-grade cohort in the Chicago Public Schools on the Iowa Test of Basic Skills reading test). We use an effect size calculated on the basis of the test scores of only students who participated in Summer Bridge to make our estimates comparable to those calculated by Harris Cooper and his colleagues' meta-analysis. Cooper et al. (2000) used an effect size calculation that is the average of the prestandard and poststandard deviation for program participants. Thus, these program effect sizes restrict the standard deviation estimate to only those students who participate in summer programs. Because our adjusted gain is estimated on the basis of a predicted latent test score which corrects for year-to-year fluctuations in performance, the standard deviation of the predicted test scores are substantially below what would be expected from one test-score administration to the next. Therefore, to be conservative, we use the poststandard deviation only.

matics (see Fig. 4.1). Across all 3 years, eighth graders experienced an increase of 6.5 months in reading and over 5 months in mathematics.

Adjusted gains are smaller and more inconsistent among third graders. In the 1st year (1997), third graders demonstrated relatively modest (2.5 months) gains in reading and a half-year gain in mathematics. Adjusted gains were significantly lower in 1998 and were higher again in 1999. Combining effects across years, third graders had adjusted reading gains of roughly 2 months. Gains for third graders were somewhat larger in mathematics, but not nearly as large as those observed for sixth and eighth graders.

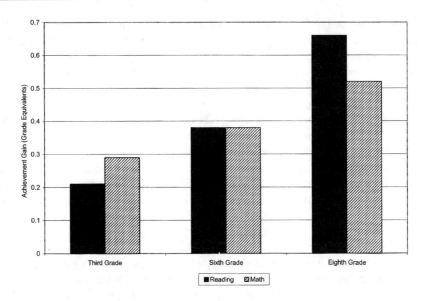

FIG. 4.1.   Summary of 1997–1999 adjusted summer achievement gains.

Chicago Summer Bridge in Comparison to Other Summer Programs

Given the length of the summer program, the adjusted test-score increases among sixth and eighth graders appear quite large. An increase of 4 months in reading for a 6-week program (1.5 months) seems impressive. These gains are also quite large when compared to results from other programs. Cooper et al. (2000) estimated that remedial summer programs produce an effect size of .25 standard deviations. The effect sizes reported in Table 4.1 convert the adjusted learning gains to an equivalent metric. In the third grade, effect sizes are in line with what other research finds—roughly one quarter of a standard deviation. In the sixth grade, effect sizes ranged from a low of .30 in reading in 1998 to a high of .44 in mathematics, also in 1998. On average, effect sizes for sixth grade suggest that students in Summer Bridge increased their test scores by over a third of the standard in achievement on the ITBS. In the eighth grade, effect sizes were approximately half a standard deviation in reading and over a half of a standard deviation in mathematics.

Relative Efficiency of Summer Bridge

A second way to understand the magnitude of the test-score increases in Summer Bridge is to ask the following: How large were these adjusted test gains compared to what these students experienced in the 40 weeks of the prior school year? There are 6 weeks of summer school for third and sixth graders and 7 weeks for eighth graders. There are also 6 weeks between the May ITBS and the end of the school year. If we assume that half of that end-of-school-year time was dedicated to instruction, then third-grade students would have about 9 weeks or 2.25 months of instruction between their May and August testing.[6] The average adjusted gain for third graders of approximately 2.1 months in reading (.21 GEs) suggests that Summer Bridge increased student scores by 1 month for each month of instruction.

Table 4.2 compares the average adjusted test-score increase of students who attended Summer Bridge to their predicted learning gains during the school years prior to the testing year (see Equation 5). These results shed a different light on the relatively poor performance of third graders in Summer Bridge. Although third graders who attended Summer Bridge seemed to increase their test scores by 1 month for a month of instruction during the summer, this was not the case during the school year. The average third grader who attended Summer Bridge gained roughly 4 months in reading during the entire 40 weeks of the school year. The school-year learning rate of sixth and eighth graders who attended Bridge was also lower than average for the system, but the difference was not as large as in the third grade.

We can look at the school-year versus summer comparison more directly by converting these into an efficiency ratio of gains per week in summer versus the school year. To obtain the summer learning rate, we divide the adjusted summer gain by 9 weeks, the number of weeks in summer school plus instructional time at the end of the school year. To obtain the school-year learning rate, we divide the predicted school-year gain by 40, the number of weeks in a typical school year. The summer-school efficiency ratio is the summer learning rate divided by the school-year rate. An efficiency score of 100% indicates that students increased their achievement test scores at roughly the same rate during the summer as in the school year. A score of 200% indicates that, in summer, the students learn at twice the rate of the school year.

The efficiency ratios presented in Table 4.2 suggest that a week in Summer Bridge provided students in all grades with greater test-score increases than a week during the school year. For example, eighth-grade students in Summer Bridge increased their reading achievement at over three times the rate during the summer as compared to the academic year. As a matter of interest, the high ratios in sixth and eighth grade reflect

---

[6]Research on the use of instructional time in the Chicago Public Schools finds that instructional time often declines significantly after testing occurs (Smith, 1998). Thus, our estimates that approximately half of the remaining time between the time of testing and the end of the school year is dedicated to instruction is based on observations that teachers in high-stakes testing environments often "stop" instruction earlier and use class time for other activities.

TABLE 4.2

Comparing Summer to School-Year Learning Rates: Summer Bridge Adjusted Gains, Predicted School-Year Gains, and the Relative Efficiency of School Year Versus Summer Iowa Test of Basic Skills Reading and Mathematics (Grade Equivalents)

	Reading			Mathematics		
	Predicted School-Year Gain	Adjusted Summer Gain	Efficiency (Summer to School Year)[1]	Predicted School-Year Gain	Adjusted Summer Gain	Efficiency (Summer to School Year)[1]
Third grade						
1997	0.438	0.254	258	0.843	0.480	253
1998	0.412	0.112	121	0.766	0.182	105
1999	0.387	0.202	231	0.819	0.259	141
Sixth grade						
1997	0.792	0.380	213	0.694	0.367	235
1998	0.781	0.317	180	0.679	0.443	290
1999	0.788	0.428	241	0.706	0.312	196
Eighth grade						
1997	0.783	0.636	325	0.713	0.472	265
1998	0.827	0.668	323	0.749	0.578	309
1999	0.851	0.666	313	0.788	0.489	248

Note. In all cases, gains are statistically significantly greater than zero at the .001 level.

[1]The efficiency ratio is calculated by comparing the learning rate per week during the school year to summer. So, the efficiency of third-grade Bridge in 1997 is 258% = (.25/9)/(.44/40).

large summer gains, whereas the high ratio in third grade reflects relatively small school-year gains.

RESULTS

This section examines the magnitude of test-score increases in the Summer Bridge program. Taken together, these results provide strong evidence that Summer Bridge has short-term positive impacts on test scores in all grades and in both reading and mathematics. Our results suggest that short-term test-score increases in Summer Bridge are greater among older students, with the largest increases occurring among eighth graders and the smallest effect among third graders. Part of the reason for the smaller relative test-score increases among third graders may be the GE metric. Older students tend to make larger test-score increases than younger students because one more item correct on the ITBS translates into a greater GE increase in the upper than in the lower grades. When we compared the adjusted test-score gains of Summer Bridge students in all three grades to their learning rates during the school year (a method that makes learning gains in Summer Bridge relative to average learning gains at that grade level), we found that the learning rate of students who attended Summer Bridge was above that experienced by these same students during the regular school year.

The finding that sixth and eighth graders in Summer Bridge experienced large test-score gains differs from previous research. Prior evaluations of summer school found that remedial summer programs that serve primary-grade students have larger program impacts than programs serving middle-grade students (Cooper et al., 2000). One hypothesis for the large test-score gains observed in Summer Bridge may be the focus of the curriculum on basic reading and mathematics skills. Cooper et al.'s (2000) analysis found that teachers in early-grade programs tended to report using the summer for more individualized and creative instruction, whereas teachers in middle-school programs tended to emphasize more general study skills in content areas. Thus, the age differences observed in previous research on the effects of summer school may be more driven by the instructional content and foci of programs across grades than by age-related differences in program effects.

A second hypothesis for the relatively large effects of Summer Bridge among older students concerns the motivational response of students. The CPS initiative relies heavily on incentives for students to work harder. Eighth graders face the greatest costs of not meeting the test cutoffs (they do not go to high school) and have the greatest capacity to shape their school performance through their own motivation and effort—including simply working harder on the day of the test itself. It might also be true that eighth graders are at a time in their development when they can more easily learn in short, intensive periods of immersion. In contrast, third graders may be less sensitive to the threat of retention, less able to shape their own learning through effort, and less likely to overcome barriers through intensive learning spurts.

The finding that Summer Bridge produced short-term test-score increases above those observed in other programs raises the following question: How can we understand the relatively positive gains of students in Summer Bridge, both in comparison to these students' school-year learning gains and to other programs? One explanation for the large test-score gains during Summer Bridge involved the high-stakes context of the policy and the high alignment between the curriculum and the test. One might argue that students increase their test scores in Summer Bridge simply because the curriculum teaches students the skills they will need to score higher on the ITBS. In addition, students may be more likely to work harder on the test and pay attention when it matters most, at the time when they face retention. In this view, the summer-school achievement gains are largely the result of "testing" and "test prep" effects and may not represent a greater fundamental mastery of skills and knowledge in reading and mathematics.

An alternative explanation is that Summer Bridge was effective because prior research suggests that many of the critical programmatic components of the program would be conducive to gains in achievement-test scores. First, there is substantial evidence that small class size produces long-term benefits, particularly for low-performing students (Finn & Achilles, 1999; Nye, Hedges, & Konstantopoulus, 1999). Second, the Summer Bridge program may produce more focused instructional time than during the school year. Smith (1998) found that poor time management and low levels of instructional time erode the opportunity to learn in Chicago elementary schools. In the most poorly managed classrooms and schools, Chicago students received about half the recommended hours of instruction. During the summer, however, teachers have few noninstructional demands on their class time, a focused 3-hour time allotment, and clearly defined objectives. The combination of focused instruction, small class sizes, and motivated students may produce more intensive learning environments. Third, the Summer Bridge curriculum may increase the pacing of instruction, giving students greater opportunity to learn. Too often students in low-achieving elementary schools cycle through the same curriculum year after year, without exposure to the skills they are expected to demonstrate on tests such as the ITBS (Smith, Smith, & Bryk, 1998). Finally, because they are hand-picked by principals, the teachers in Summer Bridge may be particularly qualified or motivated.

Variation in Achievement Gains Across Students and Schools

Our analysis so far suggests that, on average, students who attended Summer Bridge during the first 3 years of the program experienced large test-score gains in both reading and mathematics. To what extent were the gains in Summer Bridge shared equally among students of different achievement levels and demographic characteristics? Tables 4.3 and 4.4 present the results of the HLM analysis that estimates the effect of student and school demographics and prior achievement on summer gains. All of the Level 1 coefficients are grand mean centered, with the exception of the variable, "Did not fail subject in May." Thus, the intercept represents that adjusted summer gain for the average student who had to pass the exam in August. Table 4.3 presents the results for reading and Table 4.4 gives the results for mathematics. In Table 4.5, we translate these coefficients into predicted average summer gains for different groups of students, assuming that the groups are average on the other independent variables. Thus, Table 4.5 shows the predicted summer learning gains of students of different risk levels for students who are "average" on the remaining demographic characteristics.

Variation in Summer Gains Across Students

Adjusted summer gains did, in fact, differ by students' prior achievement, or risk, level, but these effects differed across grades. In third grade, students with the lowest achievement had the greatest gains in summer achievement-test scores, whereas in eighth grade, it was the lowest risk group that made the greatest gains. The predicted adjusted gain for high-risk third graders was .26 in reading, compared to only .07 for third graders who were already close to the test-score cutoff. This average gain in mathematics did not differ significantly by whether students were at high or low risk of retention in any of the grades.

Although there is some variation in Summer Bridge effects in reading by prior achievement, perhaps the most striking finding concerns the homogeneity of effects across demographic groups. For example, in the third and eighth grades, none of the coefficients on gender and race are significant. In the sixth grade, Hispanic students did significantly better as did "White or other race males." Because of high levels of immigration, many White and Asian students in the CPS are children of immigrants. Because sixth grade is the grade in which bilingual students are often included under the policy, this positive effect for Hispanics may represent an additional benefit for students transitioning out of bilingual education programs.

TABLE 4.3

Hierarchical Linear Modeling Estimates of 1999 Summer Bridge Adjusted Gains in Reading by School and Student Characteristics (Iowa Test of Basic Skills in Grade Equivalents)

	Third Grade		Sixth Grade		Eighth Grade	
	Coefficient	T-ratio	Coefficient	T-ratio	Coefficient	T-ratio
Intercept	.204	10.32	.455	23.31	.757	19.05
Student characteristics						
Age	-.015	.810	.002	.11	-.10*	3.37
Black	-.010	.17	.063	.92	.029	.22
Hispanic	.025	.41	.167*	2.58	0.40	.34
Boys	-.071	.99	.163*	2.10	.153	1.26
Black male	.010	.14	-.174*	2.11	-.130	.99
Hispanic male	.029	.36	-.190*	2.22	-.082	.61
Prior achievement						
Low risk	.079	1.03	.131	1.50	-.132	1.20
Moderate risk	.078	1.02	.018	.20	-.288*	2.76
High risk	.189*	2.43	.054	.58	-.305*	2.79
Student block group poverty	-.015	.81	-.048	1.74	-.062	1.82
Same school in summer	-.066*	1.99	-.078*	2.34	-.026	.55
Stable over school year	.049	1.80	.055	1.29	-.011	.17
Did not fail subject in May	-.215*	8.23	-.625*	22.16	-.88*	21.74

(Continued)

TABLE 4.3
(Continued)

	Third Grade		Sixth Grade		Eighth Grade	
	Coefficient	T-ratio	Coefficient	T-ratio	Coefficient	T-ratio
School characteristics						
Percentage passed in school in May	.076	.49	-.204	1.18	.207	.67
Mean student prior achievement	.114	1.01	.133	2.23	.129	.95
School concentration of poverty	.002	.03	.042	.87	.096	1.17
On probation in 1998 to 1999	.037	.59	-.093	1.38	-.027	.24
Percentage Limited English Proficient	.003	1.11	.000	.29	-.004	1.03
Predominantly Black	.081	.79	-.076	.93	-.107	.47
Predominantly Hispanic	-.052	-.58	-.176*	2.67	-.245	1.51
Predominantly minority	-.008	-.11	-.194	2.91	-.184	1.05
Racially mixed	.017	.20	-.129	1.87	-.109	.69
	Variance	p-value	Variance	p-value	Variance	p-value
School variance components						
With student predictors	0.00852	0.00	0.05418	0.00	0.30534	0.00
With student and school predictors	0.09006	0.00	0.05418	0.00	0.30011	0.00
Number of students	8,158		6,432		5,197	
Number of schools	338		316		283	

* = coefficient significant at .05 or higher.

TABLE 4.4

Hierarchical Linear Modeling Estimates of Summer Bridge Adjusted Gains in Mathematics 1999 by School and Student Characteristics (Iowa Test of Basic Skills in Grade Equivalents)

	Third Grade		Sixth Grade		Eighth Grade	
	Coefficient	T-ratio	Coefficient	T-ratio	Coefficient	T-ratio
Intercept	.256	16.09	.342	19.74	.484	17.74
Student characteristics						
Age	.049	4.48	.015	1.16	-.047	2.66
Black	-.007	.14	.046	.91	-.067	.95
Hispanic	.038	.79	.057	1.16	-.048	.72
Boys	-.084	1.60	-.088	1.62	-.191*	1.96
Black male	.011	.19	.009	.16	.167	1.64
Hispanic male	-.003	.05	-.000	.00	.179	1.70
Prior achievement						
Low risk	-.008	.39	.043	1.19	-.084	1.72
Moderate risk	-.002	.10	-.020	.53	-.040	.82
High risk	-.002	.06	-.054	1.29	-.051	.91
Student block group poverty	-.037*	2.34	.002	.13	.019	.79
Same school in summer	-.088*	3.59	-.052*	2.16	.010	.23
Stable over school year	.024	1.10	-.027	.94	.003	.07
Did not fail subject in May	.023	1.32	-.025	1.30	-.25*	9.85

(Continued)

TABLE 4.4
(Continued)

	Third Grade		Sixth Grade		Eighth Grade	
	Coefficient	T-ratio	Coefficient	T-ratio	Coefficient	T-ratio
School characteristics						
Percentage passed in school in May	-.154	1.63	.147	.964	.232	1.28
Mean student prior achievement	-.010	.1101	-.059	1.06	-.165	1.49
School concentration of poverty	-.043	1.25	-.008	.22	-.059	.96
On probation in 1998 to 1999	-.009	.23	-.044	1.00	.025	.33
Percentage Limited English Proficient	.000	.02	-.002	1.26	.001	.36
Predominantly Black	-.044	.59	-.159	1.94	-.066	.59
Predominantly Hispanic	-.052	.80	-.092	1.37	-.094	1.14
Predominantly minority	-.064	1.03	-.209*	3.21	-.051	.61
Racially mixed	.022	.38	-.028	.44	.091	.93
	Variance	p-value	Variance	p-value	Variance	p-value
School variance components						
With student predictors	0.03568	0.00	0.03918	0.00	0.13081	0.00
With student and school predictors	0.0359	0.00	0.03736	0.00	0.13069	0.00
Number of students	8,049		6,431		5,197	
Number of schools	338		316		283	

* = coefficient significant at .05 or higher.

TABLE 4.5
Estimated Summer Bridge Gains in Reading 1999 by Student
Characteristics; Hierarchical Linear Modeling Results:
Iowa Test of Basic Skills in Grade Equivalents

	Third Grade		Sixth Grade		Eighth Grade	
	Reading	Math	Reading	Math	Reading	Math
Average estimated gain	.20	.26	.45	.34	.76	.48
Achievement gap						
No risk	.07	.26	.41	.35	1.03	.50
Low risk	.15	.25	.54	.39	.90	.42
Moderate risk	.15	.26	.43	.33	.74	.46
High risk	.26	.26	.47	.30	.72	.55
Race and gender						
Total						
Boys	.17	.22	.53	.30	.83	.39
Girls	.24	.30	.37	.39	.69	.58
Black	.20	.25	.43	.34	.75	.47
Boys	.17	.20	.42	.30	.75	.46
Girls	.22	.30	.43	.38	.73	.49
Hispanic	.23	.29	.53	.35	.77	.50
Boys	.22	.25	.50	.31	.81	.50
Girls	.26	.34	.43	.40	.74	.51
White or other	.21	.25	.36	.30	.72	.54
Boys	.17	.22	.53	.25	.85	.36
Girls	.24	.30	.36	.34	.70	.56
Overage for grade	.19	.21	.46	.36	.66	.44
Summer school						
Same as school year	.19	.24	.44	.33	.75	.48
Different school	.26	.33	.52	.39	.78	.49
Did not fail subject in May	−.01	.26	−.17	.32	−.13	.34

Note. A student risk is based on the student's estimated distance from the test cutoff using their prior-year (e.g., fifth grade for sixth graders) predicted test scores. A student is at high risk if his or her prior-year test score was 1.5 or more grade equivalents (GEs) below the test-score cutoff. Moderate risk is defined as .5 to 1.5 GEs below in the grade prior, and low risk between .5 above or below the cutoff.

Other demographic measures often have the expected sign but are only occasionally significant. For example, older students and those who live in census blocks with a high concentration of poverty tend to have smaller gains than other students. The age effect is significant in third- and eighth-grade mathematics and in eighth-grade reading. We might expect that students who are overage for grade and who have experienced a prior retention would be significantly less likely to believe that participation in the summer program would pay off for them, thus lowering motivation and work effort. Being overage for grade might also be a proxy for general difficulty in school. Although this effect is significant, it does not appear substantively important. For example, the predicted summer gain for an eighth grader who is 1 year older than average was roughly 13% lower in reading and 8% lower in mathematics.

Variables indicating whether the student attended the same school during the academic year and the summer, and whether the student had to pass the exam in August, are significant and important predictors of test-score gains. First, there are consistent positive effects of traveling to a different school for Summer Bridge. In the first 2 years of the program, nearly all schools offered summer school programs. In an effort to save money on busing costs and consolidate some of the smaller programs, in 1999 roughly 15% to 20% of students attended summer school in a different school than they attended during the school year. This was a controversial decision, with many educators and parents arguing that this policy would disadvantage students who had to move because they would have to attend schools where they were unfamiliar with peers and teachers. In fact, the opposite seems to be the case. The coefficient on "same school in summer" is negative in all cases and is significant in the third and sixth grades. Third and sixth graders who traveled to different schools for Summer Bridge gained roughly .06 to .09 more than students who remained in their regular school—gains that are not large but significant. One interpretation is that students were placed in Summer Bridge because they were not successful in their home school, and may thus benefit from a new learning environment. Another interpretation, however, is that those students who attend schools other than their neighborhood elementary schools because of choice are most likely more motivated students or have more involved parents and, thus, would be more likely to do well in Summer Bridge.

There is also a clear pattern of differential gains in reading between students who needed to pass the ITBS test cutoff when they took the exam in August and those who had already reached that standard in May. If summer school gains were driven primarily by student motivation, one would expect that students who did not need to reach the cutoff would show considerably smaller, or even negative, gains. We see some evidence for such incentive effects, particularly in reading. Students who took the reading exam under a low-stakes testing scenario actually scored worse in August than in May. The effect of not having to take the exam was greatest among sixth and eighth graders and smallest among third graders. In mathematics, the effect of taking a low-stakes exam (e.g., of not having to pass that subject) had a significant negative effect only in the eighth grade. One explanation for why these effects are apparent in reading but not mathematics involves the nature of the exams in each subject. Because it requires students to read a variety of passages and answer comprehension questions, the reading exam rewards perseverance. Students who concentrate and work diligently throughout the entire testing period are able to correctly answer many more questions than students who give up more easily. In contrast, the mathematics exam consists of largely self-contained questions.

Variation in Summer Gains Across Schools

Having controlled for student characteristics, we find that there is considerable variation across schools. To get a sense of the range of Summer Bridge effects, consider the 95% plausible value range around the average Summer Bridge gain in reading for sixth graders, .455+/− (1.96 * sqrt (.054) = .455 +/− .455. This suggests that the average gain in reading among sixth graders was zero in some schools and was as high as 9 months (.91) in others. In general, very little of this across-school variation in adjusted test-score gains for Summer Bridge can be explained by standard demographic or achievement characteristics of the school, however. Racial composition, probation status, percentage of students who are LEP, and the mean prior-achievement level of the school, have no significant effect on the school's average summer achievement gains of third- and eighth-grade students in 1999. In the sixth grade, the inclusion of school-level covariates explained roughly 5% of the across-school variation (see the bottom panels of Tables 4.3 and 4.4).

One exception involves racial composition effects in the sixth grade. Students in predominantly Hispanic schools had substantially lower reading gains in sixth grade than students in other schools. For example, sixth graders in predominantly Hispanic schools gained .18 GEs less in reading than comparable students in the average school. A similar effect can be seen in predominantly minority schools (i.e., schools with a high percentage of Black and Hispanic students). In interpreting this finding, it is important to note that even predominantly Hispanic and minority schools made absolute gains in reading in Summer Bridge that were quite large. In the previous section, we also found that Hispanic sixth graders made larger-than-expected gains in Summer Bridge. We hypothesized that Summer Bridge effects among Hispanics in the sixth grade are more complicated because many more students will be exiting bilingual education and subject to the policy for the first time. This school-level effect suggests that Hispanic schools, on average, produced lower gains in the sixth grade and, thus, that Hispanic students who attend non-Hispanic schools benefit more than their counterparts who attend more ethnically homogenous schools.

DISCUSSION

This section focuses on two questions: (a) To what extent is there evidence that Summer Bridge program effects vary by student characteristics? and (b) controlling for student characteristics, is there evidence of variation in program effects across schools? For the most part, Summer Bridge has positive program effects for both boys and girls, for Black and Hispanic students, and for students who face both relatively large and relatively small learning deficits. Students with the lowest achievement had the greatest summer reading gains in the third grade, but the lowest gains in reading in the eighth grade. These across-grade differences in effects by students' skill levels might represent a curriculum effect. In third grade, the curriculum may be better targeted at the skill needs of the lowest achieving students. In the eighth grade, however, students who were farthest behind the test-score cutoff may have had skills that were so low that the curriculum did not address their needs. Eighth graders with the weakest skills may also be experiencing disengagement from school and may have had the greatest difficulty believing that they could increase their test scores and pass, resulting in much lower motivation. Taken together, the lack of any consistent differences in program impacts by student characteristics may be one of the most positive findings in this chapter because it suggests that, despite concerns about running large-scale summer programs, Summer Bridge in Chicago produced rather uniform benefits across students.

We did find substantial across-school variation in program impact, even after controlling for the demographic and achievement characteristics of students. This is particularly interesting given the highly centralized and closely monitored nature of the program. This variation cannot be explained by the demographic or achievement characteristics of the schools. This suggests that school-level decisions about staffing and administration of the program and teacher quality, as well as more general features of school organization, may play a large role in the relative success of Summer Bridge.

CONCLUSION

In an era of high-stakes testing, many school systems are looking for ways to provide extra support for students with low skills to help them meet promotional and testing standards. Summer school has become the most popular approach that large school systems use to address this problem. In light of substantial literature on summer learning loss (see Alexander, Entwisle, & Olson, this volume), summer would seem like an opportune time for intervention. Summer provides concentrated time and the ability to do more focused remedial supports without paying the costs of slowing down instruction during the school year. This chapter analyzed learning gains in Chicago's highly acclaimed Summer Bridge program during its first 3 years of implementation. Our results suggest that Summer Bridge is effective and that summer programs may be a promising approach to providing students extra instructional time and remedial support. In each of the 3 years, sixth- and eighth-grade students demonstrated substantial gains in their test scores. In all three grades, the rate of learning of students who attended Summer Bridge was above that experienced by those students during the regular school year. For the most part, Summer Bridge produced rather uniform gains across demographic and racial and ethnic groups. We do not know the extent to which these gains will be sustained. Some preliminary evidence suggests that students who attended Summer Bridge in 1997 and passed at the end of the summer maintained their learning gains, on average, over 2 years. These students continued to have lower-than-average learning growth during the school year (Roderick et al., 2000). These early results are promising. In subsequent work we will be looking more systematically at the extent to which participation in Summer Bridge produced long-term increases in test scores.

The central policy question facing school systems is this: To what extent are these findings replicable in school systems other than Chicago and, in particular, what components of the program (e.g., small class sizes, curriculum aligned to the ITBS test, and mandatory approach in a high-stakes testing environment) are critical for replication? The small class sizes and instructional support with the help of tutors and aides is the most expensive component of the program. Yet this is the programmatic component that is most supported by prior research.

A second critical question is the role of the curriculum and the high alignment between the curriculum and assessment tool, in this case the ITBS. On the one hand, critics of high-stakes testing would argue that this high alignment reflects "teaching to the test" and would lead to gains on that test that are not generalizable to other measures. On the other hand, these results might be taken as evidence that summer programs work when they have clearly defined instructional objectives and when students are being assessed on the skills they have been taught. In high-stakes testing environments, such alignment may be critical for issues of fairness. It makes no sense to hold students accountable for, and ask them to demonstrate progress on, skills for which they have not had the opportunity to practice. In addition, summer instruction may be most effective when it is focused on a clear set of instructional objectives that can be practiced in limited periods of time, and when teachers know that students will be assessed on those skills. In summation, the choice of assessment, decisions about what skills students should be working on, and the development of curriculum and materials that focus on those skills, must be thought of as a central component of the programmatic design of summer school.

The third programmatic component is the high-stakes testing environment itself. Throughout this chapter, we have highlighted how motivational responses on the part of students might play a role in the magnitude of gains we observe in this program. In particular, we find that the test scores of eighth graders increased the most over the summer. In addition, we found that those Summer Bridge students who passed their reading promotional gate in May actually experienced declines in their reading test scores over the summer, suggesting that these students might have taken the August test less seriously. Motivational responses that occur because students are working harder on a particular test would lead to overestimates of program impact. But motivational responses that occur because students are working harder and attending to their schoolwork throughout the summer would not suggest overestimates of impact but would suggest that the mandatory high-stakes testing environment in the program is critical to its impact. Would we have observed these gains if students were not required to attend? Would we have observed these gains if students did not face the threat of retention and, for eighth graders, the prospects of not going on to high school?

Our results suggest that there is substantial variation across schools in program impact that cannot be explained by the demographic and achievement characteristics of the schools. Even within the highly centralized nature of the program, schools continue to have wide flexibility in decisions about how to staff the program and in other areas of implementation. Schools that may run more effective programs, or have more highly qualified staff, may simply be better equipped to run effective instruction during the summer. Centrally developed curriculum is not teacher-proof. Variation in teacher quality will continue to affect the quality of instruction in the classroom. Centrally developed programs are also not school-proof. This suggests, however, that summer programs need to have high degrees of staff training, monitoring, and support, as well as evaluation of this variation in program impact, if they are not to reproduce inequities in school quality that students are experiencing during the school year. What is important is that our analysis suggests that this variation in program impact is not simply a result of demographic and achievement characteristics of schools.

Finally, in this chapter, we have argued that it is crucial to use more sophisticated methods than simple pretest and posttest comparisons in evaluating summer learning gains, particularly when comparing gains to the school year. Adjusted summer gains were often 50% smaller than observed gains, largely because students were selected into the program on the basis of low May scores; many would have been expected to score higher in August in the absence of any program effect. Once we adjusted for these biases, adjusted summer gains were even more impressive and school systems should not shy away from more rigorous evaluation of program impact.

ACKNOWLEDGMENTS

This research is supported by grants from the Joyce Foundation, the Spencer Foundation, and the Office of Educational Research and Improvement under the Field Initiated Studies program. The content does not necessarily represent the policy of the Department of Education and the reader should not assume endorsement by the federal government. We would like to thank the Chicago Public Schools for providing the data for this study, and, in particular, Dr. Blondean Davis and William McGowan for their cooperation. We are indebted for assistance of John Q. Easton, Miriam Engel, and Jennifer Nagaoka. Thanks to the many members of the Consortium's staff, directors, and steering committee for helpful feedback on the analysis.

REFERENCES

Cooper, H., Charlton, K., Valentine, J. C., & Muhlenbruck, L. (2000). Making the most of summer school: A meta-analytic and narrative review. *Monographs of the Society for Research in Child Development, 65*(1, Serial No. 260).

Finn, J. D., & Achilles, C. M. (1999). Tennessee's class size study: Findings, implications, misconceptions. *Educational Evaluation and Policy Analysis, 21,* 97–110.

Fordham, S., & Ogbu, J. (1986). Black students' school success: Coping with the burden of acting White. *Urban Review, 18,* 176–206.

Hess, G. A. (1999). Expectations, opportunity, capacity, and will: The four essential components of Chicago school reform. *Educational Policy, 13,* 494–517.

House, E. R. (1998). *The predictable failure of Chicago's student retention program.* Unpublished manuscript, University of Colorado, Boulder, CO, School of Education.

Johnston, R. C. (2000, September 6). Bumper summer school crop yields mixed test results. *Education Week, 6,* p. 10.

MacIver, D. J., Reuman, D. A., & Main, S. R. (1995). Social structuring of the school: Studying what is, illuminating what could be. *Annual Review of Psychology, 46,* 375–400.

Mathews, J. (2000, June 13). Hot debate on value of summer school. *The Washington Post,* p. A24.

Mickelson, R. (1990). The attitude achievement paradox among Black adolescents. *Sociology of Education, 63,* 44–61.

Nye, B., Hedges, L. V., & Konstantopoulus, S. (1999). The long-term effects of small class sizes: A five-year follow-up of the Tennessee class size experiment. *Educational Evaluation and Policy Analysis, 21,* 127–142.

Roderick, M., Bryk, A. S., Jacob, B., Easton, J. Q., & Allensworth, E. (1999). *Ending social promotion: Results from the first two years.* Chicago: Consortium on Chicago School Research.

Roderick, M., Jacob, B., & Bryk, A. S. (2002). *The impact of high stakes testing in Chicago on student achievement in promotional gate grades.* Chicago: University of Chicago, School of Social Service Administration.

Roderick, M., Nagaoka, J., Bacon, J., & Easton, J. Q. (2000). *Update: Ending social promotion. Passing, retention and achievement trends among promoted and retained students.* Chicago: Consortium on Chicago School Research.

Smith, B. (1998). *It's about time: Opportunities to learn in Chicago's elementary schools.* Chicago: Consortium on Chicago School Research.

Smith, J. B., Smith, B., & Bryk, A. S. (1998). *Setting the pace: Opportunities to learn in Chicago's elementary schools.* Chicago: Consortium on Chicago School Research.

Steele, C. M., & Aronson, J. (1998). Stereotype threat and the test performance of academically successful African Americans. In C. Jencks & M. Phillips (Eds.), *The Black–White test score gap* (pp. 401–430). Washington, DC: Brookings Institute.

Stipek, D. (1996). Motivation and instruction. In D. C. Berliner & R. C. Calfee (Eds.), *Handbook of educational psychology.* New York, Macmillan.

Suarez–Orozco, M., & Suarez–Orozco, C. (1995). *Trans-formations: Immigration, family life and achievement motivation among Latino adolescents.* Stanford, CA: Stanford University Press.

5

Summer School 2000 and 2001: The Boston Public Schools Transition Services Program

John Portz
Northeastern University

Summer school in Boston for academically at-risk students is part of a 15-month program to improve student achievement. As part of this Transition Services Program, students in grades 3, 6, and 9 receive additional math and reading instruction during the school year and, if necessary, in summer school before and after each of these grades. In Summer School 2000 and 2001, between 7,200 and 8,200 students enrolled in a 5-week intensive program to improve math skills, reading skills, or both.

In this chapter, I look at the context and experience of the summer school program in Boston. I focus initially on the Summer School 2000 experience and highlight several key program challenges from that experience that Boston and other school systems face when they implement summer programs for at-risk students. Discussion of these challenges is followed by an overview of the Summer School 2001 experience and an analysis of the changes introduced by the school department as a result of the previous summer's experience.[1]

---

[1] The author is part of a research team from Northeastern and Harvard Universities that is under contract with the Boston Public Schools to provide an ongoing, 3-year, formative and summative evaluation of the Transition Services Program. The research team includes Richard Weissbourd, Caroline Watts, and Terry Tivnan from Harvard and Glenn Pierce and James Fraser from Northeastern. The evaluation design includes interviews, survey questionnaires, district-wide student data analyses, and case studies at six schools. The views, findings, and opinions in this chapter are those of the author and do not necessarily reflect those held by the City of Boston, the Boston Public Schools, or the Massachusetts Department of Education.

THE SETTING

Boston Public Schools

The Boston Public Schools (BPS) enroll 63,500 students at 130 schools. Like many other urban school systems, the student population is predominantly Black or Hispanic: 49% of students are Black, 27% are Hispanic, 15% are White, and 9% are Asian. The learning needs of this student population are diverse. Many students receive special education or bilingual services. Approximately 13,000 students (21% of the total) receive special education services, whereas 9,300 students (15% of the total) participate in bilingual programs. The BPS provides transitional bilingual education programs in nine different languages.

In 1996, the BPS launched a 5-year reform effort called "Focus on Children." This effort included a strict promotion policy, curricular emphasis on literacy, high school restructuring, expanded use of technology, more extensive professional development, and focused services for students who are falling behind. Raising student achievement—the ultimate goal of this reform effort—is a challenge. When students took the Stanford 9 Achievement tests in the spring of 2000, 19% of them scored Level 1 ("little or no mastery") on the reading test and 37% of them scored Level 1 on the math test (Boston Public Schools, 2000a). On state-mandated tests (discussed later), student test scores were lower. In the spring of 2001, students in grades 4, 8, and 10 took the state-mandated test: 30% of BPS students failed the English language arts exam and 48% of students failed the math exam. The Transition Services Program is targeted to help these students and their classmates who face major academic challenges (Vaishnav, 2001).

Massachusetts Education Reform Act of 1993

School reform in Boston takes place within the context of an extensive state education-reform effort. The Massachusetts Education Reform Act, which was adopted in 1993, is a systemic initiative that touches nearly all parts of kindergarten through 12th grade public education. The Act included a major overhaul of the school funding formula and instructed the state to create learning standards, curriculum frameworks, and assessment tools for all subjects and grades. In the mid-1990s, state officials had established learning standards; the standards were followed by extensive and detailed curriculum frameworks to provide guidance to school districts on how to implement the standards.

For assessment, the Massachusetts Comprehensive Assessment System (MCAS) was developed as a series of criterion-referenced tests to evaluate student knowledge of the curriculum frameworks. The MCAS tests are mandatory for all public school students and are the centerpiece in the state's evaluation of student and school performance. MCAS tests have been developed in English language arts, math, science, and social studies. The tests are generally recognized as quite challenging. They include extensive reading and writing sections, with numerous open-ended and problem-solving questions.

The first MCAS tests were given in the spring of 1998 in grades 4, 8, and 10. In English language arts, the percentage of students failing ranged from 13% in grade 8 to 26% in grade 10. In math, the percentage of students failing ranged from 23% in grade 4 to 50% in grade 10. There have been slight improvements in subsequent spring offerings of the test, but the failure rate remains quite high. Beginning in 1998, the state Department of Education offered grants to school districts to assist in developing and implementing support programs for students who performed poorly on the MCAS.

The 2001 MCAS tests in English language arts and math were high-stakes tests for all 10th graders, meaning that students had to earn a passing grade to receive a diploma in 2003. Students who scored at the failing level will be given four additional opportunities to pass the test. The challenge is formidable, although the results showed considerable improvement over 2000. In English language arts, 18% of 10th graders at public schools in Massachusetts failed the test, compared to 34% in 2000. In math, 25% failed the test, compared to 45% in 2000. In the BPS, the failure rates were higher, although they also improved over the 2000 test. Among Boston 10th graders taking the English language arts exam, 40% failed in 2001, compared to 56% in 2000. Among 10th-grade students taking the math exam, 47% failed in 2000, compared to 66% in 2001.

The MCAS has generated considerable controversy. Numerous proposals are being debated, including a delay in implementation of the high-stakes element and exemptions for special education, bilingual, and vocational education students. Alternative assessment strategies and different types of diplomas also are under consideration. Although the high-stakes debate continues, it is generally accepted that a demanding assessment system will remain. To meet that challenge, Boston and other school districts across the state are developing summer and school-year programs to raise student achievement scores.

TRANSITION SERVICES PROGRAM

The Transition Services Program is the centerpiece of Boston's effort to improve student learning among academically at-risk students. Grades 3, 6, and 9 are identified as the key "transition" grades: Grade 3 students make the transition from "learning to read" to "reading to learn," Grade 6 students are entering middle school, and Grade 9 students are entering high school. Students should not be promoted from these grades unless they can read grade-level text, communicate their understandings in writing, and master grade-level content. Promotion standards were established for each grade with specific benchmarks on standardized tests, such as the Scholastic Reading Inventory, department-generated tests, and, in some instances, course grades.

The program expands learning opportunities in English language arts and math during the school year, as well as during the summer. During the school year, students targeted for transition services receive additional instructional time, a targeted curriculum, and before- or afterschool support. In the 1999 to 2000 school year, the school department hired 100 literacy specialists and 50 math specialists to work with students and other teachers in individual schools to provide extra services. These specialists taught within existing classrooms, provided student instruction in their own classes, and worked closely with other teachers to develop and implement an appropriate curriculum for transition students. The early focus in the program was on literacy. Each literacy specialist helped in the adoption and implementation of a targeted literacy curriculum to help at-risk students improve their academic skills. It is important to note that transition services were provided in small classes and with opportunities for individualized instruction.

During the 1999 to 2000 school year, approximately 6,200 students in the three grades participated in transition services in 85 schools (Boston Public Schools, 2000b). Forty percent of these students participated in both English language arts and math programs, and within each area (English language arts and math), approximately one quarter of students received more than one type of service. The largest number of students received additional assistance in the literacy block during the school day. Among participants, approximately 35% were identified as special education or bilingual education students. By race, approximately 90% of students in the program were Black or Hispanic.

In an interim assessment in the spring of 2000, the school department focused on achievement in English language arts (Boston Public Schools, 2000b). Among transition services students who failed to meet the standardized test grade-level benchmark in the fall, approximately 16% of third graders, 32% of sixth graders, and 35% of ninth graders met the benchmark during the winter test.

Summer school is the second piece of the Transition Services Program. Summer school is mandatory for students who fail to meet promotion requirements in the three transition grades, as well as for those who fail to meet promotion requirements in second, fifth, and eighth grades. Summer classes offer an intensive learning environment in a small class setting. As in the school-year component, instruction focuses on English language arts and math. If students coming from grades 2, 5, or 8 do not meet promotion requirements after the summer program, they are placed in transition services in grades 3, 6, or 9. The school-year transition services described earlier are available to assist these students in meeting promotion requirements, and students who do not meet the requirements during the school year attend another summer school session. At the end of the second summer-school experience, students who still do not meet promotion requirements will be retained in transition services in grades 3, 6, or 9.

In the summer of 1999, BPS offered the first summer school for academically at-risk students, albeit on a limited scale. Students in grades 2, 5, 6, 7, and 8 were required to attend the program if they were at risk of failing English language arts, math, or English as a Second Language (Boston Public Schools, 1999). Approximately 2,500 students attended from among the approximately 4,100 students originally required to attend. Summer school lasted for 4 weeks and students attended 4 hours per day, 4 days per week. The typical schedule included 2-hour blocks each for English language arts and math.

The Scholastic Reading Inventory was used to assess changes in student reading achievement. Based on pretest and posttest measures, between 53% (Grade 5) and 78% (Grade 7) of students demonstrated reading-score gains. Using a benchmark score to assess grade-level performance, 31% of students who were below benchmark at the beginning of the summer were able to reach the benchmark by the end of summer school. In math, scores on a BPS-produced test were available only for middle-school grades 6, 7, and 8. Among these students, between 85% and 90% posted gains from a pretest, and 24% of students below the benchmark at the beginning of the summer were able to reach the math benchmark by the end of the summer. At the end of the summer, approximately 10% of students were retained in the same grade, with 90% promoted to the next grade or to transition services in that grade (Boston Public Schools, 1999).

SUMMER SCHOOL 2000

Program Design

Summer School 2000 was the first full-scale implementation of the summer transition program. Compared to the 1999 summer experience, the 2000 summer program was longer and larger. The program continued to operate 4 hours per day and 4 days per week, but an additional week was added, bringing the total to 5 weeks. BPS also added two more grades, resulting in summer school for grades 2, 3, and 5 to 9. The program began on July 10, and a total of 98 schools were involved (Boston Public Schools, 2000c).

In the seven grades targeted for summer school, 10,800 students (approximately 31% of all students in those grades) were told they must attend summer school because they had failed to meet promotion requirements. Consistent with school policy, summer school would be for all students in the system, regardless of academic classification. Thus, of the students who were told they must attend summer school, approximately 29% were in special education and 14% were bilingual education students.

Preparation for summer school began in the spring of the year when the principal at each school designated a "summer prep coordinator," typically a teacher. The coordinator's responsibilities included monitoring student performance, entering relevant student information into a newly developed intranet data system, and contacting parents of students who were likely to attend summer school. Three fourths of these prep coordinators continued during the summer as the site coordinator to oversee implementation of the summer program in their schools. Summer teachers also were hired in the spring and given the option of attending 1 of 10 professional development programs. These programs, which were optional for teachers and were uncompensated, highlighted different math, English language arts, and English as a Second Language (ESL) curricula.

As in the 1999 summer program, not all students who were told to attend summer school actually did so. Of the 10,800 students required to attend, 2,799, or 26%, did not attend at all. In addition, 760 students were dropped during the summer because of disruptive behavior or low attendance. Final participation totaled 7,255 students—approximately 67% of those originally required to attend (Boston Public Schools, 2000c). Participation varied by grade level (see Table 5.1).

TABLE 5.1
Enrollment in Transition Summer School 2000

Grade	Required to Attend	Never Attended	Dropped Due to Attendance or Behavior	Final Enrollment
2	1,420	423	69	928
3	1,634	377	89	1,168
5	1,454	362	81	1,011
6	1,478	265	100	1,113
7	1,498	294	125	1,079
8	1,110	275	83	752
9	2,220	803	213	1,204
Total	10,814	2,799	760	7,255

The structure of the summer program included some flexibility. At the elementary grades (2, 3, and 5), students were required to attend for 4 hours, but in the middle and high school grades (6–9), students were required to attend only the 2-hour time block for the subject in which they were failing. Most students, however, did attend for the entire 4-hour period. Class sizes were generally small. Although there was variation across schools and grades, the median class size was 12 students. For a summer curriculum, teachers were given learning guidelines at the beginning of the summer, but the actual materials used in the classroom varied considerably across the system. Some teachers used materials purchased specifically for the summer, but many teachers relied extensively on curriculum materials from the school year. In general, teachers were afforded considerable flexibility to design a curriculum and lesson plans that they thought would be most successful in their classroom.

Teachers and site coordinators at each school were generally positive about their summer experience. In an end-of-summer survey, 57% of teachers rated the program as excellent or very good, 29% rated it as good, and 14% rated it as fair or poor (Northeastern/Harvard Evaluation Team, 2000). Among site coordinators, 94% rated the summer program as excellent or very good. Small class size was the most frequently mentioned strength of the program. Among both teachers and site coordinators, 59% mentioned small class size in response to an open-ended question on major strengths of the program. As one sixth-grade teacher commented, "The major strength of the Transition Summer Program is the small class sizes. Students who did not do well last year really need that personalized attention. They leave the program feeling a great sense of accomplishment and intelligence" (Northeastern/Harvard Evaluation Team, 2000, p. 15).

Teachers and site coordinators also praised the intensive nature of the program, the opportunity for focused instruction, the hard work of many students, and the collegial support among teachers. Teachers commented on the positive learning environment, the opportunities for individualized instruction, and the support of their colleagues and the site coordinator. As one third-grade teacher concluded, the summer program was a "real effort to target students in need and address their weaknesses" (Northeastern/Harvard Evaluation Team, 2000, p. 23).

Student Results

The school department used a pretest and posttest to measure the academic progress of summer school students (Boston Public Schools, 2000c). In English language arts, the Scholastic Reading Inventory was used to assess achievement in reading. The results were generally positive and indicated that a significant number of students were able to raise their achievement level. Among students who were below the reading bench-mark at the beginning of the summer, 45% were able to meet the bench-mark by the end of the summer. Across the grades, the percentage of stu-dents reaching the benchmark ranged from 59% in Grade 9 to 38% in Grade 2. In comparison, in the 1999 summer program, only 31% of stu-dents were able to meet the reading benchmark.

In math, the school department developed its own assessment instru-ment and the results were similar. Among summer school students who had not met the math benchmark during the school year, 41% were able to meet the benchmark by the end of the summer. Across the grades, the per-centage of students reaching the benchmark ranged from 59% in grade 3 to 23% in grade 6. This compares quite favorably to the 1999 summer ex-perience, in which only 24% of middle school students (the only group for whom test data are available) were able to reach the benchmark by the end of the summer.

A second outcome measure for the summer program is represented by the final promotion–retention decision for each student. On this measure, it is instructive to compare the promotion–retention decisions for students who completed summer school to decisions for students who did not complete or attend summer school, despite the fact that the school depart-ment had told them that they were required to do so because of their low school-year performance. Table 5.2 compares these two groups of stu-dents according to the decision, as of August 30, 2000, to promote, retain, or assign them to transition services in grades 3, 6, and 9 (Boston Public Schools, 2000c).

It should come as no surprise that students who completed summer school were more likely to be promoted to the next grade. In most in-stances, these students raised their reading skills, math skills, or both, to the benchmark level required in the promotion standards. Among stu-dents completing summer school, 19% were assigned to transition ser-

TABLE 5.2
Promotion and Retention Decisions for Students
Required to Attend Summer School

Decision	Completed Summer School		Did Not Attend or Complete Summer School		Total	
	Number	Percentage	Number	Percentage	Number	Percentage
Promoted	4,404	61	605	17	5,009	46
Assigned to Transition	1,353	19	888	25	2,241	21
Retained	1,491	21	2,073	58	3,564	33
Total	7,248	100	3,566	100	10,814	100

vices and 21% were retained. This retention level was higher than the previous summer program in which 10% of students were retained.

The data in Table 5.2 also reveal the complex nature of promotion decisions. Among students who were required to attend summer school, but who did not attend or complete the program, 605 students (17%) were nevertheless promoted. These students had not met the formal promotion standards but were promoted for other reasons. In some cases, special education students were promoted regardless of benchmark scores because their individual education plan called for promotion based on other criteria. In other cases, another school district policy required the student to be promoted, as with the policy that allows only one retention at each school level (elementary, middle, or high).

Among students who completed summer school, the promotion–retention decisions varied across the grades. Table 5.3 provides this information (Boston Public Schools, 2000c).

The data in Table 5.3 highlight the critical role played by the Transition Services Program. School officials are using the summer program following grades 2, 5, and 8 as an opportunity not only to assist students in improving academic skills, but also to identify students who need additional academic assistance. This is most evident in grades 2 and 5, in which more than half of the students who completed summer school were assigned to transition services in the next grade. These students receive targeted services in the following school year and are joined by other students who did not attend summer school but were assigned to transition services. In addition, students in grades 3, 6, and 9 who failed to reach benchmarks are also assigned to transition services.

Additional analysis to measure the effectiveness of the summer program is being conducted by the evaluation team hired by the school department (see Footnote 1). Test score data, promotion decisions, and other measures

TABLE 5.3
Promotion and Retention Decisions for Students
Who Completed Summer School 2000

	Grade in June and Summer						
Decision	2	3	5	6	7	8	9
Promoted	37%	66%	40%	83%	92%	58%	44%
Assigned to Transition	55%		56%			37%	
Retained	8%	34%*	3%	17%*	8%	1%	56%*

*Although listed as retained, these students will remain in transition services in their respective grades. The high retention level in Grade 9 can be attributed, in part, to the number of students who must retake one course they failed in Grade 9. Otherwise, many of these students will be in Grade 10 classes.

of student achievement and participation are being analyzed and compared to data on other students in the school system—particularly those students with relatively similar skills levels, as measured by standardized tests, who did not participate in the Transition Services Program.

PROGRAM CHALLENGES

Summer programs pose a host of challenges for school districts (see also Cooper, Charlton, Valentine, & Muhlenbruck, 2000; Harrington–Lueker, 2000). Although individual school districts have unique concerns and problems, they face a number of common challenges as well. Among these are designing a summer curriculum, connecting the summer curriculum with the school year, providing a learning environment for all students, preparing teachers for summer classes, ensuring the availability of materials and supplies, and maximizing student attendance. Each of these challenges is discussed below in the context of Boston's summer experience.

Designing a Summer Curriculum

Creating and designing a summer curriculum is a critical programmatic task. Summer programs need a curriculum and learning materials that can support accelerated student learning in a small-class environment. The curriculum from the school year may be inadequate or inappropriate for this specialized need. If that is the case, how should a summer curriculum be designed?

School districts have responded to this question in different ways. In Boston, summer curriculum design was left primarily to individual schools and teachers. The central office provided a list of learning objectives, but how those objectives would be met was up to individual teachers. Many teachers thrived in this flexible environment. They adapted materials from the school year or adopted a new approach designed more specifically for a remedial small-class setting. Some teachers, however, faced a more difficult challenge. If they were teaching a grade or subject that was new to them, they had limited experience or materials to use in their summer classrooms. Learning objectives provided some guidance, and colleagues offered support, but these teachers found it difficult to structure their summer classrooms.

In an alternative approach, adopted by Chicago and some other districts, the summer curriculum is prescribed by the central office. Curriculum specialists develop a set of materials that will guide classroom instruction, or they adopt a curriculum package developed by outside providers for use in all schools. Central office control may include prescribing actual lesson plans for each day of the summer school. This approach ensures that all students experience a curriculum designed specifically for summer classes. It may come at the cost, however, of giving teachers the flexibility to adapt materials to the needs of their individual classes.

This challenge is a classic centralization–decentralization issue that is common to large school districts. How school districts meet this challenge often depends on the practices and traditions of that district. In Boston, for example, flexibility in curriculum design is common at the school level. The school district and the state have learning standards and curriculum frameworks for each grade and subject, but individual schools in Boston are encouraged to adopt a curriculum approach that is supported by school-level teachers and administrators. In this model of whole-school reform, schools have adopted different curriculum packages, particularly in the area of literacy. The summer approach, then, is consistent with district practices during the school year. Although maintaining some local flexibility, preparations for summer school in 2001 included a review of this approach and the development of a more structured format for curriculum in summer classes.

Relating Summer Curriculum With the School Year

A related challenge involves the relation between the summer curriculum and the curriculum used during the school year. Should the summer curriculum be similar to, and an extension of, the curriculum used during the year, or should it be different and approach learning tasks in an alternative manner? One can argue that raising academic achievement calls for continuity in curriculum between the school year and summer. Alternatively, others argue that students with failing marks during the school year need a different approach to learning in the summer.

Boston sought a middle ground for its 2000 summer program, although the final outcome emphasized continuity with the school-year curriculum. In fact, 80% of summer teachers relied, at least in part, on instructional and curriculum materials from the school year (Northeastern/Harvard Evaluation Team, 2000). This reliance was as much by circumstance as by design. The late arrival of summer materials, combined with the school district's decentralized approach to curriculum design, prompted most teachers to use curriculum materials from the school year that they already knew and had available to them. Professional development workshops prior to summer school introduced some curriculum strategies for the summer classroom, but only about one third of teachers attended these optional workshops.

As with centralization or decentralization of curriculum design, meeting the challenge of relating the summer curriculum to the school-year curriculum is not a simple or straightforward process. School districts have adopted different approaches. Some districts emphasize continuity in curriculum between the school year and summer. Seeking a "seamless" experience for students, these districts extend curriculum from the school year into the summer to allow students to succeed in specific areas in which they previously failed. Familiarity and repetition are viewed as supportive of accelerated learning.

Alternatively, some districts emphasize the need for a completely different approach to learning for students who have been unsuccessful in the school-year classroom. Repeating a curriculum or instructional approach may be an exercise in futility; summer school students need a different approach to support an acceleration of learning to make up for past shortfalls. From this perspective, an alternative curriculum, combined with small class sizes, provides the best opportunity for these students.

Educating All Students in a Diverse Classroom

A third challenge involves the diversity of the summer school classroom. Although some school districts, like Boston, include special education and limited-English-speaking students in the summer school program, other districts exclude such students from their summer remedial programs. If the summer classroom is inclusive, can a curriculum be designed and teachers prepared to support learning for all students? Alternatively, if the summer classroom includes only regular education students, what arrangements are made to support accelerated learning for special education students and others with special needs?

Boston's summer program was inclusive of students in special education and bilingual programs: 27% of summer school students were in a special education classification, and 12% were in bilingual programs during the school year. As a result, the typical summer classroom included a group of students with different academic skills and learning abilities. This diverse environment, even in the context of small class sizes, posed a significant challenge for some teachers. Most teachers lacked training in special education or bilingual education, and many were not accustomed to having this range of students within one classroom.

Although the challenge is significant, Boston is committed to providing a summer learning experience for all students. After the 2000 summer program, administrators began to explore options to better support teachers in meeting this challenge. Possible options include specialized professional development or smaller class sizes for particularly diverse classrooms.

Preparing Teachers for the Summer Classroom

Summer school programs typically include a classroom environment that differs significantly from the school year, primarily in smaller class size and longer instructional periods. Are teachers adequately prepared to teach in this environment? Do they have the appropriate credentials and experiences to be successful in this setting? In some school districts, this challenge is accentuated by the difficulty of hiring teachers for the summer; many teachers are reluctant to alter summer plans to accommodate a 4- or 5-week program.

Teachers in Boston's 2000 summer program were experienced and generally taught in their area of certification. The average tenure for a summer teacher was 12 years and two thirds had a masters degree or higher. Eighty-five percent of teachers were certified to teach at the grade level they taught in summer school. Among English language arts teachers, 87% were certified in that subject; among math teachers, 65% were certified in that subject.

Teacher preparation for Boston's summer school included a choice from among 10 professional development workshops. As noted earlier, however, the workshops were optional, and teachers did not receive compensation. Only 35% of teachers attended one of these workshops. The limited number of teachers who participated lessened the impact of this professional development opportunity, although attendees rated the workshops as generally relevant for the summer classroom.

Providing Materials for the Classroom

An important administrative challenge is providing instructional materials to the summer classroom in a timely manner and in sufficient quantity. One review of summer programs nationwide noted that the late arrival of summer materials was one of the most frequent complaints of summer school teachers (Cooper et al., 2000). Meeting this challenge can be complicated by the approach taken to several of the other issues already raised, particularly the design and development of curriculum. For example, if the school district adopts a centralized approach to curriculum design, the timely delivery of instructional materials is critical. If curriculum is more decentralized and is an extension of the school-year curriculum, the delivery of materials remains important, but is less critical as a prerequisite to the start of summer school. In this case, school-year materials already at the school can be used in the summer classroom.

In Boston, basic classroom supplies were delivered to each school in a timely manner, but the delivery of curriculum materials for the 2000 summer program did not take place until after the session had begun. The delivery of materials was delayed for a number of reasons, including the late receipt of monies from state government (which funded the summer program) and a late start to planning for the summer program.

Maximizing Student Participation

A major challenge faced by Boston and other large school districts is convincing all students who need summer school to attend. In Boston, for example, 26% of students required to attend summer school did not attend. These students, totaling 2,800, had not met promotion standards and were told they would not pass to the next grade, but they still did not report to the first day of summer school. Two other Massachusetts cities, Worcester and Springfield, faced similar situations for their 2000 summer programs (Mass Insight Education, 2000). Students who fail to attend present a serious problem that undermines the goals of summer programs.

To address this challenge, school districts must convince students and parents that summer school is a critical component of a child's education. Particularly for younger students, clear communication with parents is important to raise the awareness of summer school and its educational importance. The more summer school is viewed as an integral part of the education experience—rather than as a punishment for poor performance—the more likely it is that students will participate. Connecting summer school to other summer activities, such as recreation or part-time jobs, can also make summer school a more positive experience. Failing to draw these students into the summer classroom almost certainly dooms them to falling further behind their classmates in grade and academic achievement.

LEARNING FROM EXPERIENCE: SUMMER SCHOOL 2001

In 2001, the Boston schools conducted another summer school for transition students (see Northeastern/Harvard Evaluation Team, 2001a, 2001b). As a result of what it learned from the previous year's experience, the school department made a number of changes in the program. Although there was still room for improvement, this 2nd year of a large-scale summer school effort provided an improved learning experience for students.

Summer School 2001 was similar in size and scope to the previous year's program. Over 12,000 students in grades 2, 3, and 5 to 9 failed to meet promotion standards and were required to attend. Of these students, 8,260 (66%) completed the summer program. As in 2000, the program operated for 4 hours per day, 4 days per week, for 5 weeks.

Test scores and promotion decisions indicate that a significant number of students made academic progress over the summer. Across all grades, 46% of summer school attendees who had not met the reading benchmark at the end of the school year did so after the summer program. In 2000, the comparable measure was 45%. For math, 54% of summer school attendees who had not met the math benchmark at the end of the school year did so after the summer program. In 2000, the comparable measure was 41%. A large number of students also demonstrated progress in terms of promotion. Across all grades, 68% of students who attended summer school were promoted to the next grade at the conclusion of the summer, and 15% were assigned to transition services in the next grade (grades 3, 6, or 9). The remaining 17% of students were retained in their current grade.

For Summer School 2001, BPS made a number of changes in response to the program challenges outlined previously. In the area of curriculum, the school department responded to concerns raised the previous summer by providing a more detailed curriculum with books and other materials specifically for the summer program. The school department purchased English language arts materials for each class in each grade, and it developed a scope and sequence for math that incorporated materials already being used in the school system. Most teachers adopted these materials for their summer classroom, often combining them with other curriculum materials. Teachers who used these materials responded with a generally positive assessment.

The school department also attempted to create a closer connection to the school-year curriculum, particularly in math. Summer math materials were a direct extension of materials used during the school year. This was advantageous for math teachers trained in the school-year materials, but for teachers who had not received such training, the summer math curriculum was often difficult to master effectively within such a short time period.

The availability of summer curriculum materials was itself a considerable improvement. Whereas the late arrival of materials in summer 2000 was the most frequent complaint by teachers and site coordinators, in summer 2001, this issue received only a few mentions. Most teachers received their materials in advance of the summer program, or during the first week of classes, and were able to incorporate the materials into their classrooms.

Professional development for teachers was also improved over the 2000 experience. To increase attendance while holding program costs down, the school department scheduled professional development sessions at the end of the school year, before teachers concluded their regular contractual responsibilities. Teachers planning to teach in the summer were excused from their schools to attend at least one of these sessions.

Approximately 80% of teachers attended a session, compared to only one third in the previous year. In addition, the professional development sessions were designed specifically around the curriculum materials that would be used during the summer. This provided teachers with a focused introduction to the summer curriculum and an opportunity to begin planning for their summer classrooms.

Several program challenges proved more difficult to address. For example, the diversity of student needs within the summer classroom continued to be a major challenge for many teachers. In some classrooms, one third or more of the students had special education or bilingual status. A small number of schools had special education or bilingual teachers on their summer teaching staff to provide support, but, in most schools, a teacher with regular certification was responsible for instruction. The ability of teachers to respond to this diverse environment varied by their own background, skills, and experiences in teaching diverse populations.

Another continuing challenge was increasing overall student participation in the summer program. As noted earlier, in both 2000 and 2001, 33% of students who were told they must attend summer school did not complete the program. Most of these noncompleters did not even attend the first day of summer school. In 2001, this problem was most apparent in grades 8 and 9, where 35% did not report the first day, and an additional 14% were dropped for low attendance or poor behavior. The school department has worked to improve communication with students and parents, but nonparticipation remains an important concern.

CONCLUSION

Boston's Transition Services Program joins the ranks of alternative school programs designed to raise academic achievement among students most at risk of failing. During 15 months of targeted services to each student, the program provides additional instructional time and smaller classes in the summer and during the school year to help students meet promotional standards. As an alternative to simple retention, the program allows students to move to the next grade as transition students in an environment that offers additional academic support.

Initial results are positive. Many students in the 2000 and 2001 summer programs showed improvements in their test scores, and a large number of students were promoted to the next grade. The program is young, however, and data analysis is at a very early stage. Comparison with appropriate nonparticipant groups is needed, and a closer analysis of specific transition programs and actual teaching practices in transition classrooms is also important.

Although research on this program continues, the Boston experience does raise a number of key questions which confront policymakers and administrators of summer programs. Designing curriculum, preparing teachers, and maximizing student participation are a few of the key challenges that face summer programs. Successfully addressing these challenges will be difficult, but doing so is critical in Boston and other cities that hope to raise academic achievement levels for all students.

REFERENCES

Boston Public Schools. (1999). *Boston Public Schools summer academic support program: Grades K–8.* Boston: Boston Public Schools, Office of Research, Assessment, and Evaluation.

Boston Public Schools. (2000a). *Stanford 9 achievement test: Report-part 1: Preliminary analysis, spring 2000.* Boston: Boston Public Schools, Office of Research, Assessment, and Evaluation.

Boston Public Schools. (2000b). *Boston Public Schools transition services: Interim report on student progress.* Boston: Boston Public Schools, Office of Research, Assessment, and Evaluation.

Boston Public Schools. (2000c). *Transition services summer school 2000.* Boston: Boston Public Schools, Office of Research, Assessment, and Evaluation.

Cooper, H., Charlton, K., Valentine. J. C., & Muhlenbruck, L. (2000). Making the most of summer school: A meta-analytic and narrative review. *Monographs of the Society for Research in Child Development, 65*(1, Serial No. 260).

Harrington–Lueker, D. (2000). Summer learners: Can summer school make a difference in student achievement? *American School Board Journal, 187*(3), 20–25.

Mass Insight Education. (2000). *For the first time ever: The extraordinary efforts in Massachusetts schools to get extra help to the students who need it most.* Boston: Author.

Northeastern/Harvard Evaluation Team. (2000). *Implementation evaluation of the Boston Public Schools summer 2000 transition services program.* Boston: Northeastern University.

Northeastern/Harvard Evaluation Team. (2001a). *Evaluation of Boston Public Schools' summer 2001 transition services program. Part I: Attendance, promotion status, and benchmark achievement.* Boston: Northeastern University.

Northeastern/Harvard Evaluation Team. (2001b). *Evaluation of Boston Public Schools' summer 2001 transition services program. Part II: Implementation evaluation of the Boston Public Schools' summer 2001 transition services program.* Boston: Northeastern University.

Vaishnav, A. (2001, November 2). MCAS 2001: In Boston, gains and problems. *Boston Globe,* p. A33.

6

Assessing the Effectiveness of Summer Reading Programs

Scott G. Paris
University of Michigan

P. David Pearson and Gina Cervetti
Michigan State University

Robert Carpenter, Alison H. Paris,
Jennifer DeGroot, Melissa Mercer, and Kai Schnabel
University of Michigan

Joseph Martineau
Michigan State University

Elena Papanastasiou
University of Kansas

Jonathan Flukes, Kathy Humphrey,
and Tamara Bashore–Berg
Ingham Intermediate School District

Despite remarkable invention and innovation in American history during the past 50 years, public education is the focus of heated criticism. The basic controversy is the public perception of eroding quality of education and declining achievement of American students. Although the severity, and even reality, of this crisis has been contested (Berliner & Biddle, 1997), politicians have used comparative achievement-test data to argue that too many American students are unprepared for the technological and scientific challenges of the 21st century. The attributions of blame are widespread, including the usual suspects of parents, teachers, and poverty, and the calls for reform have been equally strong and diverse. Amidst this churning sea of educational criticisms and wishful thinking for speedy reforms, there are baffled parents and frustrated teachers searching for the nearest and best lifeboats for their students. The current popularity of summer school is one of these lifeboats.

Summer school encompasses many possible programs varying in curricular focus, amount of time that students participate, quality of instructional staff, and connections to regular school programs, to name only a few key features. Over the past 50 years, summer programs for remediation, accelerated learning, and gifted students have all enjoyed periodic popularity. Why is summer school increasing in popularity now? One powerful reason is that research has revealed that disadvantaged students display "summer loss" in academic achievement. Heyns (1978) analyzed the impact of summer programs on sixth graders in Atlanta, GA, and found that White students gained about 2.5 months of annual growth (using grade norm scores) on achievement tests, regardless of whether they attended summer programs, whereas African American students who attended summer programs gained only .3 months of growth on the tests. However, this was much better than African American students who did not attend summer school; they lost an average 1.8 months. Cooper, Nye, Charlton, Lindsay, and Greathouse (1996) found that math achievement for middle-class and disadvantaged students showed similar declines over the summer, but reading achievement increased for middle-class students and declined for disadvantaged students. Entwisle and Alexander (1997) also found that students from disadvantaged schools showed greater summer achievement losses than students from middle-class schools but equal learning rates during the school year.

The Sustaining Effects Study (Carter, 1984) found that the rates of learning were lower in the summer than the regular year, although no absolute loss was observed in the summer. Heyns (1987) reanalyzed the data and found that poor and minority students showed the least academic progress during the summer. Thus, summer loss affects disadvantaged students most severely, especially for reading. In fact, Entwisle and Alexander (1997) hypothesized that the cumulative pattern of summer losses for disadvantaged students underlies the growing gap between successful and unsuccessful students. The media has referred to this growing bifurcation as the "achievement gap," but the pattern has also been called the "Matthew effect" by reading researchers because the (academically) rich get richer and the poor get poorer (Stanovich, 1986). By any name, it signals a fundamental problem in American education, and one potential solution has been summer school.

A second reason that summer programs are popular is the growing emphasis on more school attendance. Stevenson and Lee (1990) showed that East Asian students attended school more each day, each week, and each year than American students. Reasoning that more time devoted to schooling may be partly responsible for the high achievement levels of East Asian students, many people have called for revised school calendars or year-round schooling. Summer school is one way of extending "time on task," and it may be critical for low-achieving students, especially for those who spend little time using literacy skills during summer vacation from school.

A third rationale for advocating summer school is educators' general reluctance to retain students in grade. Retention in grade separates students from their peer groups, creates social stigmas, and is significantly related to subsequent school problems and dropping out (Meisels, 1992). Summer schools may provide just the dose of extended learning opportunities that will allow at-risk students to "catch up" enough to avoid retention. It is a policy that supports students with specific help, rather than punishing them with a retention that may have long-lasting negative effects.

A fourth rationale for summer programs is the identification of successful features of summer programs. During the past 30 years, there have been many goals and instructional activities for summer programs that were aimed at helping different groups of students. Some were more successful than others. Meta-analyses of these diverse programs revealed key characteristics of successful programs that may provide guidance for future programs. In a thorough review of summer school programs, Cooper, Charlton, Valentine, and Muhlenbruck (2000) presented 10 principal conclusions; the first five, following, were strongly supported, whereas the latter five were more tenuous findings:

1. Programs that focused on lessening or removing learning deficiencies have a positive impact; students completing remedial summer programs can be expected to score about .20 SDs higher than control groups on outcome measures.
2. Programs that focus on acceleration of learning (and other goals) have a positive impact on students, similar to the impact of remedial programs.
3. Summer school programs have more positive effects on middle-class students than on disadvantaged students.
4. Remedial summer programs have larger positive impacts when conducted in a small number of classes or schools or in a small community.
5. Programs that provide small-group or individual instruction produce the largest impact on students.
6. Summer programs that require some type of parent involvement have shown larger effects than those without parental involvement.
7. Remedial summer programs may have larger effects on math than on reading achievement.

124

124   PARIS ET AL.

8. The advantages gained in summer programs may diminish over time.
9. Summer programs may be more beneficial for students in early primary grades or in high school than in the middle grades.
10. Summer programs that are monitored to ensure that instruction is delivered as planned, that students attend the programs regularly, and that only students who attend regularly are included in the analyses, produce larger effects than unmonitored programs.

These insights about effective summer programs have been gleaned from many programs. Together with the other rationales for summer school, they provide motivation, suggestions, and optimism for implementing summer school programs to help students most at risk for low achievement. It is important to realize that summer reading programs are just one form of remedial action in a wide-scale approach to improving student achievement and attaining the lofty goal of preparing every child to read at grade level by third grade. Early interventions, family literacy programs, technology, professional development, higher standards, and other programs have been implemented for the same overall purpose of reducing the achievement gap—some with more success than others—but none provides the magic bullet or quick fix for which policymakers hope.

RESEARCH ON SUMMER READING PROGRAMS IN MICHIGAN

Our research is set in the context of ongoing American school-reform efforts that often include a variety of summer school programs and reading interventions. Our research examines summer school programs that are designed to help young children develop skills that will enable them to read at grade level. The Michigan Department of Education contracted us to evaluate samples of the diverse summer reading programs throughout the state. There was no single approach tested in the research because the project was commissioned as a global evaluation of the various state-funded summer reading programs. Each funded school district designed programs to fit the needs of its students, the talents of its teachers, and its available resources. In the process of evaluating representative summer reading programs, we were able to identify characteristics of successful programs and to develop procedures for evaluating literacy programs for kindergarten through third-grade (K–3) students. Both findings should be of value to educators designing summer literacy programs and to researchers who want to evaluate them.

Study 1

We began our research in the spring of 1998, only weeks before Michigan's first summer school programs were initiated under a special funding program. Six representative school districts in Michigan were selected for evaluation, but no control groups were possible. The research design included a pretest and a posttest for children who attended summer school, and we decided to administer the identical reading tasks before and after the summer programs to assess growth. Obviously, any gains might be affected by practice effects or maturation, but we assumed that those would be modest and a necessary confound given our constraints of time and testing resources. We gathered data from observations of the summer classes and interviews with teachers, as well as the data on students' reading skills.

The curricula of the K–3 summer programs varied widely—partly because this was the first year of a state-funded initiative that offered applicants wide berth in specifying their curriculum, and partly because there was little time available to plan the programs. Among our six research sites, the length of the summer programs varied from 3 to 6 weeks in duration, and the curriculum varied from a strict focus on reading to general academic remediation. The staffs at the schools included teachers who were on staff at the buildings, precertified teachers, and paraprofessionals. Some teachers knew the students well, but others did not. Our observations often revealed that supplementary motivational activities, such as field trips, pizza parties, and unstructured play in the schools, were as frequent as instructional time spent on reading. Nevertheless, we also observed many good teachers working individually with children and some programs that involved parents in the child's summer reading activities.

Choosing reading tasks to assess the impact of summer school programs is a challenge in all evaluation research, and it proved a challenge for us. Most researchers have used norm-referenced achievement tests, but we believe that these have serious problems. First, they are highly correlated with individual differences in general verbal ability, and they are relatively insensitive to teacher and curricular variables (Cross & Paris, 1987).

Second, achievement tests are rarely aligned with the curricula of summer school programs and may not assess the delivered intervention. Third, achievement tests are susceptible to special coaching, practice effects due to teaching to the test, and motivational variations of the students that may not reflect meaningful or enduring effects on children's reading. Fourth, it seems more hopeful than realistic to expect short-term summer programs to have substantial effects on children's achievement scores if the tests assess enduring characteristics of students. In fact, the meta-analysis conducted by Cooper et al. (2000) showed that the average effect size of summer school programs is only about .22 standard deviations. This is a small gain on any assessment instrument, representing a magnitude that is regarded as small by meta-analysis standards and difficult to separate from variation due to other factors. On most achievement tests, correctly answering from two to five additional questions may result in a difference of less than one quarter of a standard deviation. For all these reasons, we were reluctant to use standardized achievement tests, yet there was external pressure by policymakers to use such tests, at least in addition to other assessments.

Thus, we chose to administer more authentic reading assessments, including an informal reading inventory (IRI) adapted for our research purposes. All children in the study were initially given the graded word lists from the Qualitative Reading Inventory II (QRI; Leslie & Caldwell, 1995).

Children were given ascending levels of word lists until we could identify the highest grade level at which they could read at least 14 of the 20 words. Each child was then given a narrative QRI passage to read aloud at the level of the highest word list the child had completed successfully. The child's reading was recorded on audiotape and later analyzed for miscues, self-corrections, retelling of the selection, and answers to the QRI comprehension questions. In this manner, we were able to collect data on a child's word identification on graded word lists, oral reading accuracy of graded narrative passages, retelling, and comprehension in a relatively brief testing period. For those children who were unable to read at least 14 words on the preprimer list, we administered several tasks from the Michigan Literacy Progress Profile (MLPP), including tasks to assess phonemic awareness and concepts of print. All children were given the same tasks in the first few days and last few days of their summer school programs.

The results on the reading performance measures were straightforward. Children across the six sites increased their reading accuracy, retelling, and comprehension scores on the QRI significantly from pretest to posttest. The effects were larger at some sites than others, and greater for younger children and poorer readers, but they did not differ by gender. The distribution of children by race was confounded with grade and site, and the sample sizes were too small to analyze separately. No data on socioeconomic status were available either, so we could not test whether poor and middle-class children differed in their reactions to summer school. Despite these limitations and the lack of a control group, we were cautiously optimistic that the summer school programs had provided positive benefits for children's reading skills.

As part of the study, we also identified features of successful programs that the Michigan Department of Education used as either required or desirable criteria in evaluating requests for proposals in the 1999 competition. These features included the following:

- A minimum of 60 hours of reading instruction.
- Daily opportunities to read both easy and challenging materials.
- Daily opportunities to write authentic texts.
- Direct instruction on phonological awareness as needed.
- Direct instruction on strategies for word-reading, comprehension, and writing.
- Motivating activities to engage students in using literacy for learning.

In addition, we described desirable features of programs that we had observed. For example, summer programs that employed regular teachers from the same buildings seemed to have more continuity between past and future teachers, better records of children's summer school performance, and more alignment between instruction and assessment practices. We noted that some programs made considerable efforts to involve parents and that these programs seemed to have greater attendance and student motivation. Curricula varied widely from programmatic to haphazard, so we recommended strong curricula with thematic or coherent strands. The state incorporated these suggestions in its requests for proposals for Year 2 funding, and the effect on both the quality of the proposals and on instructional improvement in the 2nd year of summer school programs was striking.

Study 2

The major purpose of this study was to provide a more rigorous experimental test of the impact of summer reading programs throughout the state of Michigan. We also continued the development and field testing of some assessments in the MLPP. Twelve school districts were randomly selected to participate in this evaluation project. Summer programs were conducted at 19 individual schools within these randomly selected 12 districts between June and August of 1999. The evaluation of the summer reading programs was planned in three phases: pretest data collection in spring of 1999, posttest data collection in the fall of 1999, and follow-up testing in spring of 2000. The study was designed to provide evidence about the following: (a) the growth in students' reading during the summer and following year; (b) the curricula and instruction provided in summer programs (especially any features that might turn out to be associated with high growth); (c) the views of teachers, administrators, and parents about the summer programs; and (d) the usefulness of various assessment tasks and procedures for evaluating summer reading achievement.

The 19 programs focused on grades K–3, with varying emphases on reading. The length of the summer programs ranged from 16 to 34 days, with most programs operating about 3 hours per day. Students from the participating districts were selected from among those students who had been nominated as eligible for summer school by their teachers. Although the criteria varied among schools, generally the students were reading below grade level and were considered at risk for falling further behind without extra help.

In the spring of 1999, the research team visited each district and sent letters home to all the eligible students asking their parents' consent for them to participate in the project. The research team tried to include as many of the eligible students in each district as possible, aiming for approximately the same number of students at each grade level and approximately equal representation by gender. Because procedures for determining which students would attend summer school varied greatly across districts, we could only hope that about half of the students included in the pretest would actually attend the summer programs and half would not. Fortunately, this was the case, but, not surprisingly, the children who attended summer school had lower reading achievement at the start of the study than the children who were nominated but did not attend. Those were the students in the control group.

Table 6.1 shows the nearly 900 children who were considered readers, which by our definition meant that they could read at least the preprimer passage. They were given the Basic Reading Inventory (BRI; Johns, 1997) as the informal reading inventory. We also assessed their daily reading and writing habits with a survey entitled "Literacy Habits," and we surveyed Students' Opinions About Reading (SOAR) using a Likert-type response scale. Table 6.1 indicates that the 449 children in the precomparisons and the postcomparisons attended schools throughout the state, including rural, urban, and suburban settings. The diversity of the sample is representative of young children in Michigan who are at risk for poor reading achievement. Slightly more than half of the sample was boys and slightly more than half of the sample was White. The numbers are slightly lower for delayed testing in spring of 2000. The samples for Experimental and Control groups were similar in terms of gender and grade except that there were slightly more second and third graders in the Control group. This means that, among the children we tested in the spring of 1999, fewer of the older students chose to attend summer school. The distribution of race and ethnicity was also quite similar across Experimental and Control groups.

Table 6.1 also reveals a range of reading levels on the BRI from preprimer to Grade 6, indicating that not all the children were reading below grade level, at least according to the BRI. Inspection of Table 6.1 reveals that there were more Experimental children reading passages at the three lowest levels and more Control children reading passages at the

TABLE 6.1
Student Demographics by Program Status and Testing Time

	Overall		Experimental		Control	
	Pre or Post	Delayed	Pre or Post	Delayed	Pre or Post	Delayed
Gender						
Male	249	226	121	111	128	115
Female	200	181	90	84	110	97
Grade						
1	114	106	63	60	51	46
2	190	168	85	77	105	91
3	145	133	63	58	82	75
Ethnicity						
White	243	222	108	100	135	122
African American	108	96	49	45	59	51
Hispanic	59	56	27	26	32	30
Native American	26	23	17	16	9	7
Asian	6	5	5	4	1	1
Multiracial	5	4	4	3	1	1
Passage						
Preprimer	43	39	30	28	13	11
Primer	30	26	21	18	9	8
Grade 1	72	68	37	37	35	31
Grade 2	97	85	41	36	56	49
Grade 3	72	69	34	32	38	37
Grade 4	60	52	24	22	36	30
Grade 5	36	32	15	13	21	19
Grade 6	39	36	9	9	30	27
District*						
Carrollton	67	64	21	21	46	43
Cesar Chavez	48	47	15	15	33	32
Flint	34	28	7	5	27	23
Kalamazoo	21	20	5	5	16	15
Kenowa Hills	29	27	20	18	9	9
Mt. Clemens	53	43	10	9	43	34
Portage	44	41	32	31	12	10
Romulus	55	50	33	29	22	21
St. Ignace	42	37	30	28	12	9
Traverse City	14	13	7	7	7	6
Willow Run	42	37	31	27	11	10
Total	449	407	211	195	238	221

*Eleven of the twelve sample districts are reflected in this table. Data from Leslie Public Schools were not included in the Basic Reading Inventory (BRI) analysis because at one testing time these students received an alternate BRI form that was incongruent with the rest of the sample.

three highest levels. This pattern indicates that children who attended summer programs may have started out with much lower reading skills than children who did not. In other words, although we tried to ensure similarity between the Experimental and Control groups in terms of incoming achievement, there is a potential bias in the sample, with better readers in the Control group. That may be a natural occurrence in most summer school programs where the children most at risk are most likely (or at least most encouraged) to enroll. This finding, when coupled with the slight bias for fewer children in second and third grades attending summer school, means that the children in our sample of summer school students were often the youngest and poorest readers from the eligible pool of students.

Assessment Instruments

Student achievement during the summer programs was assessed with multiple measures. These assessment tasks included several of the MLPP assessments, which were administered to individual students. In addition, other data collection instruments, such as surveys of teacher and site directors, were used to gather information from each sample site. Each of the assessment tasks or tools is described later.

MLPP. The MLPP was developed by the Michigan Department of Education (MDE) and continues to be revised in response to feedback from teachers throughout the state. The version used during the summer of 1999 was the second version of the instrument and was used by MDE in professional development workshops during 1999 and 2000. It was made available statewide to school districts to be used on a voluntary basis to track the progress of readers in the primary grades. The summer 1999 version included 11 tasks, 4 of which were used in this project. They are described briefly.

Concepts of Print. Inspired by the work of Marie Clay and the Reading Recovery movement, this series of performance tasks provides information about what children have learned about the ways that printed language is used in English, such as knowing how to handle a book, where to begin reading, left-to-right directionality, the differences between pictures and text, and the concept of a word. The MLPP score sheet has 22 different indicators of understanding, so scores can range from 0 to 22.

Sight Word and Decodable Word List. This is a tool for determining which commonly used sight words children can recognize immediately or through analysis. All of the words are high-frequency words, and about half are comprised of word patterns (e.g. "-ed" as in red, "-op" as in stop, or "-ake" as in make) that are taught in most primary-grade reading programs. The word lists included 20 words at each grade level. To avoid confounding due to previous exposure, we chose to use the graded word lists included in the BRI instead of the MLPP word lists.

Phonemic Awareness. Consistent with recent research documenting the centrality of phonemic awareness as a predictor of reading success and as a fundamental prerequisite to learning letter-sound correspondences, we gave short tests for rhyme knowledge (tell me a word that rhymes with "dig"), phonemic blending (what word would I make if I put together these sounds: mmm-aaah-puh?), and phoneme segmentation (what sounds do you hear in pat?). Each of these subtests was comprised of eight items for a total score range of 0 to 24.

Oral Reading and Miscue Analyses. Records of the children's oral reading accuracy and fluency were obtained by taking miscue analyses as children read leveled passages from the BRI. We adapted the BRI to yield quantitative information about children's reading miscues, fluency, comrehension, and retelling. The BRI also provides estimates of children's independent and instructional reading levels based on oral reading accuracy. The BRI was chosen as an individual assessment of oral reading for this evaluation because it has features that are aligned with the Michigan definition of reading and the current Michigan Educational Assessment Program (MEAP) reading test. It is one of many published informal reading inventories designed to provide diagnostic information through measures of oral reading, comprehension, and memory of text. The multiple forms of the BRI allowed us to use different passages for the premeasures and postmeasures in the evaluation design to analyze student growth during the summer. Only after the data were collected did we learn that the different forms are not equivalent, but we were able to make adjustments in the statistical analyses for this shortcoming. The BRI provides an assessment format that is congruent with the MLPP; thus, it was used to assess the validity of the MLPP assessment tools.

Gates–MacGinitie Reading Test (GMRT). The GMRT is a group-administered, norm-referenced, reading test. The lowest level is PRE, and it includes four subtests: Literacy Concepts, Reading Instruction Relational Concepts, Oral Language Concepts (Linguistic Awareness), and Letters and Letter-Sound Correspondences. These subtests are similar to the MLPP assessment tasks and could provide good evidence for concurrent validity of the MLPP. We used Level PRE for prereaders and children who had the least evidence of readiness for reading. For slightly older children or better readers, we administered Level R. Level R also includes four subtests: Let-ter-Sound Correspondences (Initial Consonants and Consonant Clusters), Letter-Sound Correspondences (Final Consonants and Consonant Clus-ters), Letter-Sound Correspondences (Vowels), and Use of Sentence Con-text. All other forms beyond Level R (specifically Levels 1, 2, 3, and 4) yielded separate scores for Vocabulary and Comprehension.

Literacy Habits. The Literacy Habits interview was designed to assess the frequency of reading and writing outside of school. Each child was in-dividually administered a 10-item interview about the amount of reading and writing they did outside of school. For example, children were asked, "How often do you go to the library or Bookmobile?" Children responded with one of three options: "Hardly ever," "About once a week," or "Al-most every day." The greatest frequency was awarded 3 points and the least received 1 point. The total scale ranged from 10 to 30 points, with higher numbers indicating greater frequency of reading and writing out-side of school.

Students' Opinions About Reading (SOAR). The SOAR was given indi-vidually to children to assess their attitudes about their own reading. There were separate items regarding skills, participation, motivation, and attitudes. For children in kindergarten or first grade, the SOAR had two items for each factor, such as, "I can read out loud in class without making many mistakes." Children responded by saying the words or pointing to one of three cards depicting "smiley faces" to indicate "Not at all like me," "A little like me," or "A lot like me," with answers awarded 1, 2, or 3 points, respectively. Children in second or third grade received a version of the SOAR with four items per factor. Thus, the total scale ranged from 8 to 24 points for grades kindergarten through first and 16 to 48 points for grades 2 and 3. Higher scores indicate more positive perceptions of per-sonal ability and attitudes for reading.

Parent Surveys. To assess children's literacy practices at home, a ques-tionnaire regarding students' home reading and writing activities was given to parents or guardians whose children participated in the summer reading program at each sample site and also to parents in the Control group whose children did not attend a summer program. The question-naire included 25 multiple-choice questions about their children's reading and writing activities at home, and their attitudes about those activities. The questionnaire also asked about materials adults read at home. Parents whose children attended the summer reading program were also asked to indicate their involvement in the summer program and their satisfaction with the information they received about their children's progress.

Teacher Surveys. Three separate surveys were administered to teachers: (a) a postprogram survey of summer program teachers; (b) a survey of summer program teachers regarding their students' reading habits, skills, and attitudes; and (c) a brief survey of classroom teachers who received a student from the summer reading program in their classroom in the fall of 1999:

• *Summer Teacher Postprogram Survey.* This survey was conducted at the conclusion of the summer reading programs. Teachers at each site were asked to share their opinions regarding the following: the instructional practices implemented during the summer program, the impact of the program on students, the usefulness of the MLPP, the professional development opportunities offered during the summer, and parent involvement in program activities.

• *Summer Teacher Survey Regarding Students' Skills, Habits, and Attitudes.* The survey of teachers in the summer reading program was designed to gather feedback on what they had learned about individual students' reading habits, skills, and attitudes during the course of the program. The form consisted of 20 statements about the children's skills, habits, and attitudes both within the classroom and outside of school. This information was collected on students for whom BRI, Literacy Habits, and SOAR data were collected at both pretest and posttest.

• *Fall Teacher Survey.* In an effort to learn more about the information provided to classroom teachers who received students from the summer reading program into their classrooms in the fall of 1999, questionnaires were mailed to the fall teachers of a subsample of students who attended the summer reading programs. The form was to be completed for the specific sample student identified on the instrument. The questionnaire items asked teachers to report the following: (a) the types of information they received from both the teacher from the summer reading program and the students' classroom teacher from the previous school year (the spring of 1999), (b) the types of information they would like to receive, and (c) the priority literacy areas in which they intended to work with the student(s) for whom they were responding.

Site Director Postprogram Survey. To gather information from site directors regarding their summer reading programs, postprogram surveys were mailed to each site. The intent of this survey was to have site directors provide their perceptions and judgments regarding various aspects of their programs. These aspects included the following: the effect of the program on students' growth in literacy-related areas, parent involvement, the usefulness of the MLPP, the influence of professional development opportunities on teacher practice, and the efficacy of the program overall.

Procedures for Data Collection

To ensure uniformity and independent, objective testing, a cadre of research assistants from the University of Michigan and Michigan State University were trained in the use and scoring of the selected assessment tools. The research assistants conducted site visits to all 12 districts to administer the pretests, posttests, and the delayed tests. Teachers in each district administered the GMRT to groups of students reading at the same levels.

At each school, researchers arranged for quiet testing rooms for eligible students. In the spring of 1999 pretest, researchers began each testing session by presenting children with the word lists from the BRI at their grade level. If a child could not identify at least 14 words from the lowest BRI word list (i.e., preprimer), the child was classified as a nonreader and given the MLPP tasks. If the child was a reader, then the researcher presented successive word lists and passages until the appropriate levels were found to test each child at an instructional level. At posttest and delayed posttest, children who were prereaders were again given word lists using the same procedures to determine if they were able to read words in lists or text.

MLPP. Children who were prereaders were administered three MLPP tasks: Letter-Sound Identification, Phonemic Awareness (with separate subtests for rhyming, blending, and segmentation), and Concepts of Print. All tasks were administered according to the MLPP guidelines and performance was recorded on the MLPP score sheets.

BRI. The most difficult problem in assessing children was finding the appropriate level of text in the BRI to use to measure their reading proficiency. This difficulty was exacerbated by the lack of familiarity between the researcher and the children and the short time available for testing. It was necessary to give each child text at an instructional level to assess that child with reading material that was neither too difficult nor too easy. According to the BRI, 14 to 18 words identified correctly signifies the instructional level.

If the child had difficulty with the grade-level word list and could not identify at least 14 words, the researcher gave easier word lists. If the child correctly identified more than 14 words, then we gave lists from the next grade level until we determined the highest grade-level word list on which the child could identify at least 14 words. The subsequent passage level given to the child was equivalent to the word list on which the child identified at least 14 words correctly. If the child could read that passage level adequately, the next higher passage level was also given so that each child was administered at least two word lists and two passages, with the highest level of each being challenging. In addition, children were given a passage at their current grade level if one was not given in the regular testing events. The purpose of this procedure was to determine the number of words each child could read correctly per minute from a passage at grade level. This passage level was kept constant at all three testing points.

At the posttest in the fall of 1999, each child was given a word list and passage at the highest level from the spring pretest, but in a different BRI form. In addition, each child also read a word list and passage from the next higher level. We attempted to vary Form A and Form B at pretest, so that approximately half of each sample at each site received each BRI form. The counterbalancing was reasonably effective from pretest to posttest. At the delayed posttest, each child received a word list and passage from the highest level of fall 1999 testing but with the same BRI form as the spring of 1999. The counterbalancing was designed to prevent any child from reading the same word lists or passages at successive testing times, to use alternating BRI testing forms, and to link one passage and word list at the same level at each successive testing time.

Scoring the BRI requires careful attention and consensus about scoring guidelines. We met frequently with all the research assistants who gathered and scored data to ensure uniformity of procedures. We also assessed the reliability of the scoring procedures by having eight people independently score data from the BRI for two children. The inter-rater agreement was calculated for fluency ratings, every miscue, every self-correction, every recalled proposition, every recalled main idea, and every comprehension question. For example, if six of eight raters recorded the same miscue or gave the comprehension question the same score, there was 75% agreement on that item. Then we calculated the average agreement among all items for each dependent variable. The average percentage of agreement among the eight data scorers was 90.6% for fluency judgments, 86.7% for total miscues, 86.4% for significant miscues, 80.1% for self-corrections, 89.9% for propositions recalled, 97.4% for key ideas recalled, and 87.5% for comprehension questions.

These rates of inter-rater agreement are acceptable, but we should note that it was difficult to achieve consensus because of several problems with our methods. First, the tape recordings of children reading solved many problems and allowed us to check our scoring repeatedly, but the volume was often too soft to detect nuances in children's pronunciation. Second, children often substituted or omitted words as they read and it was not easy to determine if the miscues altered the meaning significantly. Third, self-corrections were difficult to assess for the same reasons—soft voices and subtle changes. Fourth, the rubric for judging fluency requires discussion and practice to use consistently, and it is often difficult to judge a child's prosodic features of reading. All of these difficulties were experienced with tape-recorded readings scored by trained researchers. Thus, we worry about the reliability of scoring oral reading inventories "on the spot" by individuals who may have little training and few opportunities to discuss the subtle and complex issues involved in scoring children's oral reading.

Literacy Habits. Researchers explained the purpose of the interview (to learn about the kinds of reading students did) and the response options with an example. Then researchers asked the 10 items in a random manner and recorded the child's responses directly on the form.

SOAR. The purpose of the SOAR and the response options were explained to each child with an example. Then the 8 or 16 items in the surveys were administered in random order; the responses were recorded directly on the form.

GMRT. Teachers at each site administered the GMRT to children in their classrooms, sometimes regrouping students by ability levels of the GMRT.

Surveys

Parent Surveys. Parents responded to a survey of their children's literacy activities and attitudes that closely resembled the Literacy Habits survey and the SOAR. The surveys were mailed to all parents of children in the Control and Experimental groups. There were 439 usable surveys returned; 319 from parents who had children in summer reading programs and 120 from parents whose children were in the Control group.

Summer Teacher Postprogram Survey. A total of 168 teachers were reported to have participated in the summer reading programs; questionnaires were provided to each program's site director for dissemination to these teachers. A total of 119 respondents completed the questionnaire, for an overall return rate of 71%.

Summer Teacher Survey Regarding Students' Skills, Habits, and Attitudes. Paper-and-pencil questionnaires pertaining to individual students were mailed to teachers via U.S. mail. No teacher received more than three questionnaires. Of the 208 questionnaires distributed, 99 were returned, which represents a 48% return rate. A difficulty with this data set is that due to factors such as the selection criteria for students to be included (various test data already collected) and varying return rates by site, some districts were overrepresented, whereas others were underrepresented or not represented at all.

Fall Teacher Survey. Questionnaires were sent via U.S. mail to the 1999 fall teachers of a subsample of students who attended the summer reading program. The sample drawn included 309 of the students in the summer reading program, which corresponded to a total of 139 fall classroom teachers. A total of 91 teachers (65%) responded and provided information for 196 of the subsample of students.

Site Director Postprogram Survey. Paper-and-pencil questionnaires were mailed to the site directors for each of the 12 districts in the summer reading program. Completed questionnaires were returned for tabulation and analysis by all 12 of the site directors in the Goals 2000 Cycle 8 summer reading programs.

RESULTS

The Nature of Summer Instruction

Teachers in the summer school program were asked to complete daily instructional logs for 2 weeks of summer instruction. The log was divided into 14 instructional activities: phonics and phonemic awareness, word identification, comprehension, vocabulary (meaning emphasis), fluency, writing, spelling and mechanics, oral language, shared reading-choral reading, guided reading, partner reading, and independent reading. Teachers were asked to use a 5-point scale to indicate how much time they devoted to each instructional activity during the school day: 1 to 10 minutes, 11 to 20 minutes, 21 to 30 minutes, 31 to 40 minutes, or 40+ minutes. Teachers were also asked to indicate the "grouping format" in which each activity occurred: whole class, small group, one-on-one, learning centers, or independent. Finally, for the reading and writing activities (writing, shared reading, guided reading, partner reading, and independent reading), teachers were asked to indicate the genre of the activity or materials used. The options for reading were stories, poems, nonfiction, peer writing, or mixed genre. The options for writing included stories, poems, nonfiction, personal narrative, responding to literature, journal, and other.

Because instructional activities often overlap, teachers were directed to mark all relevant instructional foci for a given period of time. For example, a 15-minute guided reading activity focused on the development of reading fluency would be coded both as guided reading time and as fluency time. Therefore, the total number of minutes reported for a given day often exceeded the actual instructional time. Teachers were also directed to mark more than one grouping and more than one genre, where applicable.

Ten of the 12 sampled districts submitted logs. One district was excluded from these analyses because the format of the program differed markedly from the others, making comparison difficult. Therefore, 9 of the 12 sample districts are included in these analyses. The number of logs submitted varied across districts and across classrooms. For these analyses, we included all classrooms from which we received logs, but selected a subset of logs from each classroom to avoid overrepresentation from some classrooms. We selected up to 10 logs from each classroom—five from the beginning of the program (roughly the 2nd week) and five from the end (roughly the 4th week). To avoid overrepresentation from districts that submitted logs from many classrooms, we calculated all overall means for time on task by averaging the district means.

Classrooms were grouped differently by grade across districts. Those logs that were submitted from mixed-grade classrooms were counted once for each grade level in analyses by grade. For example, logs for a kindergarten through first grade classroom would be counted once for kindergarten and once for first grade.

Time on Task

To simplify the time-on-task analyses, we combined the 14 instructional categories into five factors:

- Factor 1   Code-level emphasis (word identification + phonics + spelling).
- Factor 2   Meaning-level emphasis (comprehension + vocabulary).
- Factor 3   Reading (oral reading + fluency + shared reading + guided reading + partner reading + independent reading).
- Factor 4   Writing.
- Factor 5   Art and other.

For time-on-task analyses, we substituted average times for each of the time options (e.g., 5 minutes for 0–10 minutes). We are reporting the results of time-on-task analyses in terms of percentage of total reported time, rather than mean minutes per day, because there was substantial variability across districts in reporting practices. Teachers were instructed to count activities with overlapping instructional foci multiple times, where appropriate. Therefore, as previously noted, the total number of minutes reported could greatly exceed the total number of minutes in the instructional day. The extent to which reported minutes exceeded the length of the instructional day varied from district to district. Time-on-

TABLE 6.2
Percentage of Time on Task by Factor (Across Districts and Grades)

Factor	N	Mean Percentage
Factor 1: Code-level	641	25
Factor 2: Meaning-level	641	17
Factor 3: Reading	641	39
Factor 4: Writing	641	13
Factor 5: Art and other	641	7

task analyses based on total number of reported minutes would not have taken this into account. As shown in Table 6.2, students in summer school spent the most time (about 39% of the total reported time) on reading activities. More time was devoted to activities emphasizing code-level skills (25%) than those emphasizing meaning-related skills (17%). The time spent on any factor (as a percentage of reported time) varied somewhat across districts, but the overall distributions did not vary markedly. Seven of the nine districts allotted time to the activities in the same order (in descending order): reading, code-level emphasis, meaning-level emphasis, writing, and art. The two districts that differed did so only in that they spent more time on art and other activities than writing activities. Districts varied most in the amount of time devoted to code-level activities (18% to 29%) and reading activities (32% to 45%).

Grouping

In addition to characterizing the summer programs according to their instructional foci, we identified the grouping formats that teachers used most frequently in conducting the various instructional activities. Students, especially kindergartners, spent most of their instructional time in whole-class groupings during all activities except guided, partner, and independent reading. Oral reading took place in whole-class settings 90% of the time, whereas phonics activities occurred in whole-group settings 81% of the time. Overall, code-emphasis and meaning-emphasis activities tended to be taught in whole-group formats, whereas reading and writing activities were more equally distributed across a variety of student grouping arrangements.

Kindergarten students were less likely than older students to spend time in small groups during most activities—notably excluding oral reading, shared reading, and partner reading. Kindergarten students had fewer instances of small-group work for phonics, word identification, spelling, comprehension, vocabulary, fluency, guided reading, and writing, than first, second, or third graders. The only exception was that third graders had a slightly lower percentage of small-group work for phonics and spelling.

With the exception of writing, kindergarten students generally had more one-on-one time with the teacher during all of these activities than did older students. Older students (second and third graders) were more likely than younger students to work one-on-one with the teacher on writing activities. Younger students (particularly kindergarteners and first graders) were more likely than older students to spend some of their phonics, word identification, spelling, and comprehension time in learning centers.

The Relation Between Instructional Practices and Student Growth

To determine whether there was any relation between instructional practices and student achievement, we used the classroom as the basic unit of analysis to conduct computed correlations between the mean gain scores of students in each classroom and various aggregate indexes of instructional emphasis (time spent on various factors). Although there were a few moderate correlations of some interest, the overwhelming conclusion is that instructional factors, as reported by the teachers, did not predict average student growth.

Characterizing High- and Low-Growth Classrooms

In addition to looking at overall trends in summer instruction and their relation to student growth, we turned the question of achievement gain around. Instead of asking whether summer school made a difference, we located the highest growth classrooms from our sample and compared them to the lowest growth classrooms in terms of curricular emphases and instructional activities. Our goal was to identify characteristics of high-achieving classrooms. The results of these analyses are summarized briefly.

During the summer of 1999, we conducted observations in 24 summer classrooms. We selected eight of these classrooms for close analysis on the basis of students' pretest-to-posttest change scores on eight reading measures: number of words read correctly on sight-word lists, reading time on instructional-level passages, total miscues on instructional-level passages, only meaning-changing miscues on instructional-level passages, propositions recalled on instructional-level passages, comprehension questions correct on instructional-level passages, key ideas recalled on instructional-level passages, and words read correctly in 1 minute on the grade-level passages. In about half of the eight sample classrooms, students had experienced growth on nearly all of the eight reading indicators (higher growth classrooms); in the other classrooms, students lost ground on most of the dimensions, despite their attendance in summer school (lower growth classrooms). We used our observations, in addition to teachers' instructional logs, to look within and across these classrooms for factors that distinguished instruction in the high-growth versus low-growth classrooms.

Higher growth classrooms were characterized by several consistent themes and practices. In higher growth classrooms, teachers provided instruction in a variety of formats: a combination of embedded and direct skill instruction; integrated and themed instruction; and an abundance of scaffolded coaching, including one-on-one reading time with the teacher. Overall, the curricula in the higher growth classrooms exhibited a comprehensiveness that lower growth classrooms lacked. What emerges is a picture of a classroom in which there is ongoing, integrated, balanced literacy practices with support from the teacher in the form of explicit instruction, minilessons, and scaffolded support in whole-group and one-on-one settings.

Oral Reading Measures

It is possible to compare reading rates of children in this study to norms for reading rates provided by Hasbrouck and Tindal (1992). Those norms indicate that second graders at the median rate should be reading about 94 words correct per minute (wcpm), and that students in the bottom quartile read about 65 wcpm by spring of second grade. The mean wcpm for Experimental and Control second graders were 51 and 62 respectively, which were both below expected rates for children in the lowest quartile. By the spring of third grade, the means for each group had climbed to 79 and 93. These compare with the Hasbrouck and Tindal (1992) norms of 87 wcpm for the lowest quartile and 114 wcpm for the mean. Thus, we see that children in both groups were reading at rates that would place them far below their peer groups.

We chose to administer an oral reading inventory because it provides multiple indicators of reading skills. We analyzed 10 dependent variables derived from the BRI to determine if there were differences between Experimental and Control students. For the word-list data, we created a common scale to analyze children's identification of words by giving children credit for lists below the level on which they were tested. For example, if a child correctly identified 19 words on the first-grade list and 15 words on the second-grade list, the total score was 19 + 15 = 34 + 20 for the primer list + 20 for the preprimer list = 74. There were no significant differences due to summer school between spring and fall of 1999, but there was a significant effect favoring the Control children between the pretest and the delayed test. The mean gain scores (pretest to delayed test) were 24.6 for the Experimental children and 28.1 for the children in the Control group. Control children scored higher than Experimental children at every testing time, which again raises the possibility that the groups were not equal in the beginning.

We analyzed the oral reading measures in the conventional manner. That is, we compared measures such as the percentage of oral reading accuracy between Experimental and Control groups, although the measures were derived from different grade-level passages. Using analyses of variance (ANOVAs) and analyses of covariance (ANCOVAs) on the percent scores and on pretest to posttest change scores, we found no indications of differences between the Experimental and Control groups at any of the three testing times. We found a disappointing pattern of results for all of the following measures: oral reading accuracy, oral reading acceptability, prosody, self-corrections, propositions recalled, key ideas recalled, comprehension, and total reading time. We struggled with these data and the disappointing results for more than a year before discovering a statistical solution.

An Analytical Breakthrough

Perhaps the most significant point in this chapter is the solution to the pervasive problem of analyzing oral reading behavior. As oral reading measures are increasingly being used by states for K–3 reading assessment, our solution may prove useful to many states and districts. We were troubled by conventional analyses of BRI data across different passage levels because they do not provide more "credit" for performance on more difficult passages. The solution was to use analyses based on Item Response Theory (IRT) because it places all items (in this case, passages) on a common scale (see Embretson & Reise, 2000). This is the same kind of analysis used by large-scale tests such as the Scholastic Aptitude Test (SAT), the National Assessment of Educational Progress (NAEP), and Michigan Educational Assessment Program (MEAP), but it has not been used for analyses of children's oral reading inventory data. Perhaps BRI data have not been analyzed with IRT techniques because the measures were designed to be informal and formative, not summative. Because measures of oral reading performance are being used more and more often for accountability, IRT analyses may become popular for analyzing children's oral reading data on graded passages. IRT requires a large sample and multiple "items" for each subject to estimate item difficulty and individual student-ability scores simultaneously (Hambleton & Swaminathan, 1985). In our analyses, items were the different IRI passages administered across grade levels, forms, and testing times. We used a software program called Conquest to analyze the data and to create scaled scores for each child on each oral reading measure derived from reading passages.

The differences in results between IRT and conventional analyses were striking. IRT analyses revealed consistent and clear demonstrations of the positive impact of summer reading programs on many features of children's oral reading. Figure 6.1 illustrates the IRT mean values for fluency scores. Fluency was a composite score derived from accuracy, prosody, and rate measures and is best thought of as an aggregate index of oral reading fluency. Figure 6.1 shows that the two groups were similar in oral reading fluency at the initial pretest, but the Control group showed the classic summer loss by posttest. Children in the Experimental group who attended summer school showed no summer loss and both groups gained similar amounts in the following year.

Similar trends are evident for the IRT scores on reading rate and comprehension as shown in Figs. 6.2 and 6.3. Reading rate declined during the summer only for children who did not attend summer school. Comprehension for these Control group children remained level during the summer but increased modestly for children who attended summer school. Both rate and comprehension measures improved at similar rates during the following school year. These three figures illustrate dramatic positive effects of summer school that are consistent with previous research and quite different than our previous analyses with the BRI oral reading data.

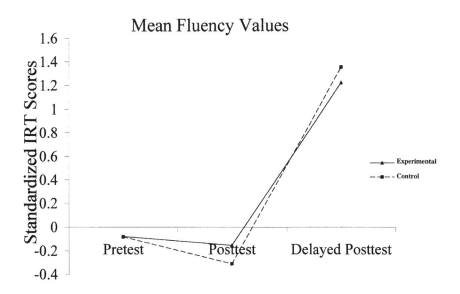

FIG. 6.1.   Mean Item Response Theory reading fluency by group and time.

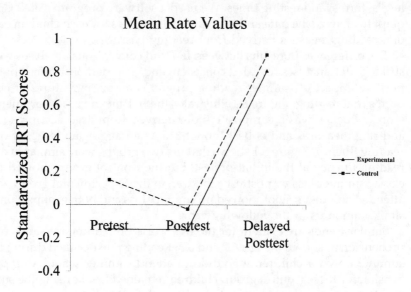

FIG. 6.2. Mean Item Response Theory reading rate by group and time.

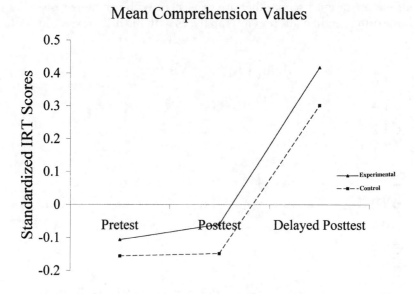

FIG. 6.3. Mean Item Response Theory reading comprehension by group and time.

From the IRT analyses, we can conclude that children who did not attend summer school in 1999 showed classic summer reading loss from spring to fall. This was evident for reading rate, fluency, and accuracy. Children who did attend summer school at the sites in our study showed no overall decline on these aspects of reading. Comprehension was the same for children in both groups. Thus, attending summer school provided a general "buffer" for the reading loss that children at risk usually experience. The buffer effect of summer school was significant at a modest but expected level.

A meta-analysis by Cooper et al. (2000) suggested that summer school has an effect size of .22, and our summer reading programs showed an effect size of .33 or a third of a school year. The buffer effect did not vary across grade levels. In first, second, and third grades, the advantages of summer school were statistically the same. The long-term benefits of summer school are evident in the fact that children in both groups achieved approximately similar levels in the spring of 2000. In other words, the children who were most at risk and attended summer school did not fall further behind or lose the gains that they made over the summer. In spring of 2000, however, they did not outperform children who did not attend summer school. Given that summer school students, as a whole, showed lower initial reading achievement, this suggests that the gap between groups was closed during the year. Thus, they caught up to the level of the Control group but did not surpass it.

Gates–MacGinitie Reading Test (GMRT)

We asked staff members in each sample district to administer the GMRT to students who had been identified by their schools as eligible for summer school. Initial examination of the GMRT scores revealed a wide range of performance at each level, which may suggest that some children were given levels of the test that were either much too easy or too difficult for them. We were concerned that the children who earned very high scores at the pretest were operating at a ceiling performance level, which might prevent them from showing improvement at posttest or delayed posttest. Thus, we removed from the analysis all children who scored more than 1.5 SDs above the mean for their grade level at pretest from the GMRT sample. Table 6.3 shows the numbers of students included in the analyses of GMRT. There were 783 children who took the GMRT in the spring of 1999; 669 of those students took the GMRT again one year later.

We conducted separate analyses of variance at each level of the GMRT—PRE, R, 1, 2, and 3. Table 6.4 shows the raw score totals for Levels PRE and R and the scaled scores for Vocabulary, Comprehension, and Total scores at Levels 1, 2, and 3. For Levels PRE, R, and 1, the Experimental

TABLE 6.3
Sample Sizes by Testing Time and Status

	Overall		Experimental		Control	
	Pre	Delayed	Pre	Delayed	Pre	Delayed
Gender						
Male	444	376	251	218	193	158
Female	339	293	178	155	161	138
Grade						
Kindergarten	101	80	54	44	47	36
1	276	228	167	141	109	87
2	237	208	125	114	112	94
3	169	153	83	74	86	79
Ethnicity						
White	455	386	241	211	214	175
African American	176	149	95	82	81	67
Hispanic	92	81	51	43	41	38
Native American	41	39	27	25	14	14
Asian	8	8	7	7	1	1
Multiracial	10	6	8	5	2	1
GMRT						
Pre	138	47	79	29	54	18
R	142	123	81	79	55	44
1	240	82	134	44	105	38
2	156	205	87	121	68	84
3	121	141	48	75	723	66
4		71		25		46
Level						
No Level	36	31	17	14	19	17
MLPP	225	185	142	119	83	66
Preprimer	86	72	58	51	28	21
Primer	39	26	26	18	13	8
Grade 1	77	63	42	37	35	26
Grade 2	108	91	48	43	60	48
Grade 3	76	75	37	36	39	39
Grade 4	56	56	27	26	32	30
Grade 5	39	34	20	17	19	17
Grade 6	38	36	12	12	26	24

Note. MLPP = Michigan Literacy Progress Profile.

group showed significantly larger gains from pretest to posttest than the Control group, but none of the gains persisted as significant advantages at the delayed posttest.

The youngest and least skillful readers in summer school made significant gains on the GMRT, but children who took Levels 2 and 3 did not. Control group children at the three lowest levels showed summer loss or modest gains on the GMRT, whereas the children who attended summer school showed significant growth from spring to fall. At most levels, the

TABLE 6.4

Means and Standard Deviations for Gates–MacGinitie Reading Test (GMRT) Scores at Pretest, Posttest, and Delayed Posttest by Status

	GMRT	Experimental			Control		ANOVA Results	
	M[a] (SD)	Pretest M (SD)	Posttest M (SD)	Delayed Posttest M (SD)	Pretest M (SD)	Posttest M (SD)	Prepost	Predelay
Pre[b]	67.0 (14.1)	71.8 (14.3)	62.1 (19.7)	68.7 (13.8)	69.5 (13.6)	64.5 (20.0)	* (F = 6.3)	* (F = 4.4)
R	37.7 (9.0)	38.7 (11.8)	55.6 (15.3)	44.2 (10.7)	43.6 (11.2)	62.8 (16.1)	* (F = 3.9)	N/S
1[c]	389.0 (34.9)	394.2 (33.6)	479.9 (178.9)	395.5 (35.3)	395.9 (38.8)	470.8 (159.1)	N/S	N/S
Scaled vocabulary 2	413.5 (30.8)	416.0 (30.4)	464.5 (111.0)	411.0 (33.3)	414.4 (32.9)	458.5 (104.6)	N/S	N/S
3	444.3 (27.1)	447.2 (36.9)	468.1 (33.3)	446.8 (31.5)	450.7 (33.4)	473.2 (31.2)	N/S	N/S

(Continued)

147

TABLE 6.4
(Continued)

	GMRT[a]	Experimental Pretest	Experimental Posttest	Experimental Delayed Posttest	Control Pretest	Control Posttest	ANOVA Results Delayed Posttest (Prepost)	ANOVA Results (Predelay)
	M (SD)	M (SD)	M (SD)	M (SD)	M (SD)	M (SD)	Prepost	Predelay
Scaled comprehension 1	348.5 (61.3)	362.7 (64.4)	478.2 (184.1)	366.2 (60.0)	371.8 (68.3)	458.8 (154.8)	N/S	N/S
2	393.2 (58.8)	410.1 (62.7)	462.3 (116.8)	395.5 (48.1)	401.7 (46.3)	460.9 (130.0)	N/S	N/S
3	421.1 (49.3)	408.5 (74.1)	453.7 (53.3)	430.3 (46.5)	438.3 (52.3)	469.0 (52.7)	** ($F = 7.4$)	MS
Scaled total 1	374.5 (42.7)	382.9 (41.6)	479.9 (180.2)	384.9 (42.0)	386.3 (47.2)	469.7 (160.8)	* ($F = 4.0$)	N/S
2	406.2 (37.1)	413.6 (38.7)	464.8 (112.2)	406.6 (33.2)	410.6 (34.5)	466.7 (126.4)	N/S	N/S
3	437.8 (30.2)	436.0 (46.6)	465.3 (36.9)	442.1 (32.8)	447.6 (36.9)	473.8 (36.3)	N/S	N/S

Note. ANOVA = analysis of variance.

[a] Pretest means differ slightly when comparing the posttest and delayed posttest because the sample was slightly smaller at delayed posttest. The pretest means reported in this column are from the posttest comparison.

[b] GMRT scores at level "Pre" and "R" are raw scores, whereas the scores at levels 1 to 4 are scaled.

[c] The level is the pretest GMRT level.

$*p < .05.$ $**p < .01.$

children in the Control group had higher scores at both pretest and posttest, but they made less growth compared to the children who attended summer school. There were no gender differences at any level. On this measure, then, we can conclude that summer reading programs had the greatest benefit for the youngest and poorest readers, at least in the short run. By contrast, whatever differences exist at delayed posttest favor the Control group—implying that any short-term advantages gained during summer school are overwhelmed by other factors in the following school year. This might imply that summer reading programs need to be reinforced throughout the following year to sustain gains students make, or it might demonstrate that the benefits of summer school are more evident on oral reading tasks than on standardized achievement tests.

Value Added Analyses

Because we had access to substantial data on program features, we were able to analyze growth on the GMRT as a function of these characteristics. We used Hierarchical Linear Modeling (HLM) to examine the impact of different program characteristics on reading gains. For the sake of simplicity, as well as in fairness to programs, our interpretation was restricted to students who had approximately 60 hours of summer school instruction—in other words, students who attended most of the summer school sessions. Two characteristics of summer programs helped to explain which sites showed greater gains over the summer, but neither factor predicted differential achievement in the subsequent year. We are cautious in interpreting these effects because there were only 19 sites in which we could observe variation in these characteristics, and because we investigated a number of additional site characteristics, raising concerns about Type I error.

The first factor was the total years of experience of the teachers in summer school, which proved a significant influence on summer-school gains in GMRT Vocabulary scores. On average, students who attended summer school at sites with more experienced teachers made significantly larger gains over the summer than students who attended summer school at sites with less experienced teachers. In fact, the average total years of experience of teachers at each site accounted for 43% of the variance in the growth of the GMRT Vocabulary scores. Invoking the appropriate cautions, we can say that sites with more experienced teachers had students who made larger gains in vocabulary than did students at sites with less experienced teachers. This finding is important because we have found that many schools have great difficulty convincing their experienced teachers to work in their summer school programs, and must often resort to hiring teachers from other districts or newly credentialed teachers who have little or no experience in running their own classrooms.

A second significant finding emerged from the HLM analysis of the GMRT Comprehension scores. The largest summer gains in GMRT Comprehension scores were evident for students at sites where teachers reported using one or another of several structured methods and approaches that were listed on a school survey of practices and programs. Teachers indicated on a survey the extent to which they used methods that are similar to the methods of structured literacy programs such as Accelerated Reader, Richard Owen Literacy Network, Reading Recovery, Success For All, and Project Read. The HLM analyses compared students in classes where teachers reported varying levels of use of such approaches (including no use). The reported use of structured literacy approaches accounted for 54% of the variance in the effectiveness of attending summer school on producing summer school gains on GMRT Comprehension scores. The analysis revealed greater gains for students at sites where structured approaches were used. In fact, in contrast to the gains of students attending a school exhibiting characteristics of one or more of these structured programs, all students at sites where teachers reported no use of structured literacy approaches exhibited the classic summer loss pattern. This loss pattern is identical to the IRT patterns reported earlier and shows that, for at-risk readers, absence of participation in a reading program with these characteristics promotes a summer loss in reading comprehension.

In addition to the cautions we raised with respect to the danger of Type I errors, we also need to caution readers not to jump to the conclusion that structure is equal to rigidity. We would point out that many of the programs in the list provided on the survey promote highly flexible and adaptable use of materials and teaching strategies. Perhaps the point is that structure, organization, and clear purposes promote a general disposition to teaching and learning that is responsible for the observed growth.

Assessments for Prereaders

The MLPP tasks that assess Phonemic Awareness and Concepts of Print were administered to all children who were unable to read words in isolation on the BRI word lists. We referred to them as prereaders. At the pretest in spring of 1999, 111 children in the Experimental group and 108 children in the Control group met the prereader criterion and were given MLPP tasks. The sample of 219 children was reduced to 129 children at the delayed posttest in spring of 2000 because many children learned to read in the interim, but a small percentage of the reduction resulted from family relocation and absenteeism.

There were more male than female prereaders in both the Experimental and Control groups overall and at each grade level. The composition of the prereader sample mirrors the general sample of readers for both treatment groups. Slightly more than half of the sample were White and approximately 25% were African American. Most of the prereaders were in kindergarten or first grade in the spring of 1999. The sample sizes of prereaders in second and third grade were small. We eliminated them from the analysis because their status as prereaders likely stems from very different etiologies than for the younger prereaders.

The results of ANOVAs comparing Experimental and Control groups (Status) for pretest versus posttest and for pretest versus delayed test revealed few differences. Blending and rhyming showed no significant effects of Grade or Status. If the change scores are examined, the Experimental Group shows a significant improvement on Blending, but not Rhyming. Segmentation revealed a significant Status × Grade interaction, indicating a small difference between Experimental and Control groups in first grade, but a significant difference favoring the Experimental group in kindergarten. The aggregated Phonemic Awareness Total Score revealed only a marginally significant grade effect and no effect due to summer school. Analyses of change scores, however, showed that kindergarten Experimental children made significantly greater gains than Control kindergarten children (2.2 vs. .7) from pretest to posttest.

The scores for Concepts of Print revealed no differences due to Status but significantly higher scores for first graders in comparison to kindergarten children. It is unclear why scores at pretest in the spring of 1999 were higher than posttest at fall of 1999. Perhaps children were all showing some "summer loss" in familiarity with books in the fall, or perhaps they were especially aware of book concepts in the spring.

Although the MLPP and GMRT data on a host of "reading readiness" measures suggest that children in the Control group were more prepared to make the transition to "reader" status in the spring of 1999, it was the Experimental students who were more likely to make the transition by the early fall (and even a year later). Table 6.5 shows that 25 prereaders in the Experimental group (23%) became readers by fall of 1999, in contrast to only 10 in the Control group (9%). Although the fact that 10 children in the Control group learned to read during the summer again suggests that they had positive literacy experiences without a summer school intervention, attending summer school helped twice as many prereaders make that important transition. The advantage of attending summer school persisted slightly even at the delayed test; 78% of Experimental students were readers 1 year later, compared to 71% of Control students. Even more remarkable is the range of reading skills that these children developed in 1 year. Thirty-seven children (33%) in the Experimental group and 38 (35%) in the Control group were reading at the primer and preprimer level.

TABLE 6.5
Reading Levels at Posttest and Delayed Posttest for Students
Who Were Classified as Prereaders at Pretest

Passage	Experimental		Control	
	Posttest	Delayed Posttest	Posttest	Delayed Posttest
Preprimer	13	13	7	20
Primer	8	24	3	18
1	1	26	0	13
2	2	12	0	12
3	1	8	0	5
4	0	4	0	4
5	0	0	0	5
6	0	0	0	0
Total	25	87	10	77

Thirty-eight children (35%) in the Experimental group, but only 25 (23%) in the Control group, were reading at first- or second-grade levels on the BRI. Perhaps most remarkable were the 12 Experimental and 14 Control students who were able to read BRI passages at third-grade levels or beyond only a year after they had been first identified as prereaders (i.e., students who were unable to read even 14 words on the preprimer word list).

Although we cannot dismiss the possibility that they were not assessed correctly at pretest, this sort of growth pattern suggests that some students might legitimately be called "late bloomers." It must be acknowledged that summer school was no more responsible for supporting the development of these late bloomers than was whatever set of activities families may have engaged in over the summer and subsequent school year. Nonetheless, the large treatment differences in the number of students who moved over the boundary from "nonreader" to "reader" certainly suggests that something positive happened in summer school— something of a catalytic nature that assisted many students in moving over this critical threshold.

Literacy Habits and Opinions About Reading

Students' Literacy Habits. There were no significant main effects or interactions on Literacy Habits scores by Status, Grade, and Testing Time. Although there were neither ceiling nor floor effects on the measure, it did not reveal changes between groups or over time.

Student Opinions About Reading (SOAR). There were no significant differences between Experimental and Control groups for either the kindergarten- through first-grade or the second- to third-grade versions of the

SOAR. In addition, there were no differences between kindergarten and first grade or between second and third grade on the same versions.

Parental Reports Regarding Student Habits and Attitudes.   Parents were asked to respond to items assessing their perceptions of their child's literacy habits and attitudes toward reading. There were 319 respondents from the Experimental group and 121 from the Control group. We compared the parents of students in the Experimental and Control groups. We found only one overall Experimental versus Control difference in students' habits. Parents of second-grade students in the Experimental group judged their children to possess superior habits in comparison to the Control group parents. When we examined the data item by item (e.g., going to the library, reading at home, etc.), we found some differences favoring the Experimental over the Control group and about an equal number favoring the Control over the Experimental. With respect to attitudes toward reading, we found no Experimental–Control differences. It was interesting to note that parental ratings of attitudes decreased steadily with the age of the students for whom they were reporting attitudes. This finding mirrors the usual age-related decline when students are queried about their attitudes.

DISCUSSION

The most important finding of this research is the demonstration that summer reading programs can provide significant advantages to young children who are at risk for low achievement. In Study 1, we showed that children who attended summer reading programs read the same passages faster, more accurately, and with greater comprehension at the end of summer school than at the beginning. The lack of controls and comparisons weakens the conclusions from Study 1, however. That is why the experimental design of Study 2 was important.

In Study 2, we tested K–3 students eligible for summer school in the spring and identified those who did and did not attend summer programs at 19 different sites throughout the state. For students who began the study as prereaders, summer school helped to move significantly more of them from prereader to reader status, meaning that they were able to read at least the lowest level text on the BRI; moreover, this gain was accelerated during the ensuing school year. The IRT analyses of data on oral reading performance showed convincingly that students who attended summer school improved their reading accuracy, rate, fluency, and comprehension by fall when compared to students who did not attend summer programs. In the following school year, students who attended summer school maintained their gains and exhibited similar rates of growth as students in the Control group—so the initial achievement gap was actually narrowed.

The same benefits of summer school were evident on GMRT standardized test scores for the youngest and most struggling readers. The HLM analyses provided more detail about the specific program features that provided the greatest gains on the GMRT scores. Programs that used structured literacy programs most frequently showed greater summer gains for students than programs that did not use structured programs as often Thus, GRMT scores indicate that summer school produced significant positive reading gains for children in primary grades and served as a buffer for summer reading loss that low-achieving students often experience.

With regard to the 10 conclusions about summer programs offered by Cooper et al. (2000), our research supports several of their points, specifically numbers 1, 5, 6, 9, and 10. In particular, our research shows that effective summer programs are remedial, focused, and programmatic—that is, structured and organized for consistent instruction. The gains were evident for children in K–3, but some analyses revealed greater gains for the youngest or most struggling readers. Regular assessment and monitoring appeared to be helpful. Successful programs had low teacher–student ratios and frequent parent involvement.

Our research did not support Cooper's point number 8 that suggested gains diminish over time (Cooper et al., 2000). In fact, our Study 2 demonstrated that the rates of learning in the academic year following summer school were parallel between children in the Experimental and Control groups. If anything, the achievement gap decreased, not increased, over the year.

There is an important lesson in this research about the kinds of statistical analyses needed to analyze summer school programs. We spent more than 2 years collecting and analyzing oral reading data from young children and analyzing the data in conventional ways. Unfortunately, traditional analyses of oral reading accuracy, fluency, and comprehension confound passage levels and text difficulty that make comparisons across students and time difficult and perhaps inappropriate. We spent months analyzing the BRI data with IRT analyses, and the results were astonishing in contrast to the traditional analyses. ANOVAs of traditional BRI measures revealed few effects of summer school between students in the Experimental and Control groups, whereas IRT analyses showed clear summer losses for most Control students and clear summer gains for Experimental students. Analyses of GMRT scores, which are also equated through IRT techniques, revealed significant advantages of summer reading programs. We think the message for researchers is clear; IRT is the most sensitive and appropriate analytical technique for children's oral reading performance data gathered from leveled books or passages. This should have profound consequences for programs such as Reading Recovery and commercial IRIs such as the QRI–II and BRI that use passages and text graded by difficulty levels. Whenever such graded oral reading-performance data are collected for assessing student growth or program evaluation, IRT analyses may be required.

Another important lesson that we learned from this research is the difficulty in using experimental methods that depend on random assignment of students to groups and equivalent groups at pretest. There is ample evidence in our data set to support the hypothesis that the sample of summer school attendees was more needy, in terms of academic skills, than the sample of students who ended up in the Control group. Despite our attempts to create comparable Experimental and Control groups by asking personnel at each site to create an omnibus pool of all students who were eligible to attend summer school, we were not able to establish strict comparability of the two groups.

It is also clear that random assignment to summer programs is not feasible because families choose whether to send their children to summer school for many reasons. We suspect that three factors account for the lack of comparability of the samples. First, although all students were eligible, teachers may well have encouraged attendance at summer school for those students who needed help the most. Second, families who make summer plans for their children that do not include summer school may provide other advantages for their children, such as alternative literacy activities or other experiences (trips and cultural events) that are equally as supportive of reading achievement and growth during the summer. Third, the 50 to 60 hours of literacy activity experienced during summer school pales in comparison to the 360 to 540 hours of instruction that students experience during the regular academic year. Given that students in the Control group may have been higher achievers and less needy than students in the Experimental group, it is even more compelling that we found strong evidence of gains over the summer for readers who were most at risk.

Another lesson that we learned from this research is about which factors affect summer gains in reading. First, we wondered whether attendance during the summer was the crucial factor, so we divided the children into high- and low-absenteeism groups to predict growth from pretest to posttest among all children who attended summer school. Attendance did not explain variations in performance gain from pretest to posttest to delayed test. Second, we compared the bottom and top 25% of both summer school attendees and Control group children to determine whether they shared any common characteristics, such as age, gender, race, site, and so forth. No clear patterns or relations emerged from this analysis. Third, the factors that did produce the most summer gains are related to the amount of time spent reading and the degree of structure in the instructional program.

Analyses of the teacher log data revealed that children spent most of their time on reading activities. Most of the instructional time was spent in whole-class groupings during all activities except for guided, partner, and independent reading. For the majority of the districts represented, the story genre was used most frequently. Instructional logs reported class groupings, genres used, and the amount of time students spent reading, which helped us to distinguish the practices of higher and lower growth classrooms. In higher growth classrooms, students read extensively in a variety of formats, including small groups and one-on-one settings with the teacher. These students received some direct instruction in reading skills, but these skills were more frequently scaffolded in the context of authentic and integrated reading activities.

The survey data revealed that all stakeholders held positive perceptions of the summer programs. Teachers and program coordinators were very satisfied with the programs they carried out, and they judged them to have high, positive impact on students' literacy and their overall well-being. Program coordinators rated the programs as either very effective or somewhat effective in improving reading skills, increasing motivation and attitudes about reading, and participation in learning for all levels of students (kindergarten through third grade). Teachers were equally as enthusiastic about the impact of summer school on student achievement and disposition. When queried about the program components that were responsible for these positive outcomes, teachers most frequently mentioned the small class size, the conceptual framework of the program, and the materials used.

One final comment is in order about Michigan's summer schools. Compared to other summer programs around the country, the summer programs in Michigan have taken the high road on evaluation. They have not, as have other programs, geared their summer programs to improving scores on the outcome measures by having students do little other than completing worksheets that mimic the posttest. Instead, they have crafted programs on sound principles of curriculum, exemplary practice, and high student engagement. The state has worked collaboratively with teachers to develop and refine the MLPP and to publicize exemplary summer programs. The significant gains on standardized tests and oral reading behaviors add impressive support to Michigan's approaches to both instruction and assessment.

In the years following our summer research project, we have documented effective summer school practices and various ways that individual schools can evaluate their summer programs and document their successes. This information was available on the Internet so that educators who were designing summer programs could build local capacity for reading assessment, summer school evaluation, and program documentation. It was a practical consequence of the collaborative research that we conducted, and it enabled other schools and districts to download our assessment materials, instructional plans, and training videos. Unfortunately, the Web site and funding for summer programs were discontinued in the economic downturn of 2002.

IMPLICATIONS FOR PROGRAM EVALUATION

Our experiences with summer school programs in the state of Michigan provided us with many insights about summer school. Therefore, we make the following recommendations for implementing and assessing effective summer reading programs:

Avoid control-group evaluation designs. As desirable as it might be from a strictly scientific perspective, we do not think schools and districts should invest in control-group evaluation designs. It is impossible to create genuine control groups because schools cannot ethically assign students randomly to experimental and control groups. Parents and teachers must retain a voice in deciding which children attend summer school; as long as these sorts of intentional decisions are a part of the process, genuine experiments cannot be achieved. When other procedures are used, it is likely that the experimental and control groups differ in many potential ways such as motivation, parent involvement, and pretest scores. Statistical methods for trying to equate groups may lead to deleting participants or transforming the data, so making equivalent groups may not be possible. Finally, it seems unfair to relegate some students to a control group when they might benefit from summer school too.

Opt for a high-quality battery of pretests and posttests. Rather than testing twice as many students (as they would with a Control group), schools should invest in better assessments for those students who do attend summer school. Other things being equal, the tests should be as similar as possible from pretest to posttest. Potential assessments include the following: oral reading fluency and accuracy; curriculum-based assessments of comprehension performance, instructional reading level, or both; and specific skill or process assessments (e.g., the tasks in the MLPP). The assessments should be directly related to the summer school curriculum or individual children's particular needs and strengths. One useful strategy might be to have one assessment that is exactly the same from pretest to posttest and a second that requires the transfer and application to a new task, passage, or situation. In that way, it would be possible to answer two important questions: (a) Did the students improve at all? and (b) how will their new learning transfer to new text or situations?

Use surveys to obtain the views of key constituents. Over the past 2 years, the surveys used in the evaluation program have provided useful information for the state of Michigan and hold similar potential for each site. We believe that surveys like those used by the evaluation team should be a part of every summer school program evaluation. As good as it is to know the perceptions of the participants, however, they must always play a supporting role in relation to data on student achievement, which must remain the basis on which summer programs are evaluated.

Provide schools with resources to help them conduct rigorous, useful evaluations. These resources may include adequate staff to collect and analyze assessment data, as well as adequate time to administer, analyze, and report assessment results. These resources may also include standardized tests, informal assessments (e.g., the MLPP assessments), information for professional development, and other materials or training required to assess children's progress. The Michigan Department of Education developed a resource, in the form of a handbook and a Web site, that local districts and schools used to help them craft credible program evaluations. We hope other state and district agencies will do everything possible to build local capacity to assess the effectiveness of summer school programs.

Use the very best personnel. There is some evidence from our experience that summer school programs are not always staffed with the best-qualified, most experienced personnel. At some sites, teachers were recruited from other districts or from the ranks of the very inexperienced to fill slots that were not taken by experienced staff. If we want summer school to become the opportunity for educational renewal that the policy community claims it to be, and that parents and the public want it to be, then we will have to recruit our very best teachers. This means active recruiting and higher salaries, for starters.

Give students the time and attention they need. The current version of summer school, with teacher–pupil ratios of 1:10, goes a long way toward providing the opportunities for one-on-one attention, scaffolding, and feedback that students most at risk for failure will require. But we can do better. Schools should do everything possible to find time for students to receive daily one-on-one attention so that instruction can be targeted to their particular needs. Some districts have been able to recruit college interns—individuals who have completed their teacher-education coursework and practica, but not yet taken full-time jobs, to provide this sort of attention and scaffolding.

Coordinate summer programs with regular school-year teachers and programs. In 1999, schools were much more successful in establishing lines of communication between summer school teachers and the receiving teachers than they were in the 1998 effort. Now it is time to establish the link on the other end, so that the regular-year teacher can provide to the summer teacher diagnostic information and any data on what has and has not worked instructionally for each child. In this way, students are more likely to go to the next grade with some level of mastery over the skills, strategies, and processes that eluded them in the previous grade.

Increase the time available for prime time instruction. Between 1998 and 1999, Michigan summer school programs made great strides in ensuring that students received a critical mass of instructional time in summer school. The goal was 60 hours. Not all programs achieved that goal. In the future, we should insist on finding ways to ensure this minimal goal, otherwise programs cannot meet the demand of the renewal role that we are asking of them. And it is not just allotted time that matters; students must be there to benefit from the time, the instruction, and the support provided. This means that parents must be brought on board to ensure high rates of attendance.

Redouble efforts to involve parents. Again and again, the research on effective school programs shows the importance of parent involvement. Achievement in high-poverty schools increases in proportion to the degree to which parents are involved, the degree to which they are invited in and made to feel welcome, and the degree to which teachers and administrators reach out to them to establish two-way communication (Taylor, Pearson, Clark, & Walpole, 2000). We must take this lesson to heart and try even harder than we have in the past to get parents engaged in their children's learning. This will increase the likelihood that students will come to school to take advantage of the rich programs the school offers and complete the sorts of home-based literacy activities that will support their summer school learning.

Ensure that summer programs are adequately funded. In today's educational milieu, we are expecting summer schools to have large influences on achievement. No longer conceived as just an enrichment activity, summer school is now considered both core instructional time and a time for renewal of the achievement and learning profiles of those students who are not faring well in the regular school year. We cannot ask teachers and administrators to meet the demands placed on them in summer school without providing the sort of support they will need to do so. They need adequate secretarial support so that they can get the materials they need and establish home contacts. They need consultants who can help them with the elaborate evaluations we ask of them. They need a specific individual—a summer school coach if you will—who can provide the instructional and professional development support they need to meet their goals.

CONCLUSION

Our research clearly shows the value of summer school for children at risk for low achievement. In separate studies with more than 1,100 children who attended a variety of summer programs, we found significant benefits of summer school for children's reading achievement—gains that were evident over the summer and maintained during the next school year. Summer school is a worthwhile educational policy for helping young children learn to read and for helping those at risk to avoid summer loss of academic skills and knowledge. It is ironic that summer reading programs have increased dramatically across America at the turn of the 21st century, but less-than-favorable economic circumstances jeopardize their continuation. If summer reading programs are regarded as supplemental or optional, then they are vulnerable to annual changes in school budgets. It would be unfortunate to discontinue summer programs now that educators have learned how to design them successfully and now that researchers are more skilled at evaluating the programs and students.

We hope that policymakers acknowledge and support the long-term benefits of summer school so that all children can maximize their educational growth during the summer and throughout the school year. For those children who are rescued in this particular educational lifeboat, it is a policy well worth the investment of time, energy, and money.

ACKNOWLEDGMENTS

The report described herein was supported under the Educational Research and Development Centers Program, PR/Award Number R305R70004, as administered by the Office of Educational Research and Improvement, U.S. Department of Education. However, the contents of the described report do not necessarily represent the positions or policies of the National Institute on Student Achievement, Curriculum, and Assessment or the National Institute on Early Childhood Development, or the U.S. Department of Education, and the reader should not assume endorsement by the Federal government.

REFERENCES

Berliner, D. C., & Biddle, B. J. (1997). *The manufactured crisis.* White Plains, NY: Longman.

Carter, L. F. (1984). The sustaining effects study of compensatory and elementary education. *Educational Researcher, 13*(4), 4–13.

Cooper, H., Charlton, K., Valentine, J. C., & Muhlenbruck, L. (2000). Making the most of summer school: A meta-analytic and narrative review. *Monographs of the Society for Research in Child Development, 65*(1, Serial No. 260).

Cooper, H., Nye, B., Charlton, K., Lindsay, J., & Greathouse, S. (1996). The effects of summer vacation on achievement test scores: A narrative and meta-analytic review. *Review of Educational Research, 66,* 227–268.

Cross, D. R., & Paris, S. G. (1987). Assessment of reading comprehension: Matching test purposes and test properties. *Educational Psychologist, 22,* 313–332.

Embretson, S. E., & Reise, S. P. (2000). *Item response theory for psychologists.* Mahwah, NJ: Lawrence Erlbaum Associates, Inc.

Entwisle, D. R., Alexander, K. L., & Olson, L. (1997). *Children, schools, and inequality.* Boulder, CO: Westview.

Hambleton, R. K., & Swaminathan, H. (1985). *Item response theory: Principles and applications.* Boston: Kluwer–Nijhoff.

Hasbrouck, J. E., & Tindal, G. (1992). Curriculum-based oral reading fluency norms for students in grades 2–5. *Teaching Exceptional Children, 24*(3), 41–44.

Heyns, B. (1978). *Summer learning and the effects of schooling.* New York: Academic.

Heyns, B. (1987). Schooling and cognitive development: Is there a season for learning? *Child Development, 58,* 1151–1160.

Johns, J. L. (1997). *Basic reading inventory: Pre-primer through grade twelve & early literacy assessments* (7th ed.). Dubuque, IA: Kendall/Hunt.

Leslie, L., & Caldwell, J. (1995). *Qualitative reading inventory-2.* New York: Addison–Wesley Longman, Inc.

Meisels, S. J. (1992). Doing harm by doing good: Iatrogenic effects of early childhood enrollment and promotion practices. *Early Childhood Research Quarterly, 7,* 155–174.

Stanovich, K. E. (1986). Matthew effects in reading: Some consequences of individual differences in the acquisition of literacy. *Reading Research Quarterly, 21,* 360–407.

Stevenson, H. W., & Lee, S. (1990). Contexts of achievement. *Monographs of the Society for Research in Child Development, 55*(1–2, Serial No. 221).

Taylor, B. M., Pearson, P. D., Clark, K., & Walpole, S. (2000). Effective schools and accomplished teachers: Lessons about primary grade reading instruction in low-income schools. *Elementary School Journal, 101,* 121–166.

III

THE IMPLEMENTATION
AND EFFECTS OF NATIONALLY
REPLICATED SUMMER
SCHOOL PROGRAMS

The chapters in Part III discuss three summer school programs that have been replicated with some success across the United States. First, in contrast to the test-driven curricula of most mandatory summer programs, the curricula developed by Voyager Expanded Learning, Incorporated is based on a hands-on, experiential approach to learning. Problem-solving and discovery-based instruction is organized into thematic historical units designed to capture students' interests. Voyager is a private, for-profit corporation that provides schools and school districts with curricula and training for use in summer school programs across the country. Beyond the contrast in curricula, the evaluation of Voyager's summer program, discussed by Roberts and Nowakowski in chapter 7, is interesting because Voyager has been so widely implemented and replicated. Voyager programs serve more than 400,000 students in more than 1,000 districts in 44 states. This evaluation is one of very few ever reported that examines summer schooling across such a diverse array of schools and locations.

One goal of this volume is to provide guidance to those educators and policymakers responsible for designing and implementing summer programs. Given the limitations on available funding for summer programs, educators have to ask which students should be targeted for summer services. One question is how programs can be most effective: Is it by targeting the most at-risk students or by being open to all students? In chapter 8, Mary Moore and David Myers present findings from a nationally representative sample of Upward Bound projects. Their results indicate limited effects overall, but significant impact on certain groups of students. Based on these findings, the authors suggest that program effectiveness for Upward Bound can be improved by maximizing services for those students for whom evidence of value-added is greatest. They present a methodology to guide program operators in targeting services toward those students who are most likely to benefit and then discuss the practical implications of targeting.

In contrast to the mandatory programs designed to help students meet the standards for promotion to the next grade and to "graduate" from summer school, the Summerbridge program is distinguished by the fact that it is voluntary and commits to working with students for more than one summer. Founded in 1978, Summerbridge is an enrichment program for high-achieving middle school students from limited-opportunity backgrounds. The 6-week summer sessions combine intensive academic coursework with a variety of leadership and recreational activities. Students must apply to participate and the selection process is competitive. In chapter 9, Jennifer Laird and Shirley Feldman report early results from their ongoing evaluation of Summerbridge. They report survey data on the affective, motivational, and behavioral indicators associated with academic achievement and focus on two issues: What are the benefits of a summer program that targets high-achieving students and provides an enrichment curriculum, and do the positive effects of the summer program last throughout the following school year?

7

Addressing the Summer Learning Loss: An Evaluation of the Voyager Summer Reading Intervention Program

Greg Roberts
University of Texas at Austin

Jeri Nowakowski
Voyager Expanded Learning

Decades of research have documented the considerable gap in achievement between children attending low-income urban schools and children from more prosperous communities. More recent research has considered possible causes of this gap and potential remedies, including summer school and extended-year programs. We consider one application of research in this area with our description of the extended-year program offered by Voyager Expanded Learning, and we present the results of recent program evaluations.

SUMMER SCHOOL AND SUMMER LEARNING LOSS

The work of Alexander and Entwisle (1996) and Cooper and his colleagues (Cooper, Charlton, Valentine, & Muhlenbruck, 2000; Cooper, Nye, Charlton, Lindsay, & Greathouse, 1996) suggests a need for school-based summer programs that target the summer learning loss of disadvantaged urban schoolchildren. Summer school as a policy recommendation may be justified and gaining strength (Borman, 2000), but debate remains over what constitutes an effective summer school program for children attending urban schools. Most agree that any reform strategy must be based on research, designed with an urban context in mind, and reflect systems' orientation (Darling–Hammond, 1993; Fullan, 1993). On the details of such an undertaking, however, there is little consensus and even less research (Borman, 2000; Cooper et al., 2000). The question remains: What types of programs are most effective for preventing summer learning loss and closing the achievement gap?

BACKGROUND OF VOYAGER

Voyager Expanded Learning was founded in 1994 by Randy Best, a corporate business leader; Admiral Tom Hayward, chief naval officer under Presidents Jimmy Carter and Ronald Reagan; and Barbara Nichols, an educator and training professional. Voyager has expanded from elementary afterschool and summer school programs to include kindergarten through eighth grade programs for school-year, afterschool, intersession, and summer school use. Voyager's extended-day programs add 135 hours to the school year, and its summer programs add 80 hours, for a total of 62% more reading instruction per year.

In 1995, Voyager worked with 11 pilot schools in Dallas, TX. By 1998, it had expanded to include partnerships with 700 sites and 40 states serving approximately 60,000 students. As of June 2000, Voyager summer programs were serving 400,000 students in more than 1,000 districts in 44 states. During the 2001 to 2002 school year, Voyager served more than 9,000 students in its Universal Literacy System, which combines extended-day and extended-year reading interventions with a kindergarten through third grade in-school core reading program.

Voyager has partnerships and collaborations with the Smithsonian Institution and The Discovery Channel. In addition, NASA and the University of Oregon provide Voyager with research and technical assistance in the development of new curricula.

THE VOYAGER TIMEWARP PROGRAM

"TimeWarp™" is a research-based, strategic summer-reading intervention series developed by a team of reading specialists for elementary and middle-school students who have fallen behind. The series, which is part of Voyager's integrated learning system, is designed to close the achievement gap and prevent summer learning loss.

The main goal of "TimeWarp™" is to use available summer hours to improve student performance and increase teacher effectiveness. The series is based on the theory that experiential learning with high-interest and academically challenging content will motivate all students to learn and will improve their reading skills and strategies. "TimeWarp™" also

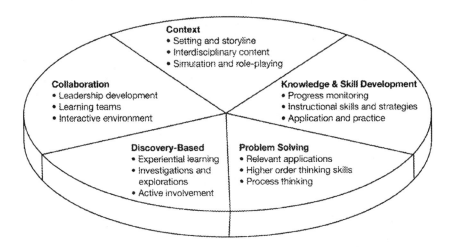

FIG. 7.1.   Voyager's Learning Framework.

actively involves students in leadership roles and cooperative learning through participation as "Team Leaders" and "Pathfinders" (paired partners and allies). Voyager's comprehensive learning framework is shown in Fig. 7.1. The Appendix gives an example of Voyager's Learning Framework applied to the "TimeWarp™ Egypt" curriculum.

THE VOYAGER LEARNING FRAMEWORK

The "TimeWarp™" model includes 4 hours of learning activities a day for 4 weeks in the summer, totaling 80 hours of instruction. The collaborative and learner-centered curriculum is designed for classes of no more than 18 students. Voyager trains teachers on curriculum and effective classroom organizational strategies to ensure faithful program implementation. Key components of the program include the following: (a) a restructured classroom that promotes collaborative learning; (b) redefined roles for teachers as colearners, guides, coaches, and mentors; (c) assessment and evaluation used as diagnostic tools to facilitate a personalized approach to learning; (d) continuous staff development focusing on standards of authentic instruction; (e) current, interdisciplinary, research-based curricula that are relevant, discovery-based, and focused on critical thinking; (f) curricula aligned with state standards and targeted to reinforce skills based on the results of state and national assessments (Table 7.1); and (g) programs that develop students' leadership skills and promote collaboration that prepares them for citizenship and the real world.

Voyager's training is designed to build instructional capacity at the district and campus levels. Districts select their teachers by expertise,

TABLE 7.1
Targeted Skills and Strategies

	"TimeWarp™ Egypt" (Grades 2–3)	"TimeWarp™ Greece" (Grades 4–5)	"TimeWarp™ The Americas" (Grades 6–7)
Concepts of books and print			
Conventions of print	•		
Book awareness	•		
Phonological awareness			
Sound and word discrimination	•		
Rhyming	•	•	
Blending sounds	•	•	
Sound segmentation	•	•	
Letter awareness and identification			
Letter recognition	•		
Letter identification and production	•		
Alphabetic principle			
Letter-Sound knowledge	•		
Decoding and word recognition	•	•	•
Sight-Word reading	•	•	•
Reading connected text	•	•	•
Spelling	•	•	•
Vocabulary development and concept awareness			
Comprehending what is read	•	•	•
Literacy response	•	•	•
Shared and independent reading			
Reading for pleasure and information	•	•	•
Listening and speaking			
Listening to spoken language	•	•	•
Oral language	•	•	•
Writing			
Forming letters and words	•		
Mechanics for writing	•	•	•
Expressing ideas in writing	•	•	•

tenure, availability, or other criteria. Teachers, site directors, and district implementation teams attend several days of mandatory training provided by Voyager and delivered by professional educators. This prepares district personnel to implement and support the program with fidelity. Training emphasizes current reading research, Voyager methodology, reading strategies associated with "TimeWarp™," and group management. Throughout the summer program, Voyager helps site directors and district implementation teams provide ongoing training and support for teachers.

A typical "TimeWarp™" day includes the following:

- Teacher-directed instruction for the whole group This provides instructional focus and encourages reading participation, while developing students' skills and strategies.
- Student learning teams grouped by reading levels Each team rotates through three learning stations. Teachers select student team leaders to facilitate group activities in the two independent learning stations. This allows teachers to lead challenge lessons with small groups of students who need additional support.
- Response and practice activities These give students a chance to reflect on what they have read and express themselves creatively by writing and creating theme-related projects which connect what they have read to real-world activities.
- A short debriefing period to review what students have learned Guides for each Voyager student's parents or guardians supply ideas on how to reinforce a child's learning success through supplemental home activities. Students are urged to share what they learn with parents, and parents are asked to make time to hear about their children's daily activities and to attend culminating activities where students demonstrate what they have learned.

EVALUATION OF THE VOYAGER SUMMER READING INTERVENTION PROGRAM 2000

Results of the evaluation of the Voyager Summer Reading Intervention Program are meaningful on several levels. First, the findings are of interest to developers and users of the Voyager curricula, and questions related to the program's impact and usability are of importance to its stakeholders. Beyond this, the findings of the Voyager evaluation may help broaden the understanding of what constitutes effective summer school programming.

The meta-analytic work of Cooper and his colleagues (Cooper et al., 2000) highlights the need for considering this issue across a range of populations and settings. A single study may be too limited in scope to address the diversity of questions on this point, and even Cooper et al.'s (2000) collection of studies left several important questions unanswered. A given evaluation can consider the program in question while also contributing to the knowledge about the class of programs to which it belongs. The Voyager evaluation was conducted with this dual purpose in mind.

Evaluation Methods

The primary question of Voyager stakeholders was as follows: Is the Voyager summer program, as implemented in schools across the United States, associated with an increase in students' reading skill levels? Voyager has collected data on program effect at several points in its history, but data have generally been gathered on relatively small samples using Voyager-developed measures. The 2000 project was the second evaluation of Voyager's extended-year program that had a national scope, and the first to use a standardized, nationally normed instrument—the Stanford Diagnostic Reading Test–IV (SDRT–IV)—to measure changes in students' reading ability.

The 1999 evaluation of Voyager's extended-year program used data collected with a Voyager-developed measure of reading skill level (Voyager Expanded Learning, 1999). The instrument was reviewed by reading specialists at the North Central Regional Educational Laboratory for readability, adequacy of format and directions, and quality of test items. Psychometric attributes of the instrument were reviewed by the Measurement and Evaluation Center at the University of Texas at Austin. The 1999 instrument was used in the 2000 evaluation with approximately 6,500 "TimeWarp™" students in Washington, DC, schools.

Measurement

The SDRT–IV is designed to diagnose students' strengths and weaknesses in the major components of reading. Sections of the SDRT–IV include Phonics, Reading Vocabulary, Reading Comprehension, and Scanning. Results from the SDRT–IV can be used to identify trends in the reading levels of students at the school or district level and to evaluate the effectiveness of instructional programs. Three levels of the SDRT–IV were used in the evaluation. Students in Voyager's "TimeWarp™ Egypt" program completed the Orange level (grade levels 2.5–3.5). Students in "TimeWarp™ Greece" took the Purple level (grade levels 4.5–6.5), and students in "TimeWarp™ The Americas" took the Blue level (grade levels 9.0–13.0) of the SDRT–IV.

Samples Used in the Evaluation

Participating schools were selected based on two criteria: their anticipated willingness to participate and their expected level of program implementation fidelity. A primary objective was to recruit schools that were willing to participate and that were already using the Voyager program according to its design. A second objective of the sample selection process was to represent the diversity of socioeconomic strata using Voyager programs.

Urban schools and suburban schools were selected. A final objective was to sample schools across Voyager's intervention series, including "TimeWarp™ Greece," "TimeWarp™ Egypt," and "TimeWarp™ The Americas." Students participating in the evaluation were characterized as low achieving (the lower quartile). Many were in danger of repeating a grade level.

A total of 13 schools agreed to participate in the evaluation. Of these, seven were located in suburban, rural, or small urban communities and six were in large urban districts. There were four middle schools and nine elementary schools in the sample. Five schools were located in the eastern and southeastern United States, five were in the Midwest, and three were in California. Eight of the schools had greater-than-average levels of economic disadvantage (more than 35% of the school population was receiving free or reduced-price lunches). Seven of the schools had a student population that was majority Black or Hispanic (greater than 50%) and another four had a plurality of students of color (no ethnic group accounted for more than 50% of the student population).

A total of 400 students from the 13 participating schools completed an SDRT–IV pretest, and 383 completed the posttest. Complete data (i.e., pretest and posttest scores on the SDRT–IV) were available for 325 Voyager students. This represents an attrition rate of about 19% (percentage of complete cases compared to pretest cases), which is not unexpected, given that the Voyager program was delivered during the summer months and a sizable number of participants were lower socioeconomic strata children living in urban settings. Children leaving the program before its conclusion tended to score less well on the pretest SDRT–IV than children with complete data (total scale score of 586 versus 611).

The findings outlined in the following sections are based on the 325 cases for which complete data were available. Attendance was not tracked, so the evaluation findings include the scores of children who attended all Voyager sessions and children who may have attended as few as two sessions (the day of pretest and the day of posttest).

RESULTS

Results from the SDRT–IV are presented using three types of scores: effect size, normal curve equivalent, and progress scores. Each of these is addressed in the sections that follow, primarily in terms of Voyager stakeholders' questions concerning program impact. Other evaluation questions, particularly those suggested by Cooper's metaanalysis (Cooper et al., 2000), are considered in a subsequent section.

Estimates of Program Effect

Effect-Size Data.   Change in test scores can be expressed in terms of effect size (ES). An ES is a value that reflects the standardized amount of change from pretest to posttest. Estimates of effect can be compared across studies and even across programs. By convention, an ES of .20 is considered a small-size effect, an ES of around .50 indicates a medium-size effect, and an ES of .80 or greater suggests a large-size effect. For educational and social programs, effect sizes in the medium-size range are relatively uncommon. More typical are programs with small-size effects or no effect.

The ES data for the Voyager program suggest considerable change in SDRT–IV posttest scores when compared to pretest scores. The ES were .41, .26, and .55 for "TimeWarp™ Greece," "TimeWarp™ Egypt," and "TimeWarp™ The Americas," respectively. The overall effect size for the Voyager program (average effect for all students on the total score for the SDRT–IV) was .42 (40% of one standard deviation)—not inconsiderable if one remembers that disadvantaged students typically lose up to a month or more of learning during the summer months (Cooper et al., 1996). The ES for the subsections of the SDRT–IV ranged from .29 for the Comprehension subtest to .45 for the Scanning subtest (Table 7.2). (As an aside, the Voyager-developed reading test used in the District of Columbia yielded similar-size effects—about .40—suggesting that the effect may be stable across measures, across implementation, or both.)

Normal Curve Equivalent Scores.   The SDRT–IV data were also considered in terms of normal curve equivalent (NCE) scores. NCE scores were originally developed to analyze and report gains in compensatory programs for educationally disadvantaged students. These scores have a mean of 50 and a standard deviation of approximately 21. This results in a scale with 99 equal-interval units. A normal curve equivalent score of 50 represents the national average of any grade level at the time of year the test was normed.

NCE scores are similar in range to percentile scores, but with more sophisticated statistical properties, and they generally prove more useful in an evaluation-related context. NCE scores can be used to compute group

TABLE 7.2
Traditional Effect Sizes

Voyager Program	Phonics	Vocabulary	Comprehension	Scanning	Total
"TimeWarp™ Egypt"	.32	.46	.27	NA	.41
"TimeWarp™ Greece"	NA	.29	.11	.33	.26
"TimeWarp™ The Americas"	NA	.18	.42	.55	.55
Totals	.32	.30	.29	.45	.42

statistics, compare the performance of students who take different levels of the same test, and compare the performance of the same student across different subject matter.

NCE scores can also be used to evaluate gains over time. NCE is scored in such a way that a year-to-year gain of zero indicates a year's academic growth in the skills measured. A positive gain indicates more than 1 year's growth; a negative gain indicates less than one year's growth. The average gains for Voyager students were roughly 8 points, 5 points, and 7 points for "TimeWarp™ Greece," "TimeWarp™ Egypt," and "Time-Warp™ The Americas," respectively. Gains of NCE points are not entirely uncommon, although generally associated with change across the school year. These data suggest that the 4-week Voyager program yields gains comparable to those of successful 9-month programs.

Average pretest and posttest scores are indicated for all Voyager programs and for all sections of the SDRT–IV in Table 7.3. The column labeled "Percentage of NCE Change" suggests the amount of improvement Voyager students experienced when compared to a representative group of same-age peers, and gains are expressed in terms of the percentage of 1 standard deviation. Using NCE data in this way is comparable to calculating an effect size. The primary difference in the ES and the NCE-based ES is the estimate of variance used to standardize the mean difference. In this case, the standard deviation of the NCE scores, approximately 21, was used as the standard unit. NCE scores increased .32 of a standard deviation for Voyager students when compared to the group of students in the SDRT–IV normative sample. Table 7.3 displays gain scores and effect sizes for groups of Voyager students and sections of the SDRT–IV.

Progress Indicator Scores. The SDRT–IV provides a progress indicator score for the Orange and Purple levels of the test. According to the *Teacher's Manual for Interpretation,* a progress indicator score can be used to "identify those students who have demonstrated sufficient competence on specific areas to make satisfactory progress in the regular developmental reading program" (Harcourt Brace & Company, 1996, p. 14). The cut scores reflect the developmental aspects of learning to read, as well as the relative importance of specific areas to the reading process.

A large percentage of students taking the Orange level of the SDRT–IV ("TimeWarp™ Egypt" students) moved from below-average standing at pretest to average or above-average standing at posttest on the Phonics portion of the test. Change was especially notable for test items addressing short vowels (+19%) and long vowels (+9%). On the Vocabulary section of the test, the percentage of students moving to average or above-average standing ranged from 7 to 14 percentage points on the Orange level of the test and 1 to 7 percentage points on Purple ("TimeWarp™

TABLE 7.3
Normal Curve Equivalent (NCE) Effect Sizes

"TimeWarp™ Egypt"

Voyager Program Level	Average Pretest	Average Posttest	Percentage of NCE Change	Number of Cases
Phonics	40.0	45.9	28%	106
Vocabulary	34.6	44.5	47%	99
Comprehension	35.7	41.2	26%	102
Scanning	NA	NA	NA	NA
Total	34.8	42.6	37%	96

"TimeWarp™ Greece"

Voyager Program Level	Average Pretest	Average Posttest	Percentage of NCE Change	Number of Cases
Phonics	NA	NA	NA	NA
Vocabulary	27.5	34.4	33%	85
Comprehension	31.7	33.7	10%	84
Scanning	29.8	35.2	26%	84
Total	26.1	31.3	25%	83

"TimeWarp™ The Americas"

Voyager Program Level	Average Pretest	Average Posttest	Percentage of NCE Change	Number of Cases
Phonics	NA	NA	NA	NA
Vocabulary	28.3	30.1	9%	124
Comprehension	27.5	33.1	27%	125
Scanning	29.0	36.9	38%	96
Total	27.3	34.0	32%	95

Total Across All Cases

Voyager Program Level	Average Pretest	Average Posttest	Percentage of NCE Change	Number of Cases
Phonics	40.0	45.9	28%	106
Vocabulary	30.1	36.1	29%	308
Comprehension	31.3	35.9	22%	311
Scanning	29.4	36.1	32%	180
Total	29.5	36.2	32%	274

Greece"). In Comprehension, as many as 16% of students moved from below-average to average or above-average levels (paragraphs with questions, textual reading, and interpretation).

Table 7.4 presents the percentage of students at or above average (i.e., at or above the cut score) at pretest and at posttest on the different skill ele-

TABLE 7.4
Progress Scores for Comprehension Subtest

Comprehension	"TimeWarp™ Egypt"		"TimeWarp™ Greece"	
	Pretest	Posttest	Pretest	Posttest
Cloze	76%	81%	NA	NA
Paragraphs with questions	43%	59%	NA	NA
Recreational reading	62%	74%	51%	52%
Textual reading	38%	54%	61%	63%
Functional reading	50%	60%	35%	43%
Initial understanding	48%	50%	51%	58%
Interpretation				
Critical analysis	46%	62%	44%	52%
Process strategies	61%	75%	NA	NA
Critical analysis	NA	NA	47%	50%
Process strategies	NA	NA	62%	67%

ments included in the comprehension subtest of the SDRT–IV. The progress indicator scores support the conclusions suggested by the effect-size data and the NCE data; the Voyager program had a considerable impact on students at participating schools.

Differences in evaluation methods can confuse findings related to more substantive factors, such as program, student, and outcome characteristics. When the focus is across a number of related studies, as in meta-analyses, it is often possible to control for differences in method and analyze the effect of these more substantive elements. This was the case in the Cooper (Cooper et al., 2000) data; they were able to adjust the effect size of studies in their sample for differences due to method, thereby eliminating the confound of methodological variables and substantive variables. (This does not eliminate the confound due to intercorrelation among substantive variables.)

That said, it should be noted that the Voyager effect-size estimates for the set of moderators in Table 7.4 are not adjusted in this way (and they could not be without including the Voyager data in a reanalysis of the Cooper [Cooper et al., 2000] studies). If apples are to be compared to apples, the unadjusted Cooper estimates should be used. The oranges (the adjusted effects) are included as an additional point of reference.

COMPARISON WITH RESULTS OF COOPER ET AL.'S (2000) META-ANALYSIS

Cooper et al.'s meta-analysis of summer school effects provides an insightful summary of the collective knowledge in this area. Their findings also offer a meaningful backdrop against which to consider the results of the Voyager program evaluation. The remainder of this chapter is devoted to this task.

The mean program effect across the 99 independent samples in the Cooper et al. (2000) study was .26 (assumes a fixed-effects model), and the median effect was .19. The values reflect the impact of all extended-year programs in Cooper's sample. Regardless of type, summer school increases student outcomes by about .25 of a standard deviation when compared to students' average preprogram score or to the average score of students who did not attend summer school.

The Voyager program effect across all curricula and for the total score on the SDRT was .42 when posttest scores were compared to pretest scores, and the Voyager program effect was .32 when gain scores were considered in terms of NCE units. The Voyager pretest to posttest ES estimate (.42) is 62% greater than the Cooper average, and it ranks in the upper 25% of Cooper's distribution of effect-size values. Cooper's effect sizes range from −.22 to 2.7, and most cluster around the median (.19) with almost one half (47%) falling between .01 and .29.

Variables Moderating Effect Sizes

The Cooper meta-analysis considers a number of moderating variables, which they organize (Cooper et al., 2000) according to several categories, including student characteristics, program context, methodological features, and program features. Table 7.5 displays the first two of these categories and, within each, several moderators that are relevant to a discussion of the Voyager results. Methodological features are not included in Table 7.5, although they are relevant to the present topic and warrant brief mention as well.

TABLE 7.5
Progress Scores for Comprehension Subtest

| | Cooper | | Voyager |
	Unadjusted	Adjusted	Voyager
Student characteristics			
Grade Level			
Kindergarten through third grade	.24	.19	.41
Fourth through sixth grade	.19	.17	.26
Seventh through twelfth grade	.29	.35	.55
Program Context			
Type of community			
Large urban	.28	.29	.35
Other	.38	.34	.42

Methodological Features. The Cooper (Cooper et al., 2000) ES estimate for programs evaluated using a one-group pretest to posttest design was .24. As indicated earlier, when Voyager posttest scores were compared to pretest scores, the estimated effect size was .42. For programs in the Cooper sample using a two-group design, the effect size was .07. Of these, studies using randomized treatment and control groups had an average effect of .14, whereas nonequivalent-group studies had an estimated effect size of .05 (these values do not significantly differ from each other). The Voyager NCE-based effect size involved comparing Voyager students to the normative sample of the SDRT. This two-group design is similar to studies in the Cooper set of nonequivalent-group evaluations, suggesting that the .32 Voyager estimate can be evaluated in relation to Cooper's value of .07.

Student Characteristics and Program Context. The effect sizes for different-age Voyager students were .41, .26, and .55 for primary, intermediate, and middle-school students, respectively. This compares to effect sizes of .24, .19, and .29 for similar-age students in the Cooper sample. The Cooper data suggest that age and the effect of summer school may be U-shaped in nature. Summer programs tend to be more helpful for younger and older students and less effective for students falling between the two. Cooper speculated that the curvilinear relation of age and summer school effect may be due largely to differences in the instructional approaches used with the different age groups. The Voyager data do not support this assertion. Voyager's program is very similar in philosophy and instructional focus across its different levels, suggesting that the U-shaped nature of the Voyager data may not be entirely due to grade-related instructional differences. This question deserves further attention.

"Program context," the other category in Table 7.5, considers attributes of the community in which the program was delivered. In the Cooper et al. (2000) sample, the effect sizes were .28 and .38 for "Large urban" and "Other" categories, respectively. The effect sizes for the Voyager data are .35 and .42, again for "Large urban" and "Other," respectively, where "Other" includes suburban and rural school districts. The trend in the Voyager data is in the same direction as the Cooper data; effects of summer school were greater in schools other than those in large urban districts. The percentage difference (difference in "Other" and "Large urban") in the Voyager data differed somewhat from the Cooper data, however. In the Cooper sample, "Other" was 36% larger than "Large urban," and in the Voyager sample, "Other" was 20% larger. The gap between large urban schools and schools in suburban and rural districts was less prominent in the Voyager data than in the Cooper study.

Many of the methodological, student, and programmatic attributes discussed as moderators in Cooper's meta-analysis did not vary in the Voyager evaluation because they are embedded in the Voyager program model. For instance, Voyager is generally delivered to classes of no more than 20 students for 80 instructional hours. Although it is possible to compare the total program effect for Voyager to Cooper's moderated effects, such comparisons are perhaps less meaningful than ones that allow analysis within and across Voyager and Cooper (the comparisons outlined in the foregoing section). Readers interested in comparisons not presented in this chapter are referred to the Cooper et al. (2000) study.

DISCUSSION

The Voyager program had an effect on the reading ability of students across the United States during the summer of 2000. The size of the Voyager effect can be described as considerable; it is in the upper quartile of program effects reported by Cooper et al. (2000), and it appears to be relatively stable across Voyager program sites and instruments used to measure skill gains.

Several questions are suggested by the evaluation findings for Voyager. Notable in this respect is the question related to the internal validity of studies in this area of research. A randomized group design was not used in the Voyager evaluation, and the results should be considered with this in mind. However, alternative explanations for the effects evident in these data are less than compelling. Participants were not attending school while participating in Voyager, thus minimizing the possibility of school effects as a causal factor. Maturation effects seem unlikely because the Voyager program lasted about a month—a relatively brief span of time. The Voyager program is the most likely candidate for explaining the effect.

In the Cooper et al. (2000) sample, a one-group design is associated with considerably greater effects than a two-group study, suggesting the following question: Aside from maturation and school effects, what factors other than Voyager may have contributed to the difference in pretest and posttest scores? We must also consider the more general question: What threatens the internal validity of summer school studies with non-randomized-group designs? Addressing these questions will require further meta-analysis using program data coded according to type of validity threat. Again, this highlights the importance of considering program evaluation at various levels. The program in question is but one focus for evaluators working in this area.

The notion of applying an isolated set of evaluation findings beyond the boundaries of a program is a hallmark of "theory-driven models of program evaluation," an approach that will continue to inform the evaluation of Voyager programs. Theory-driven approaches assume that evaluation of an effective program built on well-tested psychological, social, and learning theories is enhanced when those same theoretical frameworks are embedded in the evaluation design. The research-based Voyager program is built on recent work on effective instruction, student learning, and the essentials of beginning reading. Ongoing evaluation will consider ways of further enhancing these research-based elements in the Voyager programs.

The summer implementation of Voyager embodies many of the factors that recent research suggests are critical to effective use of, and positive results for, extended-year programs (see Borman, 2001). Summer programs are most effective when they involve parents, remain small in size, undergo careful scrutiny for treatment fidelity, contain substantial academic components aimed at teaching reading and math, and coordinate summer school experiences with those that occur during the regular school year. Voyager programs include all of these identified components. Continuing evaluation of Voyager's summer program will model the interrelations of these critical components and evaluate their relative effect in improving student achievement and narrowing the gap in achievement.

Future evaluation of the Voyager program will address questions of a longitudinal nature as well. Multigroup studies of Voyager's long-term effect are presently underway in the Washington, DC, school district. The data will address the sustainability of the Voyager program effect, the effect of combining Voyager summer school with the Voyager after-school program, and the effect of attending Voyager over consecutive summers. The goal is to gather solid data that will help to improve Voyager programs while also providing input to the wider community of researchers and service providers. The most current evaluation of the Voyager Universal Literacy System—including core, extended-day, and summer reading programs—is available on Voyager's Web site (www. voyagerlearning.com).

APPENDIX

Voyager Learning Framework Example Using "TimeWarp™ Egypt" Curriculum

"TimeWarp™ Egypt" is an example of how the curricula use Voyager's framework of learning in context, knowledge and skill development, problem solving, discovery-based instruction, and opportunities for collaboration among students.

Learning Context

In the "TimeWarp™ Egypt" curriculum, Voyager students ("Voyagers") search for their Time Tracker counterparts—fictional students who disappeared through a time warp to ancient Egypt. To bring the Time Trackers back home, students study archaeology, history, geography, and fine arts, as well as literacy skills and strategies. Voyagers learn about Egyptian hieroglyphs, ancient etiquette and fashion, and mummies and the mummification process.

Knowledge and Skill Development

Teachers monitor the progress of Voyagers using the preassessment tool, periodic performance assessments, observations, student reflections, and the postassessment tool. Instructional skills and strategies are targeted to help students comprehend text, analyze words, use graphic sources, and write to communicate with others. The curriculum correlates with the highest state and national grade-level standards.

Multiple opportunities for application and practice are supplied through the curriculum's instructional framework, including Instructional Focus, Reading Experiences, Learning Stations, teacher-directed Challenge Lessons, Word Making and Word Sorting, and Response sections.

Problem Solving

Voyagers learn problem-solving skills by investigating how the Egyptians may have moved massive stones to construct pyramids and by researching which items were considered essential for a pharaoh in the afterlife. Higher-order thinking skills are strengthened by practicing metacognitive reasoning in "Think-Alouds," formulating advice for the Time Trackers, and evaluating Egyptian toys and games.

Students learn process thinking as they record the details of the Time Trackers' mysterious disappearance, chart the steps in making mummies, and follow written steps to simulate an authentic archaeological dig.

Discovery-Based Learning

Experiential learning is integrated throughout "TimeWarp™ Egypt" as Voyagers take on the roles of archaeologists and Egyptologists. Students get their hands wet constructing a model of the River Nile. An Ancient Splendors videotape takes them on a virtual field trip to Egypt, and Ancient Egyptian Bingo helps them learn to use context clues. Voyagers are actively involved in every segment of a lesson, often working in small learning teams and engaging in interactive discussions.

Collaborative Learning

Voyager's format gives students opportunities to develop collaborative and leadership skills throughout the curriculum. The Voyager teacher's role is to act as a guide or facilitator, encouraging leadership and collaboration among students. Students work in pairs and act as "Pathfinder" partners for each other. Small-group learning teams help students learn to work effectively with others. Voyagers are grouped and regrouped to gain experience, and they may become "Team Leaders" who direct their groups through an activity.

REFERENCES

Alexander, K. L., & Entwisle, D. (1996). Early schooling and educational inequality: Socioeconomic disparities in children's learning. In J. Clark (Vol. Ed.), *James S. Coleman: Falmer sociology of education series 1* (pp. 63–79). Hampton, England: Falmer Press.

Borman, G. D. (2000). The effects of summer school: Questions answered, questions raised. *Monographs of the Society for Research in Child Development, 65*(1, Serial No. 260).

Borman, G. D. (2001). Summers are for learning. *Principal, 80,* 26–29.

Cooper, H., Charlton, K., Valentine, J. C., & Muhlenbruck, L. (2000). Making the most of summer school: A meta-analytic and narrative review. *Monographs of the Society for Research in Child Development, 65*(1, Serial No. 260).

Cooper, H., Nye, B., Charlton, K., Lindsay, J., & Greathouse, S. (1996). The effects of summer vacation on achievement test scores: A narrative and meta-analytic review. *Review of Educational Research, 66,* 227–268.

Darling–Hammond, L. (1993). Reframing the school reform agenda: Developing capacity for school transformation. *Phi Delta Kappan, 74,* 52–61.

Fullan, M. (1993). Getting reform right: What works and what doesn't. *Phi Delta Kappan, 73,* 744–752.

Harcourt Brace & Company. (1996). *Stanford diagnostic reading test: Teacher's manual for interpretation.* San Antonio, TX: Author.

Voyager Expanded Learning. (1999). *Solutions that impact performance: Voyager research base and results.* Dallas, TX: Author.

8

Translating Results From Impact Studies Into Changes in Operating Programs: Improving Upward Bound Through Targeting More At-Risk Students

Mary T. Moore and David E. Myers
Mathematica Policy Research, Inc.

An ongoing evaluation of the Upward Bound program, which the U.S. Department of Education funds, has recently shown that the program has large impacts on students who may be more at risk of academic failure and few if any impacts for students who are less at risk (Myers & Schirm, 1999).[1] Furthermore, findings from the evaluation suggest that Upward Bound may have an impact on outcomes for only about half the students it serves (see Table 8.1 for a complete summary).

Upward Bound is a federal program designed to help economically disadvantaged students prepare to enter and succeed in college. The program was established in 1965, and, in terms of its budget, is the largest federal program (other than student financial aid programs) to help high school students attain a postsecondary education. In early 2000, program statistics indicated that about 44,000 students were participating in more than 560 local Upward Bound projects.

Students typically enter the program during their freshman or sophomore year of high school and can remain in the program through the summer after high school graduation; however, only half the students stay in

---

[1] This evaluation collected data from students through the end of 2002. With the newer rounds of data, we will be able, for example, to describe the program's impact on outcomes such as college attendance and completion.

TABLE 8.1

Summary of Findings on the Impacts of Upward Bound on Selected Student Outcomes

	Overall	Expectations		Sex		Race or Ethnicity			LIFG Status[a]			At-Risk Status		Grade at Application	
		Higher	Lower	Girls	Boys	African American	White	Hispanic	LIFG	FG	LI	Lower	Higher	Ninth Grade	Tenth Grade
Educational expectations (years of schooling)															
Students	T		T			T	T	T	T			T	T	T	
Fathers			T		T	T	T			T			T	T	
Mothers			T		T	T				T			T	T	
High school credits															
Nonremedial English			T		T		T	T	T		T		T		T
Nonremedial social studies	T		T	T	T		T	T	T		T		T		
Nonremedial math	T		T	T	T		T		T		T		T		T
Nonremedial science			T		T		T		T		T				
Nonremedial foreign language			T		T			T			T		T		
Nonremedial total for five major subjects			T		T			T	T		T		T		
Nonremedial vocational education							T				T				
Nonremedial computer science			T		T		T		T		T		T		
Nonremedial other		T	T		T		T						T		T
Total nonremedial			T			T	T				T		T		
Total AP or Honors, all subjects			T		T	T					T		T		T
Total credits, includes remedial			T				T						T		T

Satisfied New Basics curriculum

Cumulative grade point average

High school status

Still in high school

Dropped out

Graduated

School status

Attend college[b]

Attend 4-year college

Attend 2-year college

Attend vocational school

Credits earned

Four-year college

Total nonremedial

Total remedial

Two-year college

Total nonremedial

Total remedial

College selectivity

[a]LIFG refers to students' low-income or first generation status when they apply to participate in Upward Bound. LIFG means both criteria were met; FG indicates students did not meet the low-income criteria but they were potential first generation college students; LI indicates that they were from a low-income family, but they were not potential first generation college students. Note: T indicates a significant positive impact at the .10 level was found.

[b]Not computed for ninth- and tenth-grade applicants when analyzed separately.

the program more than 19 months. Local projects give students a range of services that include the following: academic instruction in subjects such as math, science, English, social studies, and foreign language; tutoring; and counseling. Projects offer these services during an intensive summer program, which is generally a 6-week residential program, and, to a more limited extent, throughout the school year. The average annual cost per Upward Bound participant is about $4,000, which is about two thirds the annual expenditure per pupil for elementary and secondary school students (Smith, Aronstamm Young, Bae, Choy, & Alsalam, 1997).

When policymakers consider what it costs to serve a student in Upward Bound and the findings concerning the share of students influenced by participating in Upward Bound, it is important to identify strategies for translating the impact findings into practices that will help to ensure that Upward Bound serves the students it is most likely to affect.[2] We propose a method for adjusting the mix of students served by Upward Bound so that the program may obtain, on average, significant impacts while still preserving some of its general character. After describing the approach, we illustrate how this method may be used and show potential adjustments Upward Bound projects might consider when recruiting and selecting students. We conclude with a discussion of issues concerning the implementation of changes in targeting practices at the federal and local level.

It is important to emphasize that this chapter explores potential changes in policy and practice suggested by findings to date from the national evaluation. Its purpose is to illustrate the translation of current findings on impacts at the subgroup level into a national program goal with local project ramifications. Any actual change in targeting should await conclusion of the national evaluation and evidence that demonstrates the sustained nature of the subgroup effects that have characterized Upward Bound's impacts in the high school years.

AN APPROACH FOR INCREASING
OVERALL PROGRAM IMPACTS THROUGH
CHANGES IN TARGETING

Our goal is to develop an approach that can be used to adjust the targeting of Upward Bound, so that the program can achieve substantial overall program impacts. One may consider a variety of approaches for defining

---

[2]Other evaluations, such as the evaluation of the Career Academies program, have shown that students who are more at risk of academic failure experience larger impacts on academic outcomes when participating in the intervention than other students less at risk (see, e.g., Kemple & Snipes, 2000).

what qualifies as a substantial program impact; however, for purposes of this analysis, we define such an impact as one that is statistically significant.[3]

To meet the U.S. Department of Education's (ED's) requirements concerning the characteristics of the students served, local projects must select students so that two thirds of their participants are from low-income families and are potential first-generation college students. The other one third may come from either the low-income group or from the group of potential first-generation college students. In addition to meeting these requirements, projects must select students who demonstrate a need for academic support.

Because the ED allows projects considerable flexibility in how they define need, and the evaluation found that the size of the impacts varied according to this dimension, we focus our analysis on two potential measures of academic need: (a) students' educational expectations before entering the program, and (b) academic performance in the ninth grade. There are other factors that one might consider when making changes in targeting, such as emphasizing specific demographic subgroups; however, changes along these lines may run into strong opposition or legal challenges. With the flexibility that projects currently have in defining which students need academic support, use of measures such as educational expectations and academic performance are probably most appropriate.

Setup

The setup for this analysis is based on two relationships. The first relationship is that between overall program impacts and impacts for subgroups of students, such as students with lower and higher educational expectations, or students who demonstrate poor academic performance before entering the program.[4] (To simplify our presentation in the remaining sec-

---

[3]Alternative levels of statistical significance and formulations of the alternative hypothesis can be used. For example, one may decide to use a critical value of 1.65 or 1.96 when assessing whether an impact is significant, or use a one- or two-tailed test.

[4]Impacts were computed from a randomized design where eligible Upward Bound applicants were randomly assigned to Upward Bound and a control group. Actual estimation of the impacts was carried out by estimating separate regression models for each subgroup. The regression models included as covariates the estimated propensity score of being in the treatment group and an indicator for treatment status. The propensity score is the probability of being assigned to the treatment group and was predicted on the basis of a large number of student characteristics which were measured before random assignment (see Rosenbaum & Rubin, 1983, 1984). We included the propensity score as a covariate to help minimize potential biases that may occur by chance during the randomization process. The sample of students was drawn from a complex sample design (i.e., 67 Upward Bound projects were selected with known probability and students within projects were randomly

tions of this chapter, we always use a shorthand and refer to the two groups of students as students who are more at risk and less at risk of academic failure.) The second relationship is that between estimated program impacts and our measure of a statistically significant impact.[5]

We can express the relationship between the overall impact, as defined by the difference between a treatment group mean and a control group mean, and the subgroup impacts as a weighted average:
where $\bar{Y}_T$ is the average for an outcome for the Upward Bound group (treatment

$$\bar{Y}_T - \bar{Y}_C = (\bar{Y}_T - \bar{Y}_C \mid AR = 1)P(AR = 1) + (\bar{Y}_T - \bar{Y}_C \mid AR = 0)P(AR = 0) \quad (1)$$

group); $\bar{Y}_C$ is the average outcome for the control group; the difference in means on the right-hand side of the expression are conditional differences for the group more at risk ($AR = 1$), and the group less at risk ($AR = 0$); $P(AR = 1)$ is the proportion of students served by the program who are more at risk; and $P(AR = 0)$ is the proportion less at risk. We can state the relation between program impacts and our measure of a significant impact as follows:

$$t = \frac{I_{AR=1}P(AR = 1) + I_{AR=0}P(AR = 0))}{\sqrt{\hat{\sigma}^2_{AR=1}P(AR = 1) + \hat{\sigma}^2_{AR=0}P(AR = 0)}} \quad (2)$$

where t is the standard t-statistic;
$I_{AR=1} = (\bar{Y}_T - \bar{Y}_C \mid AR = 1)$, $I_{AR=0} = (\bar{Y}_T - \bar{Y}_C \mid AR = 0)$, $\hat{\sigma}^2_{AR=1}$ is the estimated variance of the subgroup impact estimate for the group more at risk; and $\hat{\sigma}^2_{AR=0}$ is the estimated variance for the subgroup that is less at risk. By using the identity $P(AR = 0) = 1 - P(AR = 1)$, we can express the relationship between the proportion of students we need in a program who are more at risk and our measure of a significant overall program impact:

$$P(AR = 1) = \frac{\hat{\sigma}^2_{AR=0}t^2 + I_{AR=1}I_{AR=0} - I^2_{AR=0} - \sqrt{-\hat{\sigma}^2_{AR=1}\hat{\sigma}^2_{AR=0}t^4 + \hat{\sigma}^2_{AR=0}t^2 I^2_{AR=1} + I^2_{AR=0}\hat{\sigma}^2_{AR=1}t^2}}{\hat{\sigma}^2_{AR=1}t^2 + \hat{\sigma}^2_{AR=0}t^2 - I^2_{AR=1} + 2I_{AR=1}I_{AR=0} - I^2_{AR=0}} \quad (3)$$

---

assigned to Upward Bound and a control group), and standard errors for the impact estimates were computed using the bootstrap method. In doing so, 5,000 replicate bootstrap samples were formed each time 67 projects were drawn at random and with replacement.

[5]When using our approach, we make several important assumptions. For example, we assume there are no peer effects or that any peer effects that do exist are preserved by maintaining a mix of students. The approach also assumes that the average costs of serving more at-risk students are about the same as serving students already in the program. Finally, we assume that by shifting the mix of students in the program, other costs, such as the cost of recruiting students, will not change from their present levels. In the future, we plan to look at other approaches that may allow us to relax one or more of these assumptions.

TABLE 8.2
Inputs Used to Compute Percentage of At-Risk Students Needed
to Serve to Achieve Statistically Significant Overall Program Impacts[a]

Groups	More At-Risk	Less At-Risk	More At-Risk	Less At-Risk
Lower and higher educational expectations[b]	.68	−.002	.28	.22
Higher and lower academic risk[c]	.33	−.13	.13	.12

[a]Impact in the context of this article refers to the impact of Upward Bound on all students whom Upward Bound intended to treat and not just those who decided to participate when given the opportunity.
[b]Students with lower educational expectations include those who expected to complete less than a 4-year college degree and those with higher expectations who expected to complete at least a 4-year degree.
[c]Academic risk is derived from a composite score that includes grade point average in ninth grade and credits earned in five core subjects in ninth grade.

After solving for $P(AR = 1)$, we can assess how large an overall impact this will result in by returning to Equation 1 and substituting into the equation the size of the impacts for the subgroups and the value for $P(AR = 1)$ derived from Equation 3.

Illustrations

Two examples help to describe the extent to which targeting in Upward Bound would need to be adjusted to find significant impacts with reasonable certainty. In these illustrations, we focus on a single early success score that is a composite of nine items; these items include students' cumulative high school grade point averages, credits earned in five core subjects, educational expectations, and whether a student had applied to, or enrolled in, college.[6] The composite score has a mean of zero, ranges from −4.76 to 3.26, and has a standard deviation of 1.42. Most students in the evaluation were selected for Upward Bound in 1993, and we measured the outcomes used in this analysis at the end of the 1996 to 1997 school year.

To assess the proportion of at-risk students one might want to include in Upward Bound, we performed a simulation that looked at a range of values for our measure of significant impacts and the associated values showing the mix of students included in the program (model inputs are shown in Table 8.2). Using a cutoff of about 1.7 for the critical value of a t-statistic, we find from the results of the simulation experiment that Up-

[6]The composite score was formed using a principal components analysis. Principal components analysis is a statistical technique that allows us to construct an index (composite score) from a set of items by estimating a statistical model, which can then be used to generate an index score for each student.

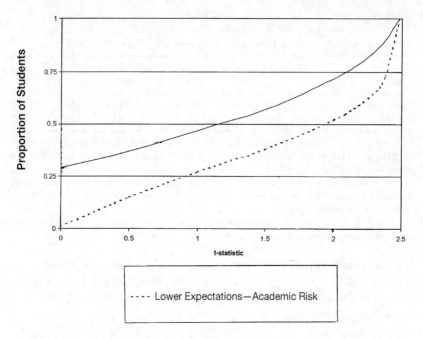

FIG. 8.1. Figure shows, for example, that as the proportion of students with low expectations in an Upward Bound project approaches 0.40, that a statistically significant impact is obtained.

ward Bound could adjust its recruiting targets to achieve statistically significant overall impacts by ensuring that at least 40% of all served students have lower educational expectations or that 70% or more are classified as academically more at risk (see Fig. 8.1).[7] Based on information from the year 2000, the program serves about 44,000 students; less than 20% of these students have lower educational expectations and 50% of them fall within the poorer academic performance category.

How large an impact would we expect to see on an outcome, such as the index we used in our analysis, when the population served by Upward Bound changes as we have already suggested? Using the impacts shown in Table 8.2, we find that increasing the percentage of students in

---

[7]Besides simply varying the size of the t-statistic and assessing the proportion of at-risk students that would need to be served to obtain significant impacts at the program level, we can obtain some results from our model that are not particularly intuitive by adjusting other inputs in the simulation. We can show that, as projects reduce the variability in impacts, a smaller number of students will need to be shifted from the less at-risk group to the more at-risk group to achieve significant impacts.

projects with low expectations from about 20% to 40% produces an overall impact of almost 0.30; the current impact is 0.10. In terms of an effect size, the change in population composition would increase the overall impact from 0.07 to 0.19 standard deviations.[8] Similarly, shifting the composition so that more students who are at greater risk of academic failure are served produces an overall impact of 0.20, or an effect size of 0.13.

The results so far have focused on changes in the overall composition of the students served by the program. Given the structure of the program, with its more than 500 local projects, one must also consider what these adjustments would mean for each project. Typically, Upward Bound projects accept about 20 to 25 new applicants each year. To increase the share of students who have lower educational expectations, for example, will require that a project find, on average, 8 to 10 such students, rather than the usual 4 or 5. Furthermore, if the academic risk criteria are used, it will mean that local projects need to include 14 to 18 students with grade point averages of around 2.0 (or C), instead of the 10 students in that category they normally would invite to attend.

MAKING CHANGE HAPPEN: ALTERING THE MIX OF STUDENTS THAT PROJECTS SERVE

Improved targeting of programs is not an uncommon recommendation of evaluation studies that address impacts or effectiveness. As noted earlier, the reasons for this are quite straightforward: more often than not, clusters of services and intervention models have stronger results for particular subgroups of students. Consequently, a potentially powerful way to improve a program's effectiveness is to maximize services going to the populations for which there is evidence of added value. This kind of redirection in the group composition of programs such as Upward Bound, however, triggers a number of concerns for federal program proponents and local practitioners, who face the prospect of serving a population that is more at risk than the one they have previously elected to serve.

This section addresses the question of how the changes we recommend for targeting a more at-risk population of youth can be translated into action. First, using data from case studies we conducted of Upward Bound projects, we summarize the barriers and concerns that targeting changes

---

[8]An effect size is defined as the impact divided by the standard deviation of the outcome; in this case the outcome is the index score. Generally, an effect size smaller than 0.20 is considered small. Larger effect sizes, such as .4 and .8, are viewed as medium and large impacts, respectively.

create for program staff at both the federal and project levels.[9] Second, we recommend several fruitful paths that will address many, if not all, of the barriers and concerns faced by local projects and national decision makers. After considering the issues involved in translating impact findings related to Upward Bound, we conclude that two overarching and enduring challenges accompany efforts to change to a more optimal mix of targeting program resources:

- A pervasive mindset continues to tie programs for students who are more academically at risk to remedial approaches. This mindset may be extremely damaging in light of research that suggests using challenging content to improve the educational performance of these students.
- The growing emphasis on projects' outcomes as indicators of effective performance can hamper efforts to retarget program services to improve performance.

Barriers to and Concerns About Increasing the Proportion of At-Risk Students in Upward Bound

What makes the Upward Bound program and individual projects reluctant to take on larger numbers of more academically at-risk youth, when the unchallenged purpose of the program for its 30-year history has been to improve access and completion of college for disadvantaged populations? The most common answer we have heard in response to this question is that risk for students from low-income and minority homes entails many dimensions besides the academic. In the minds of many program staff members, these risks may not be evident in the high school and the early college experiences of these youth; these risks, which are due to poor self-concept or the lack of tacit knowledge that better-off families or communities provide, may become much more evident as students move into the later years of college and their early adult lives. Personal testimonials from individuals who were former Upward Bound students help to sustain these views among local program staff. As we continue to follow students in the treatment and control groups through their early 20s, it is also

---

[9]These case studies focused on nine projects that were identified as having achieved higher impacts on four outcomes of early success. The outcomes relate to students' accomplishments during the high school years and include the following: cumulative grade point average; academic credits earned; expected years of education 2 years after entering Upward Bound; and application to, or enrollment in, college. These higher impact projects varied in the proportion of low-educational expectation and at-risk students they served.

possible that the future national Upward Bound study may find some support for these contentions.

Other important reasons beyond the definition of risk lie behind staff's reluctance to serve a higher proportion of academically at-risk students. Later we list the principal concerns that operate as strong disincentives. As readers will quickly recognize, many of the concerns are interrelated.

Peer Influences. The composition of students in a project, or peer effects, may be an influential factor in helping students with lower academic performance to improve. Evidence from other programs, such as Title I, have indicated that high poverty concentration in a school adversely affects the performance of individual children within the school. At this point, we simply do not know how peer effects, such as the proportion of low academic achievers, may play out in Upward Bound projects.

Project staff members clearly perceive a benefit in achieving a desirable mix of students, but often they articulate this as simply getting a "diverse blend of kids" who are properly motivated toward college, rather than a specific mix between students with low and high educational expectations or between low academic performers and high performers. Staff members generally agree that Upward Bound is not a program designed to rescue "troubled youth." Staff members are especially worried about the effect on Upward Bound's image if larger numbers of lower achieving students were to be admitted. They fear that, in time, a stigma will become attached to Upward Bound, and that the end result will be to erode overall expectations within the project and attract fewer applicants who aspire to college.

Dilution of the Academic Character of Upward Bound. Many Upward Bound project staff members anticipate the need to alter program services and instructional approaches to address what could be classified as a more academically disengaged population. Increasing this population gives many project staff members concern because they feel they will have to provide more remedial help with basic skills to get these students through their high school course work. Historical perspective is helpful in explaining these views. In the past, Upward Bound has been criticized by some because it was perceived as not placing sufficient attention on academic preparation. Project staff members feel they now have addressed this criticism, and our research supports the view that the program has evolved into one offering a heavy dose of academic instruction (in contrast to the remedial basic skills and self-esteem program described by evaluation evidence from the late 1970s). Furthermore, to serve a more at-risk population, some staff members anticipate having to add components to their programs that entail considerable career counseling and selling the importance of a college education to students.

As they contemplate what changes may be required to serve more students who are struggling academically, or who have lower academic expectations, the views of Upward Bound staff members are at odds with what research has to say about the impact of participating in Upward Bound programs on students who are most at risk. The programs in place for college-oriented students, which are the focus of most local projects, are the programs that the national evaluation results indicate are working more effectively for less well-performing students. We turn to this contradiction later in this section, when we address steps for altering the mix of students in projects.

Difficulties in Identifying At-Risk Students Likely to Benefit. Staff members face both a logistical and perceptual problem when they attempt to find higher risk applicants who are likely to benefit from Upward Bound. Projects rely heavily on the initial recruitment efforts of classroom teachers and guidance counselors in the schools they serve. Communicating the profile of an "appropriate Upward Bound student" to staff in the schools—staff who must address the needs of many students from troubled school or family backgrounds—is a challenging task. Project staff members report that it takes many iterative attempts and a very solid working relationship to achieve this level of communication. Project staff members complain that schools often want to send the more troubled youth to them as a way of finding any form of help, but they see many of these students as unlikely to benefit from a college-prep program that consists of a weekly set of contacts during the school year and an intensive summer on a college campus. Project staff members note the number of special education students and students with disciplinary issues whom schools send their way—inappropriately in their minds, given the resources they have to apply and the challenges students face when they live on a college campus during the summer. Occasionally, school staff will reinforce the selectivity preferences of Upward Bound staff. Many principals and guidance counselors endorse having a "reward" such as a referral to Upward Bound for students who are working hard and successfully in schools that serve large proportions of families from disadvantaged homes.

Project efforts to find academically less-troubled students are understandable. Most Upward Bound programs have existed for many years (often 20 or more), and the staff feel they have acquired a good sense of whom they can help and whom they cannot. They base this knowledge on the types of students who stay in the program, go on to college, and stay in touch with the program. These acquired understandings, not surprisingly, have fostered considerable skepticism among many project staff members about the national evaluation's findings that Upward Bound primarily benefits more at-risk youths.[10]

The Upward Bound project staff may be on target in emphasizing that the program is not designed to address the needs of many youth with major difficulties in school or in the outside community. It is important to note that the more at-risk students in the national evaluation study had been selected from a larger pool of students because they did, in fact, show project staff that they possessed some promise for postsecondary pursuits. The upshot of these various observations is that it will be a major challenge for project and school staff to become skillful in selecting a larger number of particular at-risk students for whom the program is likely to make a difference.

Less Duration Among More At-Risk Students. To date, findings from the national evaluation suggest that students who stay in the program for a longer time are more likely to benefit from it. More at-risk students, however, whether measured in terms of lower academic performance or educational expectations, are those least likely to persist. It will be a major challenge to keep more at-risk students in the program longer. That such students are "harder to serve" and may require greater attention is confirmed by a few projects that attempt to serve such students. Upward Bound programs will face a challenge in how projects' retention performance is perceived by federal reviewers. Specifically, if projects serve a more at-risk population, student retention rates will decline initially.

Reliance on Program Outcomes to Show Success. Conventional wisdom among project staff and the public holds that positive outcomes for students in Upward Bound (or other) programs are evidence that the program is working. Consequently, the program is seen as accomplishing its goals when high percentages of participants go on to 4-year colleges, have high grades, and receive other accolades in high school. It will be much more difficult for the public and policymakers to accept that lower rates of college attendance and other less impressive outcomes than what Upward Bound exhibited in the past may mean the program is having more impact. Further complications stem from routine indicators of program performance, which—thanks to such laws as the Government Performance

---

[10]Before the pool of eligible student applicants was randomized, Upward Bound project directors were asked to identify those whom, in the absence of the evaluation, they were most likely and least likely to accept. It is noteworthy that the national evaluation has not shown any significant difference in impacts for the pool of student applicants project directors indicated they would have picked versus the students who actually entered the program.

and Results Act of 1993—are limited to, at best, a longitudinal tracking of participating students' outcomes.

The political reality is that if Upward Bound shifts to a more at-risk population of students, it is likely to decrease the program's outcomes as currently reported to Congress. Many stakeholders fear that unwarranted negative conclusions will be drawn about the program's usefulness and effectiveness. In a related vein, individual projects will have difficulty meeting the current set of goals they have specified as a requirement for receiving their grants. A decrease in the positive outcomes they report may jeopardize their refunding by reducing the extra "priority points" that incumbent projects earn in subsequent grant competitions for outcome-based evidence of meeting their stated goals and objectives.

RECOMMENDATIONS

To successfully translate the targeting findings from the national evaluation's impact analyses, it is necessary to take seriously the various concerns and barriers that fuel the reluctance of most project staff; their concerns provide a source of critical guidance. Following, we articulate three major steps that the national program and individual project staff members might take to help the program improve its overall impact through targeting a more academically at-risk population.

1. Resist the impulse to adopt remedial instruction   Despite considerable research evidence that discredits an emphasis on remediation as an effective instructional tool, mention of serving a population at greater academic risk almost immediately prompts project staff to conclude that more remediation in basic skills will be necessary in their programs.[11] This is surprising in light of the fact that the students who were at greater risk profited from the programs that projects in the national evaluation already had in place—programs which, by and large, focused on instruction that paralleled and enriched the material covered in students' academic-track high school courses. It is equally noteworthy that our efforts to find program features common to higher performing Upward Bound projects revealed few striking differences distinguishing academic offerings in the projects with the highest percentages of students with low educational expectations. In fact, the level of academic challenge in these projects was

---

[11]A heavy emphasis on remediation tends to lower students' performance expectations and to dwell on only a narrow band of the skills important to cognitive development and subsequent performance (Hopfenberg, Levin, & Chase, 1993; Means & Knapp, 1991; Resnick, 1987; Singham, 1998; Steele, 1992; Triesman, 1992).

similar to that in projects with noticeably fewer students who had lower educational expectations.

2. Expand efforts to find more at-risk youth who can benefit from Upward Bound   Staff in most projects will have to search more extensively and direct more resources to the selection process if they are to identify the more at-risk students for whom Upward Bound is a reasonable and appropriate intervention. As noted earlier, school staff tend to refer students with a wide range of problems to Upward Bound, as part of finding any source of help for these students.

One of the higher performing projects we studied in-depth provides insight into how other projects might adjust their recruitment and selection processes to find appropriate at-risk students. For this project, nearly three fourths of its students met the criteria for low expectations and academic risk we have discussed here. The project defined its target group as students who have the ability to succeed academically, but who are underachieving. After obtaining referrals from guidance counselors, parents, current participants, and sometimes probation officers, the project leaders conducted one-on-one interviews with each applicant. Staff members looked for students who were aware of their academic standing (i.e., they knew their grade point averages and what credits they needed to graduate), who were not more than a few credits behind, and who had done well in at least one subject in school. A short essay contributed further relevant information about whether, in the words of the project director, the student had "some spark of ability and sense of the future."

Finding students who fit the desired profile was not an easy task even for this successful project. The staff found they had to interview roughly three times as many students as the number of available openings. They also expressed surprise when they learned they had achieved higher impacts than other projects on outcomes such as credits earned in high school and plans to attend college—remarking that they did not recall the students who came into the project during the course of the study as having noteworthy outcomes. (This reaction again underscores the point that observed outcomes are often incorrectly accepted as a valid indicator of how effective is a program.)

3. Educate key parties, including the federal program staff, Congress, and local communities, that Upward Bound's effectiveness rests on (a) serving higher numbers of youth who are more at risk, and (b) interpreting outcome results for this specific population of students   The third step in translating the Upward Bound targeting findings into practice involves considerable education at the national and local levels. Projects need to be held accountable and rewarded for taking in larger percentages of more at-risk youth. Their performance measures, as contained in goal statements and performance reports, need to be rebenchmarked to reflect

drops in outcome levels that will occur as a result of changes in the population Upward Bound serves. Similarly, those reviewing grant proposals for ED need to consider the change in project populations when interpreting outcome results from ongoing projects.

Educating Congress and the general public is unlikely to be as simple as a one-time informational sweep. Many members of Congress are likely to be unfamiliar with the changes in targeting that yield less impressive outcomes than those reported in the past. Similarly, local schools and community groups will require explanations and multiple reminders that high rates of college attendance are not necessarily indicative of a successful program. These points will need to be repeated across the years to many audiences if the changes examined in this article are to be implemented effectively.

ACKNOWLEDGMENTS

An earlier version of this article was presented at the October 2000 annual meeting of the Association for Public Policy and Management, Seattle, WA. The opinions presented in the article do not necessarily represent those of the U.S. Department of Education or Mathematica Policy Research. The authors would like to acknowledge the work of Julia Chan who implemented many of the analyses described in this article.

REFERENCES

Hopfenberg, W., Levin, H., & Chase, C. (1993). *The accelerated schools resource guide.* San Francisco: Jossey-Bass.

Kemple, J., & Snipes, J. (2000). *Career academies: Impacts on students' engagement and performance in high school.* New York: Manpower Demonstration Research Corporation.

Means, B., & Knapp, M. (1991). *Teaching advanced skills to educationally disadvantaged students. Final report.* Washington, DC: U.S. Department of Education.

Myers, D., & Schirm, A. (1999). *The impacts of Upward Bound: Final report for phase I of the national evaluation of Upward Bound.* Washington, DC: U.S. Department of Education, Planning and Evaluation Service.

Resnick, L. (1987). *Education and learning to think.* Washington, DC: National Academy Press.

Rosenbaum, P., & Rubin, D. (1983). The central role of the propensity score in observational studies for causal effects. *Biometricka, 70,* 41–55.

Rosenbaum, P., & Rubin, D. (1984). Reducing bias in observational studies using subclassification on the propensity score. *Journal of the American Statistical Association, 79,* 516–524.

Singham, M. (1998). The canary in the mine: The achievement gap between Black and White students. *Phi Delta Kappan, 80,* 9–15.

Smith, T., Aronstamm Young, B., Bae, Y., Choy, S., & Alsalam, N. (1997). *The condition of education 1997* (National Center for Education Statistics, Publication No. NCES 97–388). Washington, DC: U.S. Government Printing Office.

Steele, C. (1992). Race and the schooling of Black Americans. *Atlantic Monthly, 269,* 68–78.

Triesman, P. (1992). Studying students studying calculus. *College Mathematics Journal, 23,* 362–72.

9

Evaluation of the Summerbridge Intervention Program: Design and Preliminary Findings

Jennifer A. Laird
American Institutes for Research

S. Shirley Feldman
Stanford University

The benefits of a college education are large and varied (Levy & Michel, 1991; Mishel & Bernstein 1994; Topel, 1993; U.S. Bureau of the Census, 1996; U.S. Department of Education, 2000; Wilson, 1991). Unfortunately, the United States has been plagued by a persistent education gap. Children from low-income and ethnic minority backgrounds are (a) more likely to attend poorly funded, less rigorous elementary and secondary schools; (b) less likely to graduate from high school; and (c) less likely to attend and graduate from college (Baker & Velez, 1996; Berkner & Chavez, 1997; Gamoran, 1987). Despite overall increases in college attendance during the last three decades, the proportion of ethnic minority and low-income students attending college still lags behind the rates for White and more affluent students (Bankston & Cladas, 1997; U.S. Department of Education, 2000). Educators, policymakers, and parents have searched for ways to combat these troubling statistics. Summerbridge is a program that has the potential to improve the educational experiences and outcomes of the students it serves. This chapter describes the Summerbridge program, as well as the design and preliminary findings from the multifaceted evaluation effort that is currently being undertaken to assess the effectiveness of the program.

WHAT IS SUMMERBRIDGE?

Summerbridge is a tuition-free academic enrichment program for young adolescents from limited-opportunity backgrounds who are performing at or above grade level. It was founded in San Francisco in 1978 at University High School and has since grown to 27 sites in 16 states and Hong Kong. The program differs from traditional summer school by using innovative cross-age teaching that pairs high school- and college-age teachers with talented middle school students. The program consists of high-spirited afterschool and summer sessions intended to inspire both groups toward learning and achievement. Middle school students are asked to make a 2-year commitment that typically begins the summer after sixth grade and ends the summer after eighth grade. The summer sessions are designed to be intense, but joyful, 6-week sessions in which students take courses in core academic subjects, such as literature and mathematics, as well as elective courses that reflect the interests and talents of the young teachers, including foreign languages, art specialties, music, and sports. The sessions are intended to give Summerbridge students the academic, leadership, and organizational skills they will need to compete with students of more privileged backgrounds. Academic classes are complemented by many spirited group activities that demand participation and help students learn to be effective public speakers and advocates for themselves. The activities include daily all-school meetings, field trips, and an end-of-summer event to celebrate what students have learned.

Summerbridge seeks to maintain the renewed interest and enthusiasm for learning that develops in the unique summer sessions by holding afterschool sessions, Saturday school sessions, or both, during the school year. Like the summer sessions, these sessions are taught by high school- and college-age teachers and are designed to complement and expand on what the middle school students are learning at their regular schools. The leadership and organizational focus continues in the school-year program. Students are taught about important aspects of academic learning (including study skills) and the values of keeping commitments, follow-through, and promptness. Summerbridge also has a high school advocacy component that helps parents to explore alternative high school options because many of the local high schools their children attend do not have rigorous college preparatory tracks. Many Summerbridge students decide to attend selective public high schools (e.g., academic magnet schools), and a small percentage receive scholarships to independent private schools.

Summerbridge teachers are recruited through an online teacher recruitment process that attracts applicants from over 300 colleges and universities across the country. High school students are recruited locally and make up about 25% of the faculty. Applicants for teaching positions fill out an extensive application and are interviewed by the program director. Summerbridge selects an ethnically diverse teaching faculty to correspond to the student population.

Students are introduced to Summerbridge in recruitment assemblies at their schools, during which the Summerbridge program director explains the program and invites students to apply. Interested students must fill out a rigorous application. The elements of choice and application are important aspects of the Summerbridge model.

The program structure is designed to support the cross-age dynamic in two ways. First, class sizes are supposed to be held to seven students. Second, the young faculty is organized into departments by subject area, and each department has its own Department Chair. A professional teacher who teaches that subject mentors the department. Summerbridge teachers begin preparing for their summer of instruction in the spring after they are selected and participate in a week of training before the middle school students arrive. The young teachers submit their lesson plans to the mentor teachers for approval. They are also observed and provided with feedback from mentor teachers, the program director, and their peers. The faculty meets daily, and the young teachers learn from each other and from curriculum or pedagogy sessions held by the professional mentor teachers.

Most Summerbridge programs are hosted at independent private schools. Summer sessions are held on the independent school campus with the goal of exposing Summerbridge students to an environment rich in educational resources and opportunities. The programs use buses and cars to pick students up and transport them to the independent school campus, where they spend the day in classes and other related activities, and where breakfast and lunch are served. To avoid the need for transportation, the school-year sessions are held at the students' regular schools. Local Summerbridge programs raise money annually to cover the expenses of staff salaries, materials, food, and transportation. Each program is run by two or three full-time staff members, typically a director, school-year coordinator, and alumni coordinator. Summerbridge teachers receive modest stipends for summer teaching, but school-year teaching is done on a volunteer basis. The professional mentor teachers are paid.

Summerbridge National was created in 1991 to help establish new sites and to support the existing local Summerbridge programs. In 2000, the local programs became a formal national collaborative of affiliate sites and selected a new name—The Breakthrough Collaborative. Given that the program operates year-round, the new name more accurately portrays the program. It was also chosen to reflect testimonials of student alumni and former teachers who claim that the program was a "breakthrough" experience for them. Student alumni have described "breakthrough" experiences in which they realized that learning is fun, that it is "cool" to be smart, and that they wanted to attend college. Summerbridge is in a 3-year, phased process of changing its name. Affiliate sites will use the new name and logo and commit to implementing the best practices of the model, working toward a common level of excellence.

Geographic and institutional differences, as well as changing Summer-bridge site directors and leaders of the host schools, affect the way the model is implemented at each location The description of the program as given in this section is that of the optimal program as implemented at the original site. Although each site has made a commitment to the original model as described in the Affiliation Agreement, there are discrepancies from site to site. For example, although the program is designed to cover two summer sessions, student attrition from the first to the second sum-mer session is disappointingly high at some sites. Furthermore, the use of mentor teachers is not consistent across the collaborative. At some sites, mentor teachers are active, integral participants. At others, they are more peripheral.

Perhaps the greatest source of variation is the school-year program. Some sites have well-established programs that meet 3 or 4 days a week, whereas others meet only once or twice a month and are poorly attended. Summerbridge National is working with sites to identify weaknesses in individual programs and considers the evaluation described in this chap-ter as a valuable diagnostic tool for that effort.

THE GOALS OF SUMMERBRIDGE

Summerbridge has a dual mission of improving the educational opportu-nities of motivated middle school students and encouraging talented high school and college students, the Summerbridge teachers, to pursue ca-reers in education. The goals for the middle school students consist of both long- and short-term goals. The long-term goals are to improve the educational trajectories of these students, including completion of rigor-ous, college-preparatory high school programs and entrance into colleges. To achieve these long-term goals, short-term goals are necessary. The short-term goals of the program focus on those behaviors, attitudes, and motivations that are supportive of learning and education. The short-term goals also include strengthening basic skills associated with reading, writ-ing, and mathematics that are necessary for later educational success.

As this chapter describes, we are conducting an 8-year longitudinal evaluation to study the impact of the Summerbridge program on stu-dents. The evaluation will ultimately assess Summerbridge's success at achieving both its short- and long-term goals. At this stage of the evalua-tion, however, only data pertaining to Summerbridge's short-term goals are available. Information on these intermediary steps toward the long-term objectives is important both because (a) it will be years before valid data on the long-term impact of Summerbridge is available, and (b) it will be important to know at what point the program's impact waned if the long-term findings are disappointing.

OVERVIEW OF THE ASSESSMENT

In April 1999, Summerbridge National contracted with us to conduct an evaluation of the Summerbridge program. The organization is committed to a rigorous evaluation of the program's impact on students, teachers, and directors. Fiscal constraints led to a decision to delay indefinitely the evaluation of the program's effect on directors, however. Data have recently been collected on former Summerbridge teachers from five sites to determine the extent to which Summerbridge is successful in encouraging them to pursue careers in education. This chapter, however, reports only on the student evaluation.

The student assessment is two-pronged. One prong is survey-based and is designed to collect data on the affective, motivational, and behavioral indicators known to be associated with academic achievement. The second prong is an assessment of students' mathematics and reading skills based on standardized tests. This chapter first details the survey component of the student evaluation, followed by a presentation of the assessment of academic skills.

The Student Survey Assessment

Table 9.1 presents the Summerbridge student survey assessment schedule. The survey assessment of students includes three separate cohorts. That is, students who begin Summerbridge in the years 2000, 2002, and 2003 are assessed. In addition, we follow students from Cohort 1999, which was initially designated as a pilot cohort. By studying groups of students from different years, the assessment is protected from the possibility that, in any given year, the program may experience atypical circumstances, such as an extremely high rate of director turnover, which can affect the effectiveness of the program.

Students are first surveyed before their first summer at Summerbridge, which is typically the summer between sixth and seventh grade (the students are noted as "rising seventh graders" in Table 9.1). Students from each cohort are surveyed at many points, including before and after the two summer sessions (noted as "before SB" and "after SB" in Table 9.1), and approximately every 2 years thereafter. With the exception of Cohort 2003, all cohorts will be followed at least until the fall following their scheduled graduation from high school. This will permit an examination of college matriculation rates. Cohorts 1999 and 2000 will also be surveyed

TABLE 9.1
Schedule of Summerbridge (SB) Student Assessments

Assessment Year	1999	2000	2001	2002	2003	2004	2005	2006	2007	2008
Cohort 1999	Before SB *Intervention After SB Intervention Rising seventh graders	Before SB *Intervention *Comparison After SB *Intervention Rising eighth graders	Fall *Intervention Ninth graders		Fall *Intervention Eleventh graders		Fall *Intervention Recent high school graduates		Spring *Intervention Two years past high school graduation	
2000		Before SB *Intervention *Comparison After SB *Intervention Rising seventh graders	Before SB *Intervention *Comparison After SB *Intervention Rising eighth graders	Fall *Intervention *Comparison Ninth graders		Fall *Intervention *Comparison Eleventh graders		Fall *Intervention *Comparison Recent high school graduates		Spring *Intervention *Comparison Two years past high school graduation
2002				Before SB *Intervention *Comparison After SB *Intervention Rising seventh graders	Before SB *Intervention *Comparison After SB *Intervention Rising eighth graders	Fall *Intervention *Comparison Ninth graders		Fall *Intervention *Comparison Eleventh graders		Fall *Intervention *Comparison Recent high school graduates

Note.   Before SB = assessment occurs at the beginning of the Summerbridge session; After SB = assessment occurs at the end of the Summerbridge session; Intervention = intervention students assessed; Comparison = comparison students assessed; Rising seventh = students will enter the seventh grade in the fall.

2 years after high school graduation to determine whether students remain in college.

Except for the pilot cohort, each cohort includes two groups: a group of students who attend Summerbridge—referred to as the "intervention group"—and a comparable group of students who applied to but did not attend Summerbridge—referred to as the "comparison group." A comparison group is essential in order to attribute changes over time to the intervention rather than to other unrelated factors. An appropriate comparison group should be comparable to the Summerbridge attendees in important socioeconomic and educationally relevant characteristics. Ideally, random assignment would have been the preferred method for obtaining a comparison group, but this was not a viable option, as the site directors felt it would have taken away too much local control.

Thus, a comparison group was constructed from those students who were applicants to Summerbridge in 2000 but who were not admitted to the program. Using incentives generously provided by a board member, the assessment team was able to give all applicants gift certificates for completing the survey before the applicants knew whether they had been admitted to Summerbridge. A concern with the comparison group strategy was that the comparison and intervention groups might not be comparable—that is, that Summerbridge directors rejected applicants for systematic reasons.

A comparison of the intervention and comparison groups revealed that the groups contained approximately equal numbers of students—approximately 750 in each group. Of even greater importance, the groups were found to be alike in most important characteristics. The intervention and comparison groups were compared on 30 educationally relevant and socioeconomic characteristics and found to be alike on 27. The only differences (at $p < .05$) were that the comparison group was a little younger (by 1 month), contained more girls, and reported reading outside of school somewhat more than children in the intervention group. Overall, the findings suggest that it is appropriate to include students who applied to Summerbridge but did not attend the program as comparison students.

Current Status of the Student Survey Assessment

Survey data are currently available for Cohort 1999 and Cohort 2000 (see Table 9.2 for a summary of the assessment data currently available). Cohort 1999 is comprised only of an intervention group. Given that it was the first year of the evaluation, and that the assessment team did not have adequate lead-time to collect data from students who had applied but did not attend Summerbridge, there is no comparison group for this cohort. It is also important to point out that, although Cohort 1999 was originally

TABLE 9.2
Summerbridge Assessment Data Currently Available

	Summer 1999 Session		Summer 2000 Session	
	Before	After	Before	After
Cohort 1999				
Intervention Group	√	√	√	√
Cohort 2000				
Intervention Group			√	√
Comparison Group			√	

designed to be a pilot cohort to enable testing of the evaluation instruments and processes, the Board of Trustees has urged the assessment team to continue following these students. Analyses of the data from the 1999 surveys identified minor problems with a few of the measures. Those problematic questions have been improved. However, refining the questions means that it is not possible to fully assess how students change on those measures from 1999 to 2000 and subsequent years. Nevertheless, the majority of the 1999 questions performed well and were retained in identical form in the 2000 surveys. Cohort 1999 has been assessed four times: before and after the 1999 summer session, and before and after the 2000 summer session.

Cohort 2000 is comprised of both an intervention group (students who attended Summerbridge) as well as a comparison group (students who applied but did not attend Summerbridge). The intervention group of Cohort 2000 has been assessed twice: before and after the 2000 summer session. The comparison group of Cohort 2000 has been assessed once: before the 2000 summer session.

Key Questions of the Student Survey Assessment

The current data from the Summerbridge student survey assessment enable us to examine the following key questions:

1. What is the effect of the first Summerbridge summer session on students?
   - Is the first Summerbridge session equally effective for different groups of students?
   - Do the effects of the first Summerbridge session last during the school year or do they erode?
2. What is the effect of the second Summerbridge session on students?

- How does the magnitude of the effects of the second session of Summerbridge compare to the magnitude of effects of the first session?

This chapter addresses each of these key questions, and their subquestions, in turn. Before doing this, however, we explain how the assessment was conducted, as well as present descriptive information on the students who participated in the assessment.

The Student Survey Assessment Design

Data for the assessment were collected through student surveys. In 1999, both the "before Summerbridge" surveys and the "after Summerbridge" surveys were administered at the Summerbridge sites (31 sites participated in 1999). The "before Summerbridge" survey was administered in the first week of the program and the "after Summerbridge" survey was administered in the last week of the program.

In 2000, the procedures for the "before Summerbridge" survey administration were changed to collect information from students in the Cohort 2000 comparison group. Following the application deadlines, site directors sent to the national office lists of names and addresses of students who applied to their programs (26 sites participated in 2000). Surveys were then mailed to the homes of all of these students. This was done before students were notified about whether they had been accepted to the program. It was important that students not think that their answers would affect whether they were admitted into the Summerbridge program. Thus, students were instructed to return the surveys and consent forms to Dr. Feldman at Stanford University, rather than to the Summerbridge National office. The introduction letter explained that surveys were being sent to students who were applying to a variety of summer programs. To increase the likelihood that students would complete and return the surveys, two incentives were offered to all students who returned a survey and consent form: (a) a $25 gift certificate to a popular national clothing store, and (b) a chance to win one of five new iMac computers.

In addition to the initial mailing of the "before Summerbridge" survey to Cohort 2000, the intervention students from Cohort 2000 were asked to complete a survey, if they had not already done so, when they went to their Summerbridge site. Also, a second survey mailing was sent to the comparison students from the Cohort 2000 who had not yet sent back a survey. Cohort 1999 completed the "before Summerbridge" surveys during the first week of the session. Both Cohort 1999 and Cohort 2000 (intervention group only) completed "after Summerbridge" surveys at the sites during the last week of the session.

During the summer of 2000, the rate of return of the surveys was relatively low. From Cohort 2000, 62% of intervention students provided the
assessment team with usable data (defined as both "before Summerbridge" and "after Summerbridge" data). The rate of return from Cohort
1999 was even lower: 48% of students from this cohort provided the assessment team with usable data. The assessment team has worked with
Summerbridge National and site directors to identify factors which contributed to these low rates of return and have developed procedures designed to improve return rates in future assessment years. In fact, for data
collected in the summer of 2001 (not reported in this chapter), the rate of
return was 87% for the "beginning of Summerbridge" assessment.

We conducted analyses to investigate whether the sample loss for Cohort 1999 (the pilot sample) was random. Thirty-eight Time 1 scores (at
entry into Summerbridge) were compared for two groups: (a) the 218
youth who had usable data from all four assessments, and (b) the 381 students who had missing data from one or more assessment periods. Fortunately, the two groups were alike on 35 of the 38 Time 1 scores. Those with
complete data differed from those with incomplete data only in that students with complete data were more likely to be in a lower grade, be
White or Hispanic American, and to describe their regular classroom
teacher as more supportive of learning. On the remaining 35 measures, including socioeconomic and education-related measures, the two groups
were alike. Thus, sample loss was random and should not influence the
validity of the conclusions of this assessment.

Constructs Assessed in the Student Survey

Before drafting the student survey in 1999, the assessment team studied
the goals of the organization by reading promotional materials and talk-
ing with the staff of Summerbridge National. After identifying the program's goals, we outlined a set of constructs that corresponded to these
goals and which could be reliably assessed through a survey. When possible, we incorporated established measures of the constructs developed by
other researchers (in either identical or modified form) into the survey.
When measures were not available, we developed our own.

As stated earlier, analyses of the 1999 data indicated that a few items
needed to be modified. Based on this information, the problematic items
were either improved on or dropped from the 2000 surveys. Table 9.3 lists
the constructs assessed in the 2000 surveys, indicating whether they were
asked in identical form in 1999 (thereby allowing comparisons across the 2
years). The last column of the table identifies the source of the measure.
Measures developed by the authors for this evaluation are noted as

TABLE 9.3
Constructs Assessed in the 1999 and 2000 Surveys

Constructs Assessed in 2000	Definition	Constructs Assessed in 1999	Source
Effort and involvement in school			
Effort	Assesses how much students pay attention in class, participate actively in class, try as hard as they can, and are actively engaged in their school work.	√	Dornbusch, Ritter, Mont–Reynaud, and Chen (1990)
Preparation	Assesses how frequently students come to class with their homework done and with their books and pencils.	√	Dornbusch et al. (1990)
Homework	Assesses the amount of time per day students reported spending on homework on all subjects combined and on math.		Dornbusch et al. (1990)
Educational goals			
Aspirations	Refers to the amount of education students hope to achieve.	√	Glasgow, Dornbusch, Troyer, Steinberg, and Ritter (1997)
Expectations	Refers to the amount of education students expect to achieve.	√	Glasgow et al. (1997)
Personal characteristics			
Assertiveness in the classroom	Assesses whether students speak up in class and feel comfortable talking with teachers or asking questions when they do not understand something.	√	Feldman and Laird (1999)
Acceptance of being smart	Assesses how comfortable students feel in being identified as "smart" (in peer contexts where "smart" is often seen as undesirable).		Arroyo and Zigler (1995)

(Continued)

TABLE 9.3
(Continued)

Constructs Assessed in 2000	Definition	Constructs Assessed in 1999	Source
Personal characteristics			
Academic self-concept	Refers to students' perceptions of themselves as capable students.		Nicholls (1984)
Willingness to follow rules	Assesses how often students do what the teacher asks them to do.	√	Wentzel (1993)
Acceptance of diversity	Refers to students' perceptions that it's OK to have friends from different ethnic groups, that students can learn from and get along well with others from different ethnic backgrounds.		Feldman and Laird (1999)
Helpful to classmates	Assesses how often students help other students.	√	Wentzel (1993)
Perceptions of school			
Teachers as supportive of learning	Assesses the extent to which students describe their teachers as helpful and academically supportive.	√	Johnson, Johnson, Buckman, and Richards (1985)
Classmates as supportive of learning	Assesses the extent to which students perceive other students in their classrooms as being supportive of them in learning contexts.	√	Johnson et al. (1985)
School-related hassles	Assesses the frequency of aggravations experienced at school or about school-related matters.	√	Kanner and Feldman (1987)

Feldman and Laird (1999). Copies of the survey can be obtained by contacting the authors.

The information collected through the student surveys will vary across the assessment years so that it is appropriate to students' age and grade level. For example, when students are in grades six through eight, the surveys assess a variety of different measures of effort, motivation, and behaviors known to be associated with good school performance, as well as behaviors known to undermine school achievement. When students are in grades nine through twelve, the surveys will collect information on students' grade point averages, grade retention, academic track (e.g., advanced placement, honors, general, remedial), the kind of mathematics and science classes in which students are enrolled, students' knowledge of college admission requirements, as well as measures of motivation, classroom effort, school suspension, and the type of high schools students attend. When students graduate from high school, the surveys will assess their college enrollment status and college persistence.

Description of the Students

As noted previously, survey data has thus far been collected from two cohorts of Summerbridge students: Cohort 1999 and Cohort 2000. Table 9.4 presents demographic information on intervention students from these cohorts. The two cohorts are quite similar. There are more girls than boys in both cohorts. The cohorts are ethnically diverse, with African American students comprising the largest group. Slightly over half of students live with both of their biological parents. Students range in age from 10 to 13; most are 11 to 12 years old. When students entered Summerbridge, most had just completed the sixth grade, but substantial proportions of students had just completed either grades 5 or 7.

Descriptive analyses reveal that students from both cohorts describe themselves in very positive terms as they enter Summerbridge. The vast majority both wants and expects to graduate from college. Similarly, almost all students report grade point averages of B or better. They perceive themselves as strong students and indicate that they "often-to-usually" put in a lot of effort into their schoolwork. Seldom do they come to class unprepared. Furthermore, they describe their teachers at their regular school as being quite supportive of learning, although they perceive their classmates in these schools as somewhat less so. On average, students in both cohorts report reading things such as magazines, newspapers, and books at home less than once a month. Virtually all students from both cohorts typed on a computer in the last year and most did so more than 10 times. Few students reported looking for information on the Internet more than once or twice, and still fewer reported using e-mail more than once or twice.

TABLE 9.4
Description of Summerbridge Students

	Cohort 1999	Cohort 2000
Number of respondents	594	605
Gender		
Girls	58%	64%
Boys	42%	36%
Ethnicity		
African American	43%	42%
Asian American	9%	9%
Hispanic American	17%	19%
White	13%	15%
Other (e.g., Biracial)	18%	13%
Family background		
Lives with both parents	54%	53%
Lives in a blended family	22%	17%
Lives with a single parent	24%	30%
Age		
10 years	9%	12%
11 years	34%	41%
12 years	49%	38%
13 years	7%	8%
Grade just completed		
Fifth grade	24%	25%
Sixth grade	66%	58%
Seventh grade	10%	16%

T-test analyses were conducted to examine the extent to which boys and girls who enter the Summerbridge program are alike or different. Generally, for both cohorts, boys and girls are quite similar. Differences, when they exist, are very modest and consistent with established sex differences reported by others. Overall, girls tended to perceive their school environments as more supportive and themselves as weaker students, despite the fact that they received higher grades than the boys. Girls also reported that they were more likely to follow rules and to be more helpful toward other students.

Chi-square analyses were conducted to examine the extent to which there were ethnic differences among entering Summerbridge students. Generally, the four largest ethnic groups (African American, Asian American, Hispanic American, and White) were more alike than different. However, significant ($p < .01$), albeit modest, differences were apparent across the two cohorts. Asian Americans and Whites reported higher grade point averages than African Americans and Hispanic Americans; and White students, who used computers more often during the last year, perceived themselves as stronger students compared to the other ethnic groups. Hispanic American students tended to read less often at home, and African Americans and Whites indicated that they take more initiative in the classroom. Asian Americans were less likely to come to class unprepared, to engage in misconduct, and to experience hassles at school (such as conflicts with teachers), but they were more likely to indicate that they hid their academic success from their peers.

Although there were some sex and ethnic differences as students entered Summerbridge, these differences were very modest. Overall, in both 1999 and 2000, Summerbridge succeeded in attracting relatively strong, motivated students, regardless of gender or ethnicity.

There are two important consequences that follow from starting an intervention program with students who evaluate themselves so positively: (a) It is difficult to document increases in education-related scores, no matter how effective the intervention program, given that students are already scoring at the top end of these scales; and (b) decreases in education scores may even be found, as students interact with and compare themselves to other bright, motivated students, and as they encounter higher academic standards and challenges than they experience in their regular schools.

As we turn to the results that address the key questions outlined earlier, it is important to keep in mind the consequences of beginning with strong students. In addition, it is important to point out that students enter Summerbridge before they are fully engulfed by adolescence—a period when the peer group becomes more salient and students often experience strong detractors from education, such as pressure to appear attractive, to be "cool," and to experiment with alcohol, drugs, and delinquency. Thus, maintaining high levels of educational effort and aspirations, for example, may itself be a success. Until longitudinal data is collected on comparison students, however, the assessment is unable to evaluate whether Summerbridge students are more likely to maintain their status as strong students as compared to similar students who do not attend Summerbridge.

Key Question Number 1: What Is the Effect of the First Summerbridge Session?

The first set of findings addresses the critical question of what types of changes the first Summerbridge session brings about in students' lives. To examine this, students' assessments of their behavior in, and perceptions of, their regular classroom were compared to their behavior in, and perceptions of, their Summerbridge classrooms. This was done by analyzing students' responses in the first-year "before Summerbridge" survey and contrasting those to their responses in the first-year "after Summerbridge" survey. Table 9.5 presents the results of paired *t*-test analyses that include all intervention students from Cohorts 1999 and 2000. The table reports *p*-values of less than .05, .01, and .001; however, we consider findings as significant only if they are at $p < .01$. Unless otherwise noted, the sample sizes for these analyses were approximately 1,199 students (sample size varied slightly for each analysis due to missing data on specific measures).

There are several important points to note from Table 9.5. First, reports of changes refer to statistically significant findings, usually of modest magnitude, as is to be expected in a large sample. However, these changes are important in human terms (not just statistical terms). Second, the findings validate the general effectiveness of Summerbridge. Students perceive Summerbridge as more supportive of learning and education than their regular classroom. They spend more time on homework and are more prepared when they come to class. They feel more comfortable with speaking up, answering questions, and asking the

TABLE 9.5
Effects of the First Summerbridge (SB) Session
(Data From Combined Cohorts 1999 and 2000)

	Means		
	Before SB	After SB	t test
Effort and involvement in school			
Effort	2.50	2.48	−1.46
Preparation	3.47	3.52	2.78**
All homework[a]	3.33	3.54	4.26***
Math homework[a]	1.90	1.82	−1.80
Educational goals			
Aspirations	3.89	3.90	0.46
Expectations	3.82	3.83	0.80
Personal characteristics			
Assertiveness in the classroom	3.14	3.27	6.42***
Acceptance of being smart	2.41	2.39	−1.07
Academic self-concept[a]	3.27	3.19	−4.23***
Follows class rules	3.37	3.33	−2.42*
Acceptance of diversity[a]	3.71	3.77	3.86***
Helpful to classmates	3.08	3.01	−3.45***
Perceptions of school			
Teachers as supportive of learning	3.55	4.68	38.64***
Classmates as supportive of learning	2.33	2.48	2.99**
School-related hassles	0.53	0.47	−6.18***
School-related uplifts			

Note. $N \approx 1,199$.
[a]Data from Cohort 2000 only ($N \approx 612$).
*$p < .05$. **$p < .01$. ***$p < .001$.

teacher for assistance, and they become more accepting of ethnic diversity while at Summerbridge.

As expected, Summerbridge did not change all aspects of students' school-related behaviors and attitudes. The 6-week Summerbridge session did not change students' already very high educational aspirations and expectations, the effort they reported putting into learning, or their acceptance of being smart. Furthermore, some of the changes were the opposite of what we expected. Perhaps as a result of the demanding academic Summerbridge programs, the small-group instructional setting, and being surrounded by other smart and motivated peers, students showed decreases in their academic self-concept. They also reported that they were somewhat less likely to help classmates at Summerbridge than they do in regular school—perhaps because there was less need in a setting with one teacher for every seven or so students.

In answer to the first question, What is the effect of Summerbridge summer session on students new to Summerbridge? the findings indicated that Summerbridge succeeds in creating a benign educational environment where

- Students undertake more homework and come to class better prepared than they do at regular school.
- Students feel more comfortable in class and with the teacher than they do in regular school.
- Teachers and peers are seen as supportive of learning.
- Acceptance of ethnic diversity increases.

Is the First Session Equally Effective for Different Groups of Students?

Additional analyses addressed the question of whether Summerbridge has equally beneficial effects for all kinds of students, or whether some kinds of students benefit more than others. This is an important question, because in an era of scarce resources, Summerbridge might want to target the intervention to those most likely to benefit. Alternately, Summerbridge may want to modify the program so that it benefits a group that is currently not benefiting maximally.

To address this question, we conducted two-way multivariate analyses of variance to compare the effects of Summerbridge on 15 outcomes for a variety of different groups. The findings are shown in Table 9.6. P-values of less than .05, .01, and .001 are noted, but interpretations are only made when the p-value was less than .01. Unless otherwise noted, the sample sizes for the analyses were approximately 1,199 students (sample size varied slightly for each analysis due to missing data on specific measures).

TABLE 9.6
Data to Address the Question of Whether Summerbridge
Affects Some Groups More than Others[a]
(Fs From Two-Way Analyses of Variance (ANOVAs))

	F-Values for Interaction Terms			
	Sex X Time	Ethnicity[b] X Time	Age[c] X Time	GPA[d] X Time
Effort and involvement in school				
Effort	ns	2.90*	ns	8.80***
Preparation	7.30**	ns	ns	ns
All homework[e]	4.80*	ns	ns	ns
Math homework[e]	ns	ns	ns	ns
Educational goals				
Aspirations	ns	ns	ns	ns
Expectations	ns	ns	ns	ns
Personal characteristics				
Assertiveness in the classroom	ns	ns	ns	3.39*
Acceptance of being smart	ns	ns	ns	14.00***
Academic self-concept[e]	ns	ns	ns	6.40**
Follows class rules	8.04**	ns	ns	ns
Acceptance of diversity[e]	3.80*	3.70*	ns	ns
Helpful to classmates	ns	ns	ns	ns
Perceptions of school				
Teachers as supportive of learning	ns	ns	3.70**	ns
Classmates as supportive of learning	ns	ns	ns	8.20***
School-related hassles	ns	ns	3.30*	ns

Note. N ≈ 1,191.
[a]Assessed by interaction term in two-way ANOVA.
[b]Ethnic groups: White, African American, Hispanic American, Asian American.
[c]Age: 10 versus 11 versus 12 versus 13 years old.
[d]Grade point average: High versus mid versus low, as determined by high = mostly As; mid = ½ As, ½ Bs; low = Bs or lower.
[e]Data from Cohort 2000 only ($N ≈ 612$).
*$p < .05$. **$p < .01$. ***$p < .001$.

Overall, and with only a few exceptions, Summerbridge was equally effective for boys and girls, a finding of importance because boys (compared to girls) are at greater educational risk of dropping out, and because children and teens often see educational interventions as more suitable for girls than for boys. In 2 of 15 areas, however, Summerbridge was more effective for girls. Specifically, girls showed greater improvement in being prepared for class than did boys, and girls were more likely to follow rules than were boys (who actually declined in this regard while at Summerbridge).

African American, Asian American, Hispanic American, and White students derived similar benefits from Summerbridge. This finding was gratifying because, without intervention, Hispanic Americans are more likely to drop out of high school than are other ethnic groups, and minority youth of color are, in general, at greater educational risk than are Asian American or White youth (Kaufman, Klein, & Frase, 1999).

Summerbridge also succeeded in bringing about similar gains for the four age groups we considered (10, 11, 12, and 13), although the oldest students (13-year-olds) were more likely than younger children to show increases in their perception of teachers as supportive of learning.

In one set of analyses, Summerbridge showed greater differential effectiveness as a function of students' prior characteristics. Specifically, in 4 of the 15 outcomes, Summerbridge was significantly more likely to have positive effects on students with relatively low grade point averages at entry into the program than on those who entered with average or high grade point averages. Youth with the lowest grade point averages showed larger gains in effort, academic self-concept, pride in success, and the perception of classmates as supportive of education. In some instances, youth with higher grade point averages at entry actually showed declines over the same period. The conclusion that Summerbridge is particularly effective for youths with relatively low grade point averages must, of course, be tempered by the knowledge that Summerbridge programs do not accept students with very low grade point averages, but select average- or high-achieving youth who are motivated to learn. Within this range, the somewhat weaker students seem to benefit more than the others from the enrichment and nurturing provided by the intervention program.

Do the Effects of the First Session Last During the School Year?

Because we surveyed Cohort 1999 during both their 1st and 2nd year in the program, it is possible to address the important question of whether the gains made at the first Summerbridge summer session were maintained when children returned to their regular classrooms, or whether the gains eroded over time. This issue is important because the positive effects of intervention programs are frequently not sustained after the intervention has ended. That is, intervention studies frequently report significant erosion of gains over time (Cooper, Charlton, Valentine, & Muhlenbruck, 2000). Summerbridge's primary goal, however, is to teach knowledge and skills that become part of the child's permanent repertoire and that alter the educational trajectories of students from limited-opportunity backgrounds. Summerbridge does not merely seek to effect change while students are in the highly supportive and structured setting of the summer session, but to change their long-term educational outcomes.

To address the question of erosion of effects, we examined data from Cohort 1999. This group of students had completed both the intense Summerbridge program during the summer of 1999 and the variable and less intense year-long program provided by Summerbridge during the academic year 1999 to 2000. Paired *t*-test analyses were used to examine whether students' scores in the spring of 2000 were similar to their scores 9 months earlier at the end of their summer enrichment program. To be included in these analyses, Cohort 1999 students needed complete data from the 1999 and 2000 summer assessments. The sample size for these analyses was approximately 218 (sample size varied slightly for each analysis due to missing data on specific measures). We interpreted results with a *p*-value of less than .01.

The findings indicate that, like other intervention programs, some of the gains brought about by the summer program were eroded modestly, but significantly, over the school year, as shown in Table 9.7. As students returned to their regular large classrooms in middle schools where neither teachers nor other students are particularly supportive, we found erosions in students' perception of the classroom as a benign setting. In other words, it is entirely likely that students' perceptions and academically related behaviors were responsive to their environments—and most stu-

TABLE 9.7
Erosion of Gains From First Summer

	Means		
	End of First Summerbridge	Start of Second Summerbridge	t test
Effort and involvement in school			
Effort	2.53	2.38	4.59***
Preparation	3.47	3.37	2.66**
Educational goals			
Aspirations	3.92	3.89	0.83
Expectations	3.85	3.83	0.50
Personal characteristics			
Assertiveness in the classroom	3.27	3.17	2.42*
Acceptance of being smart	2.50	2.47	0.93
Follows class rules	3.35	3.21	3.95***
Helpful to classmates	3.05	2.95	2.02*
Perceptions of school			
Teachers as supportive of learning	4.76	3.33	27.80***
Classmates as supportive of learning	3.72	2.14	24.00***
School-related hassles	0.56	0.50	4.46***
School-related uplifts			

Note. N ≈ 218.
*p < .05. **p < .01. ***p < .001.

dents returned to environments that were apparently less demanding and less nurturing of student achievement than Summerbridge had been.

Although effort and preparation for class, like other school-related behaviors, are responsive to environmental demands, it is nonetheless disconcerting that they declined when students returned to their regular schools. Effort and preparation for class are characteristics which are, to some degree, internal to the student, and the goal of Summerbridge is that students will carry over to the regular classroom the motivation, effort, and organizational skills (such as being prepared for class) that they had been taught during the summer.

Although the findings of erosion of effects over time are clear-cut, the interpretation of those findings is not. The absence of a comparison group does not permit an evaluation of competing interpretations. For example, it is entirely possible that Summerbridge had a modest beneficial effect in limiting the extent of erosion that typically occurs as children enter adolescence, with its many distractions and new opportunities for self-exploration. Previous literature has found that entry into adolescence, and the transition into the wider world of middle school (with its more extensive social scene), often serve to undermine educational objectives and motivation, especially for children of limited-opportunity backgrounds (Eccles, Wigfield, & Schiefele, 1998; Entwisle, 1990). Whether Summerbridge students experienced less erosion of motivation and effort than did their classmates who did not attend Summerbridge remains to be investigated in future years, as we collect more data from the Cohort 2000 comparison group.

Key Question Number 2: What Is the Effect of the Second Summerbridge Session?

To address the question of whether Summerbridge remains effective when students attend for a second summer, we compared students' scores at the end of their second Summerbridge session to their scores at the beginning of that session.

Paired t-test analyses, summarized in Table 9.8, reveal that Summerbridge continued to have positive educational effects in the 2nd year. Specifically, Summerbridge succeeds in reversing the erosion that occurred during the academic school year. In the face of high academic demands and Summerbridge's supportive, small-group instructional setting, students spent more time on homework, came to Summerbridge classes more prepared than at their regular middle school, and were more assertive in Summerbridge classrooms. They also perceived Summerbridge classmates and teachers as more supportive of education, and saw themselves as more helpful to classmates and as more accepting of ethnic di-

TABLE 9.8
Effects of the Second Summerbridge (SB) Summer

	Means		t test
	Before SB	After SB	
Effort and involvement in school			
Effort	2.34	2.36	0.83
Preparation	3.35	3.48	4.12***
All homework	3.15	3.45	5.05***
Math homework	1.69	1.66	−0.62
Educational goals			
Aspirations	3.92	3.92	0.16
Expectations	3.82	3.86	2.00*
Personal characteristics			
Assertiveness in the classroom	3.17	3.30	4.36***
Acceptance of being smart	2.44	2.36	−2.75**
Academic self-concept	3.26	3.19	−4.12***
Follows class rules	3.17	3.22	1.78
Acceptance of diversity	3.75	3.82	3.64***
Helpful to classmates	2.93	3.04	3.51***
Perceptions of school			
Teachers as supportive of learning	3.32	3.59	6.42***
Classmates as supportive of learning	2.13	2.50	6.83***
School-related hassles	0.56	0.51	−4.25***
School-related uplifts			

Note. $N \approx 420$.
*$p < .05$. **$p < .01$. ***$p < .001$.

versity. They also experienced fewer school-related hassles. However, both students' pride in being smart and their academic self-concept decreased during the second summer.

How Do the Effects of the Second Session Compare to the Effect of the First Session?

We investigated whether the effects from the second summer session were comparable in magnitude to the effects of the first summer session. Only those students who participated in all four assessments were included in these analyses—that is, students from Cohort 1999 who completed a "before" and "after" survey during the summer of 1999 and who also completed a "before" and "after" survey in the summer of 2000 ($N = 225$). Furthermore, we compared outcomes only for those scales that were identical across the four assessments. Paired t-tests were conducted on 10 different measures (see Table 9.9). It is important to note that, because

TABLE 9.9
Comparison of Gains of First and Second Summerbridge (SB) Sessions

| | Mean Change | | |
	First Session	Second Session	t test
Effort and involvement in school			
Effort	0.17	−0.01	4.00***
Preparation	0.10	0.15	−0.92
Educational goals			
Aspirations	0.05	0.03	0.46
Expectations	0.06	0.02	0.86
Personal characteristics			
Assertiveness in the classroom	0.19	0.16	0.43
Acceptance of being smart	0.02	−0.10	1.99*
Helpful to classmates	−0.04	0.07	−1.91
Perceptions of school			
Teachers as supportive of learning	0.15	0.27	−1.80
Classmates as supportive of learning	0.58	0.30	2.64**
School-related hassles	−0.06	−0.01	1.64

Note. N ≈ 225.
*p < .05. **p < .01. ***p < .001.

these analyses were carried out on a smaller subset of students (students who participated in four assessments), the findings differ from results presented in previous tables.

In 8 of the 10 comparisons, the change scores were similar in magnitude (only findings significant at $p < .01$ are interpreted). In two comparisons, however, one change score was larger than the other (see Table 9.9). The findings presented in Table 9.9 indicate that on two measures, students made larger gains during the first than second Summerbridge session, suggesting something of a modest 2nd-year slump. Summerbridge is still effective, but somewhat less effective than in the 1st year. Perhaps the novelty of Summerbridge has worn off, as the 2nd-year program is often a repeat of the 1st-year program. Alternately, the smaller gains of the 2nd year may result from the fact that some of the students have entered adolescence, a stage of life where educational endeavors sometimes take second place to such teen interests as flirting, focusing on appearance, being accepted by other parties, and other peer activities.

To summarize the results from the student survey assessment, Summerbridge is successful in improving some of students' education-related attitudes and behaviors. These changes tend to erode, however, once students return to their regular schools. The second Summerbridge summer appears to reinvigorate students, although the effects are somewhat weaker than the effects of the first summer.

ASSESSMENT OF ACADEMIC SKILLS

The overall goal of Summerbridge is to improve the educational trajectories of students from limited-opportunity backgrounds, including preparing students in terms of the academic skills necessary for success in educational institutions. There are two ways in which Summerbridge seeks to
achieve this goal. First, it seeks to prevent "summer slide" in basic skills,
which tends to be greater in poor and minority students than in middle-
class students (Cooper, Nye, Charlton, Lindsay, & Greathouse, 1996).
Second, a more ambitious goal is to strengthen basic skills involved in
reading, writing, and mathematics in a relatively short period of intense
instruction, so that students may benefit from educational opportunities
in their middle and high schools. This goal is ambitious because Summerbridge seeks to change skills developed over 6 or 7 years in a few short
summer sessions. In light of these goals, a pilot study was undertaken in
the summer of 2001 to assess the effectiveness of Summerbridge in improving basic academic skills of the middle school students. It is regarded
as a pilot study because only a few sites, rather than the full Collaborative,
participated in the academic assessment.

Site Selection and Sample for the Assessment
of Academic Skills

Five sites, with a total enrollment of 416 students, were selected for the academic skills assessments. The sites came from 11 programs that had vol-
unteered to take part in the assessments, which were conducted in the first
few days of the summer program and again during the last week of the
program. The sites were selected with a number of criteria in mind. First,
given that Summerbridge exists in 16 states, geographic diversity was desirable. Two of the selected sites were located in the East, two in the West,
and one in the Southwest. Second, relatively well-established sites with
considerable continuity of leadership were selected. Third, sites were selected so that the aggregate of sampled students would be diverse in
terms of ethnic background. In this regard, the sample consisted of 49%
African American students, 29% Hispanic American students, 12% White
students, and 10% classified as "Other" (a category which included Asian
American, Pacific Islander, Native American, and Middle Eastern students). All sites at Summerbridge, including the sites in this pilot study,
have multiyear summer programs. In the pilot sample, 50% of students
were attending their first Summerbridge session, 40% their second, and
10% their third session. The sample contained 59% girls and 41% boys.

The Achievement Tests

The selection of achievement tests was influenced by diverse considerations. First, because there is no common curriculum across the different Summerbridge sites, it was important to locate a test of general underlying skills and abilities, rather than achievement tests matched to a particular program of instruction. Second, because the students attending the five sites came from many different school systems, each of which administered achievement tests to its students on at least an annual basis, we sought a reputable test that was not widely used across the nation. Third, because the evaluation is interested in change over time, we looked for an assessment that would provide mastery scores (how much the student actually knew), rather than simply report percentile scores (which compares children to others at their grade). Given these criteria, we chose Achievement Level Tests in reading and mathematics from Northwest Evaluation Association (NWEA).

NWEA levels tests yield both mastery scores and percentiles. Mastery scores (called RIT scores by NWEA for the test theory from which they were derived) are given for each student for each subject matter and can range from about 180 for a typical 2nd-grade level to about 240 for the 10th-grade level. A typical year's growth for sixth graders is 5.0 points for reading and 7.0 points for mathematics; for seventh graders, the growth during a school year, on average, is 4.0 points for reading and 6.5 points for mathematics. Percentile scores are also available based on a normative sample of 500,000 students from kindergarten through 12th grade (for details about the NWEA levels tests, see Kingsbury, 1997; Kingsbury & Hauser, 2001).

After Summerbridge directors received training from NWEA on test administration, they oversaw teachers at each site who administered to their students two untimed tests in reading and mathematics (in addition to a short locator test which placed students in the appropriate level of operational test). Alternate forms of these levels tests were administered to the students during the last week of Summerbridge summer session. The reading tests assessed fundamental grade-appropriate reading skills, including the following: word meaning (context clues, synonyms–antonyms–homonyms, multiple meanings), literal comprehension (ability to recall details, sequence details, classify facts, recall main idea), and interpretive concepts (ability to draw inferences, recognize cause and effect, predict events, summarize). The mathematics test assessed age and grade-appropriate concepts, such as the following: number–numeration systems (whole numbers, fractions, decimals, percentages), operations–computation (addition, subtraction, multiplication, division, fractions, decimals, percentages), problem solving, measurement (linear, time, money, capacity, weight), and applications (applied problems from all content areas).

Academic Skills Results

The data presented here are based on students with valid scores at both testing periods. Students with invalid scores were eliminated from the analyses. Scores were considered invalid when it was determined that the test was not well-suited to the student's level of ability, despite the use of a locator test, or when the student did not take the time to complete the test, as judged by more than six omitted items.

The loss of students from the sample due to incomplete or invalid data was high: 37% for reading and 41% for mathematics. Chi-square tests were used to examine whether invalid data were randomly distributed across the different groups or were more prevalent for some socioeconomic groups rather than others. The findings indicate that invalid reading scores occurred equally often among boys and girls, among the three main ethnic groups, and among sixth, seventh, and eighth graders. Invalid data for mathematics, however, varied with grade level, with more invalid data among eighth graders than those in lower grades. The amount of invalid data for both reading and mathematics differed by site.

To assess whether Summerbridge students improved in reading and mathematics skills, we conducted a series of two-way analyses of variance (ANOVAs), some of which permitted us to consider whether changes in achievement varied by sex, ethnicity (African American vs. Hispanic American vs. White), grade (sixth vs. seventh vs. eighth grade), and year at Summerbridge (1st vs. 2nd vs. 3rd). These analyses were carried out separately for reading and for mathematics scores and for mastery scores and percentile scores. The results are summarized in Table 9.10.

As shown in Table 9.10, students did not show change in mastery scores of either reading or mathematics over the course of the 6-week summer session. Furthermore, interaction terms from the two-way ANOVAs revealed that the absence of change held equally for boys and girls, for each of the three ethnic groups, for the three grade levels, and for students who were in their 1st, 2nd, and 3rd year of the program. For reading mastery scores, there was a significant interaction term between site and time of testing. Specifically, at one site, students improved significantly, whereas at another site, students declined significantly in reading scores over the summer. At the remaining three sites, students showed no change in reading mastery scores.

To further investigate the finding of no change in mathematics and reading over the course of summer instruction at Summerbridge, we examined the subscores for each of these tests. It seemed possible that Summerbridge instruction might focus more on some areas than others, and thus effects of growth might be limited to select areas. A methodological caveat is in order before presenting the results of the analyses, however. Because subscores are necessarily based on fewer items than the to-

TABLE 9.10

Mean Scores for Pre-Summerbridge (SB) and Post-Summerbridge
Achievement Assessments (Overall and Subareas) and Results
of Evaluating Whether Summerbridge Improves Mathematics
and Reading Performance[a]

	Means (Standard Deviations)		F-test/t test
	Before SB	After SB	
Mastery scores			
Reading	217.2	216.8	1.54
	(10.8)	(11.8)	
Word recognition, fluency	216.7	217.1	<1
Vocabulary	(11.5)	(14.8)	
Comprehension	217.4	217.1	<1
	(11.8)	(12.4)	
Literary analysis	218.9	217.4	2.35*
	(13.7)	(12.8)	
Mathematics	223.1	223.1	<1
	(14.9)	(14.7)	
Number sense	222.7	225.9	−3.57***
	(17.3)	(17.4)	
Computation	223.3	226.4	−3.36**
	(14.5)	(16.2)	
Patterns, functions	227.9	226.3	1.87
	(17.1)	(15.3)	
Geometry, spatial analysis	226.4	225.7	<1
	(17.3)	(16.2)	
Measurement	225.6	223.3	2.77**
	(16.4)	(17.8)	
Data analysis, statistics	225.8	227.0	−1.45
	(18.8)	(17.7)	
Problem solving, reasoning	224.7	221.7	3.61***
	(17.2)	(16.4)	
Percentile scores			
Reading	47.7	49.9	7.88***
	(23.5)	(25.2)	
Mathematics	48.0	50.1	10.21***
	(24.9)	(25.9)	

Note. Reading $N = 270$; Mathematics $N = 251$.

[a]Analysis of reading and mathematics overall conducted by two-way analysis of variance with repeated measures, with time the within-subject measure (T1 vs. T2) and site (five locations) the between-subject measure. Analysis of subareas conducted by t tests.

*$p < .05$. **$p < .01$. ***$p < .001$.

tal scores, they have lower reliability; however, large samples offset lower reliability. Thus, we analyzed the subscores, but we limited our analyses to the combined sample. The data related to changes over the course of the summer session in subscores on the mathematics and reading tests are shown in Table 9.10.

The analysis of subscores reveals that some scores improved, some declined, and others remained the same over the summer period. The reading subscores show a decline only in literary response and analysis, whereas word recognition, fluency, vocabulary, and reading comprehension scores remain constant. More differentiated results are found for the mathematics subscores, presumably because mathematics is more responsive to teaching and requires practice to be maintained. Two mathematical skills, number sense and computation, improved as a result of Summerbridge instruction. Two subscores, measurement and problem solving and reasoning, declined over the summer. Three other mathematical skills remain unchanged. Thus, the total scores mask a pattern of improvements and declines which may be of importance. It would be interesting to see if the pattern of changes maps onto areas of instruction at Summerbridge. This material is not available at this time.

Overall, it is clear that despite an intense period of instruction, Summerbridge did not succeed in raising the overall reading and mathematics mastery scores during the course of the summer, although it did succeed in select areas. Although some students showed large overall gains, an equal number showed large losses. None of the demographic characteristics that we explored were related to the pattern of gains and losses.

The percentile scores have the potential to address the issue of "summer slide." Similar mastery scores obtained at the beginning and end of summer will yield somewhat different percentile scores because the fall (or end of summer) norms reflect that students tend to forget material during extensive breaks from school. The data of Table 9.10 shows that although there were no gains in mastery scores over the summer, there were increases in the percentile scores in both reading and mathematics. In other words, the instruction of the Summerbridge program seemed to prevent summer slide.

CONCLUSION

Our analyses suggest that Summerbridge is successful in meeting some of its short-term objectives and unsuccessful at meeting others. The intensive, well-structured educational program, organized around small-group instruction by older high school and college students, and interlaced with many engaging activities, does improve some education-related attitudes and behaviors of youth from limited-opportunity backgrounds. These changes, however, are not immune from erosion when the intense summer program ends, although a second "dose" of Summerbridge once again brings the desired effects.

The 6-week summer session does not lead to substantial growth in reading or mathematics performance as measured by standardized achievement tests, although students did experience small gains in two mathematics subareas. Summerbridge does, however, help students avoid the "summer slide" phenomenon. Nevertheless, the results of the assessment of academic skills are both surprising and disappointing for Summerbridge, although perhaps not surprising for analysts of other intervention programs. Given the dedication, hard work, and enormous amount of time and effort invested in teaching and enrichment, Summerbridge would have liked to see more consistent and stronger improvements, especially in the mastery scores. The evaluation is being used as a diagnostic tool to improve programs, however, and especially to help sites articulate clear goals in the teaching of academic skills to limited-opportunity youth. In response to the disappointing achievement results, Summerbridge National is committed to exploring ways to provide increased teacher training for both the professional mentor teachers and the high school- and college-age teachers. Furthermore, Summerbridge National is working to identify specific skills to be taught and materials to be used in mathematics and reading instruction. The evaluation of Summerbridge will continue to monitor the educational trajectories of the students served by the program.

ACKNOWLEDGMENTS

The authors wish to acknowledge the valuable support they have received from the Summerbridge site directors, teachers, National staff, Board of Trustees, and, in particular, the Summerbridge Executive Director, Jan Berman. Summerbridge has consistently demonstrated its commitment to this independent evaluation by dedicating time and other resources for the study. Without their sustained cooperation, and without the leadership of Ms. Berman, the evaluation would not be possible.

REFERENCES

Arroyo, C., & Zigler, F. (1995). Racial identity, academic achievement, and the psychological well-being of economically disadvantaged adolescents. *Journal of Personality and Social Psychology, 69,* 903–914.

Baker, T., & Velez, W. (1996). Access to opportunity in postsecondary education in the United States: A review. *Sociology of Education, 69,* 82–101.

Bankston, C., & Cladas, S. (1997). The American school dilemma: Race and scholastic performance. *Sociological Quarterly, 38,* 423–429.

Berkner, L., & Chavez, L. (1997). *Access to postsecondary education for the 1992 high school graduates.* Washington, DC: U.S. Department of Education, National Center for Education Statistics.

Cooper, H., Charlton, K., Valentine, J. C., & Muhlenbruck, L. (2000). Making the most of summer school. A meta-analytic and narrative review. *Monographs of the Society for Research in Child Development, 65*(1, Serial No. 260).

Cooper, H., Nye, B., Charlton, K., Lindsay, J., & Greathouse, S. (1996). The effects of summer vacation on achievement test scores: A narrative and meta-analytic review. *Review of Educational Research, 66,* 227–268.

Dornbusch, S., Ritter, P., Mont–Reynaud, R., & Chen, Z. (1990). Family decision making and academic performance in a diverse high school population. *Journal of Adolescent Research, 5,* 143–160.

Eccles, J., Wigfield, F., & Schiefele, O. (1998). Motivation to succeed. In N. Eisenberg (Ed.), *Handbook of child psychology* (Vol. 3, pp. 1017–1095). New York: Wiley.

Entwisle, D. (1990). Schools and the adolescent. In S. S. Feldman & G. R. Elliott (Eds.), *At the threshold: The developing adolescent* (pp. 197–224). Cambridge, MA: Harvard University Press.

Feldman, S., & Laird, J. (1999). *Evaluation of Summerbridge summer program: Findings from the first year.* San Francisco: Summerbridge National.

Gamoran, A. (1987). The stratification of high school learning opportunities. *Sociology of Education, 60,* 135–155.

Glasgow, K., Dornbusch, S., Troyer, L., Steinberg, L., & Ritter, P. (1997). Parenting styles, adolescents' attributions, and educational outcomes in nine heterogeneous high schools. *Child Development, 68,* 507–529.

Johnson, D. W., Johnson, R. T., Buckman, L. A., & Richards, P. S. (1985). The effects of prolonged implementation of cooperative learning on social support within the classroom. *The Journal of Psychology, 199,* 405–411.

Kanner, A. D., & Feldman, S. S. (1987). Uplifts, hassles and adaptational outcomes in early adolescence. *Journal of Early Adolescence, 7,* 371–394.

Kaufman, P., Klein, S., & Frase, M. (1999). *Dropout rates in the United States, 1977.* Washington, DC: U.S. Department of Education, National Center for Education Statistics.

Kingsbury, G. (1997). *Achievement level tests: Technical manual.* Portland, OR: Northwest Evaluation Association.

Kingsbury, G., & Hauser, C. (2001). *Student growth on levels tests and MAP.* Portland, OR: Northwest Evaluation Association.

Levy, F., & Michel, R. (1991). *The economic future of American families: Income and wealth trends.* Washington, DC: Urban Institute Press.

Mishel, L., & Bernstein, J. (1994). *The state of working America.* New York: Economic Policy Institute.

Nicholls, J. (1984). Achievement motivation: Conceptions of ability, subjective experience, task choice, and performance. *Psychological Review, 91,* 28–346.

Topel, R. (1993). What have we learned from empirical studies of unemployment and turnover? *American Economic Review, 83,* 10–115.

U.S. Bureau of the Census. (1996). *How we're changing: Demographic state of the nation.* Washington, DC: U.S. Department of Commerce, Economics and Statistics Administration.

U.S. Department of Education. (2000). *Digest of educational statistics* (GPO Publication No. 065–000–01323–1). Washington, DC: U.S. Government Printing Office.

Wentzel, K. R. (1993). Social and academic goals at school: Motivation and achievement in early adolescence. *Journal of Early Adolescence, 13,* 4–20.

Wilson, J. (1991). Studying inner-city social dislocations: The challenge of public agenda research. *American Sociological Review, 56,* 1–14.

IV

COMBATING SUMMER LEARNING LOSS HEAD ON: PROGRAMS AND PRACTICES

How can families, school calendars, and summer school programs be designed to address the summer learning loss phenomenon head on? This is the issue we turn to in Part IV. In chapter 10, Geoffrey Borman and his colleagues discuss early results from their ongoing 3-year, longitudinal study, which investigates the long-term impact of multiple summer interventions on the academic achievement of low-income students. Kindergarten students who applied to Teach Baltimore, a largely volunteer-based program, were randomly assigned to summer school or a control group. Rather than intervening after children fall behind, this program focuses on fostering summer learning early (beginning in kindergarten) and often (providing services over three consecutive summers). This approach attacks directly the problem suggested by Entwisle, Alexander, and Olson's (2001) "faucet theory." Rather than turning on and off the schooling faucet with each beginning and end of the 9-month academic year, this study asks the following: What would happen if we kept the faucet running during each summer of students' first 3 years of school? The authors provide a detailed description of the Teach Baltimore program components and discuss the results and implications from the study's first 2 years.

Although researchers have accumulated evidence documenting and describing the summer loss phenomena, very little is known about how the characteristics of students and their families, teachers, and their regular school-year classrooms affect summer and school-year learning outcomes. How, for example, might different instructional approaches during the school year affect summer learning? Is summer loss lessened if teachers teach reading with a phonics or a whole language approach? With respect to math, does the use of manipulatives during the school year increase retention of math skills and concepts during the summer? Using data from the national Prospects study, Meredith Phillips and Tiffani Chin answer these questions in chapter 11 by combining survey data and achievement test scores. From the results, the authors draw summative conclusions and offer recommendations for policy and practice.

A recent report by the National Education Commission on Time and Learning declared that schools' time schedules have several important design flaws. Among those flaws is a design that offers 9 months of formal instruction with 3 months of vacation. Although the purpose of the traditional calendar was very clear 100 years ago, that purpose is now all but obsolete for today's students. In chapter 12, Charles Ballinger critiques the traditional school calendar and outlines how a year-round school calendar might be designed to combat the problem of summer learning loss. Ballinger agrees that the long summer vacation has both educational and social drawbacks, but suggests that we should think beyond summer school for intervention, remediation, and enrichment. More specifically, he outlines how a year-round school calendar might be designed to combat the problem of summer learning loss and to allow for periodic pauses for intervention and enrichment, leading to more efficient and sustained educational improvements.

REFERENCES

Entwisle, D. R., Alexander, K. L., & Olson, S. (2001). Keep the faucet flowing: Summer learning and home environment. *American Educator, 47*, 10–15.

10

Can a Multiyear Summer Program Prevent the Accumulation of Summer Learning Losses?

Geoffrey D. Borman
University of Wisconsin–Madison

Laura T. Overman
Johns Hopkins University

Ron Fairchild, Matthew Boulay, Jody Kaplan
Teach Baltimore

Researchers have established that the summer achievement slide has a particularly harmful impact on poor children's reading achievement (Entwisle, Alexander, & Olson, 1997; Cooper, Nye, Charlton, Lindsay, & Greathouse, 1996; Heyns, 1978). Although middle-class children's test scores essentially plateau during the summer months, poor children's reading scores tend to show marked declines. Evidence from the meta-analysis by Cooper et al. (1996) suggests that during the summer, the reading skill levels of poor children fall about 3 months behind those of their middle-class peers. This represents a difference that is equal to a third of the typical amount of learning that takes place over the course of the regular school year.

Although the specific reasons behind this summer learning difference remain somewhat unclear, the "faucet theory" of Entwisle, Alexander, and Olson (2001) helps explain the general phenomenon. That is, when school is in session, the resource faucet is turned on for all children, and all gain equally. When school is not in session, however, the school resource faucet is turned off. Middle-class families can make up for the school's resources to a considerable extent, but poor families are unlikely to have that ability.

These socioeconomic-based learning differences are disconcerting. But perhaps even more distressing is that summer learning losses by poor children may accumulate over the elementary school years (Alexander, Entwisle, & Olson, 1997; Alexander, Entwisle, & Olson, 2001; Phillips, Crouse, & Ralph, 1998). According to Entwisle's and Alexander's (Entwisle, Alexander, & Olson, 2001) long-term Beginning School Study of Baltimore children, if one were simply to add the gap that existed at the beginning of elementary school to the gaps that are created when school is not in session during the summer, that would account for virtually the entire achievement gap between middle-class and disadvantaged students at the end of elementary school.

The primary question of this ongoing, 3-year, longitudinal evaluation is as follows: Can a community-based, multiyear, summer school intervention, which uses collegiate volunteers as instructors, counteract the cumulative effect of the summer slide on low-income students' reading outcomes? The Teach Baltimore Summer Academy's design and evaluation represent practical responses to Karl Alexander's and Doris Entwisle's (Entwisle et al., 2001) findings from their Baltimore-based study of seasonal learning. That is, if we turn on the resource faucet through the consistent delivery of a multiyear summer school program, beginning after the kindergarten year, can the accumulation of summer learning losses be prevented?

BACKGROUND

Summer school programs clearly are growing in popularity across the United States—perhaps doubling in prevalence over the past quarter century (Borman, 2001). The vast majority of these programs, however, are reactionary and intermittent efforts, which provide students extra help only after they have fallen behind. The volunteer-based Teach Baltimore Summer Academy is a proactive and preventative intervention that begins early, before students have had the opportunity to fall so far behind as to be threatened with retention. Rather than being reactionary, Teach Baltimore offers disadvantaged students continuing opportunities, summer after summer, to avoid the characteristic summer slide and to catch up with their more advantaged peers.

As Cooper et al. (1996), Heyns (1978), Worsnop (1996), and others have argued, summer losses may be mitigated by continuing schooling opportunities over the summer months. Evidence of the effectiveness of summer programs, however, has typically been of poor quality. For instance, although Austin, Rogers, and Walbesser (1972) concluded that summer compensatory programs in elementary math and reading have generally promoted modest achievement gains, the authors noted that, because none of the evaluations employed random assignment, maturation remained a threat to validity. In addition, Austin et al. (1972) asserted that few summer programs established clear goals that were easily evaluated, and many projects claimed funding arrived too late to allow for proper evaluation. More optimistically, through their meta-analytic work, Cooper and his colleagues identified 93 studies of summer school that were amenable to quantitative synthesis, and indicated that the average effect size for remedial summer programs was nearly one fifth of one standard deviation (Cooper, Charlton, Valentine, & Muhlenbruck, 2000). Nevertheless, few studies reviewed by Cooper and colleagues employed rigorous experimental or quasi-experimental designs.

Beyond research on summer learning loss and the effectiveness of summer programs, the potential impact of volunteer programs is also of considerable policy relevance. With the America Reads Initiative, the federal government has focused national attention on making volunteerism an essential and explicit part of a nationwide literacy campaign to help students read well and independently by the end of third grade. Funding through the Federal Work Study program and America Reads helps to ensure that college students will continue to play a central role in this literacy effort. Although the enthusiasm and impetus to involve volunteers in the literacy effort exists, there are surprisingly few empirical findings that link volunteerism with the hoped-for increases in student achievement (Wasik, 1997).

Thus, although past research linking student achievement to summer programs and volunteerism is less than optimistic, the studies suffer from methodological shortcomings, and the programs themselves have had significant limitations. Using a well-developed volunteer-based summer instructional program and a rigorous experimental design, we hope to respond to both of these problems.

THE INTERVENTION: WHAT IS TEACH BALTIMORE?

Founded in 1992, the mission of Teach Baltimore is to create high-quality summer learning opportunities for all students in Baltimore City. Based at Johns Hopkins University, the Teach Baltimore program is designed to reduce summer learning loss and to improve teacher recruitment and retention in Baltimore City. To date, Teach Baltimore has provided summer instruction to over 2,100 Baltimore City public school students and has recruited and trained 287 college students from 45 institutions of higher education and a wide variety of majors. These instructors have contributed more than 54,000 hours of service to area youth. In the past 2 years,

21 Teach Baltimore alumni have accepted full-time teaching positions in Baltimore City public schools through an innovative partnership with the Johns Hopkins University Graduate Division of Education, the U.S. Department of Education, and the Baltimore City Public School System.

The Teach Baltimore Summer Academy program begins with 3 weeks of preservice training, in which the volunteer instructors receive training in reading curricula, lesson planning, and classroom management. Two days after training ends, the 7-week summer program begins. The Teach Baltimore day begins with a breakfast for all students. After breakfast, instructors provide 3 hours of intensive reading and writing instruction. In addition to using phonics-based instructional materials, Teach Baltimore instructors help students develop vocabulary and reading comprehension skills through engaging read-aloud activities. At the conclusion of the morning session, staff members serve lunch to all program participants. After lunch, students participate in physical activities, hands-on math and science projects, educational games, arts and crafts, and enrichment activities. The following represents the typical daily schedule at a Teach Baltimore site:

8:30–9:00 AM	Breakfast.
9:00–9:15 AM	Circle Time—Discussions about weekly goals and themes.
9:15–10:00 AM	Read-Aloud and Think-Aloud activities using the *KidzLit* program.
10:00–11:30 AM	Open court phonics-based instruction.
11:30–12:00 PM	Lunch.
12:00–12:20 PM	Physical activities.
12:25–12:45 PM	"Drop Everything and Read."
12:45–1:10 PM	Writing activities–Literature circle.
1:15–1:45 PM	Hands-on math activities.
1:45–2:30 PM	Enrichment activities (i.e., science investigations, arts and crafts, foreign language, music, and drama) organized by weekly themes.

Students also learn new skills and knowledge through weekly field trips to museums and participation in cultural events offered throughout the Baltimore community. Instructors integrate these outings with classroom activities and help students extend their experiences beyond their classrooms and neighborhoods. Although the locations vary by year, trips to places such as Port Discovery Children's Museum, the Museum of Natural History, the Smithsonian Environmental Research Center, and recreational activities, including bowling and swimming, help provide a good balance of experiential learning and fun. In addition to these field trips, students participate in a daily activity block that rotates music and drama, foreign language, physical education, and arts and crafts. There are also initiatives to capitalize on the diversity of the Teach Baltimore instructors' talents and experiences. For example, instructors have taught Spanish, Swahili, costume design, and dance during the activity period.

Teach Baltimore has three main goals: (a) to prevent summer learning loss, thereby promoting the academic achievement of children from poverty, with a particular emphasis on reading and writing; (b) to transform collegiate volunteerism into a focused and effective commitment; and (c) to create a successful prototype that can be easily and cost-effectively replicated.

PREVENTING SUMMER LEARNING LOSS AMONG LOW-INCOME STUDENTS

Research on summer learning loss and the potential for high-quality summer programs to help close the achievement gap provides an important foundation for Teach Baltimore's Summer Academy program. Given the summer effect's disproportionate impact on low-income children, Baltimore City public school students are at a considerable disadvantage. Using free and reduced-price lunch qualification as an indicator of low socioeconomic status, 86% of the students at Teach Baltimore sites were eligible during the 1999 to 2000 school year, compared with 75% of the students in Baltimore City and only 35% of students across Maryland. Baltimore students, like students from many other urban centers, also perform at considerably lower academic levels. For instance, only 15% of third-grade students at Teach Baltimore sites performed satisfactorily on the 1999 to 2000 reading section of the Maryland School Performance Assessment Program, compared to 19% in Baltimore City and 39% statewide.

TRANSFORMING COLLEGIATE VOLUNTEERISM

With the 1997 Presidents' Summit for America's Future, the America Reads Initiative, Federal Work Study program expansion, and ongoing funding for AmeriCorps national service programs, there has been tremendous impetus to increase the involvement of college students in the movement to promote literacy among America's children. Capitalizing on this movement, the Teach Baltimore program recruits, trains, and supports the development of collegiate volunteers. Teach Baltimore instructors need not be education majors, but must be positive, motivated individuals who are willing to look for and expect the best from their students. All instructors are provided a $1,400 living allowance for the summer. Instructors between the ages of 17 and 25, who teach for two consecutive summers, also receive an education award of $2,300 through a Teach Baltimore partnership with Civic Works, a Baltimore-based AmeriCorps program of national service. This award can be used to repay student loans or to pay for tuition.

Because there are generally two times as many applicants as there are positions available, the selection process is competitive. It consists of a written application with essay questions, a written recommendation from an employer or professor, and an interview with Teach Baltimore staff. Successful applicants must be committed to children and to education as a means of providing opportunity and overcoming poverty. Importantly, Teach Baltimore staff members look for candidates who are willing to work hard to challenge themselves and their students. First-time teaching experiences are difficult; therefore, instructors must be able to overcome initial frustrations and remain committed to their students.

Being a Teach Baltimore instructor is time consuming and requires a great deal of work. Instructors are expected to do the following to be most effective and to provide the best possible experience for themselves and their students: (a) actively participate in the 3-week preservice training program, as well as ongoing weekly meetings and support workshops; (b) prepare and implement daily lesson plans in reading and writing, as well as an afternoon enrichment activity; (c) work closely with Baltimore City mentor teachers and their Teach Baltimore partner teachers; (d) provide ongoing communication with parents; (e) document student progress by maintaining work folders and completing weekly progress reports; and (f) maintain ongoing contact with students throughout the school year.

For the college-student-as-novice-teacher, the Teach Baltimore summer experience provides real-world classroom experience in a controlled and focused environment. The program's two distinguishing characteristics are (a) a manageable class size (maximum eight students per Teach Baltimore teacher), and (b) extensive support and mentoring from experienced teachers in the Baltimore City Public School System (BCPSS). During a time in which school systems across the country are experiencing, or are expecting, teacher shortages, the Teach Baltimore model provides a means for inducting and preparing nontraditional teachers for work in the public schools.

CREATING A SUCCESSFUL PROTOTYPE THAT CAN BE EASILY AND COST-EFFECTIVELY REPLICATED

In their meta-analysis of summer program effects, Cooper et al. (2000) noted several program components that are related to improved achievement effects for summer program attendees. All of these activities are strong components of the Teach Baltimore prototype, and include the following:

- Small-group or individualized instruction.
- Early intervention during the primary grades.
- Parent involvement and participation.
- Careful scrutiny for treatment fidelity, including monitoring to ensure that instruction is being delivered as prescribed and monitoring student attendance.

In addition, other reviews of summer programs by Ascher (1988) and Austin et al. (1972) suggested that failed summer programs may share several of the following characteristics:

- Short program duration.
- Loose organization and little time for advanced planning.
- Low academic expectations.
- Discontinuity between the summer curriculum and the regular school-year curriculum.
- Teacher fatigue.
- Limited academic focus.

The program is designed to address each of these respective concerns. First, Teach Baltimore provides considerable instructional time, as well as sufficient vacation time, in that it implements a full-day (8:30–2:30), 7-week program that runs from the week after school dismisses for the summer through mid-August. Second, because Teach Baltimore staff members are focused solely on the summer program, time and resources for planning the Summer Academy program are utilized throughout the year. Third, an important criterion in selecting volunteer instructors is that they have high expectations for student learning. Fourth, the selected curricula provide instruction in areas that are parallel, or complementary to, school-year curricula. Fifth, Teach Baltimore recruits and trains college students to serve as summer instructors. Having been students rather than teachers all year, these instructors are obviously not prone to burn-out. Finally, student achievement is the primary program focus and with 2½ hours of reading and writing per morning, Teach Baltimore provides more instructional time than do many regular school-year classrooms.

In addition to the potential strengths of its design, the program is easily and cost-effectively replicated. Estimates, excluding in-kind support, evaluation costs, and the "true" Master's Program costs, indicate that the average cost per student for Teach Baltimore was approximately $815.

Teach Baltimore receives approximately $700 per student in in-kind donations of space, books, free lunch, AmeriCorps education grants, BCPSS supervisors and mentors (paid by the school system), and Federal Work Study funding. Relying in large part on college students who are paid a small stipend, and federal and local in-kind support, the program is inexpensive for communities to operate. In addition, the replicability of the program was demonstrated during the summer of 1999 by initiating services at four new sites serving eight new schools. The overall concept of the Teach Baltimore program also may be replicated in other districts. Urban school districts and local universities may form mutually beneficial relations, which provide training opportunities for prospective and nontraditional teachers and summer instruction for urban students.

RESEARCH QUESTIONS

The analyses in this chapter focus on the procedures used to retain the 1999 and 2000 treatment students in the Teach Baltimore program. Along with a description of the procedures, we provide 2- and 3-year retention data. Because the primary goal of Teach Baltimore is to prevent children from falling farther and farther behind due to the cumulative effect of the summer slide, the primary substantive questions involve the longitudinal treatment effects. This report tracks the treatment effects across each testing time point: from 1999 through 2001 for the 1999 kindergarten cohort, and from 2000 through 2001 for the more recent 2000 cohort of kindergarten students.[1]

METHOD

The 3rd year of the evaluation began during the spring of 2001, when we engaged in various efforts to retain the 1999 and 2000 cohorts of Teach Baltimore students in the multiyear program. At the same time, in preparation for the spring 2001 testing of control and treatment students, we compiled updated student rosters for each of the 10 participating schools and identified the schools to which transfer students had moved. After concluding these activities, the Comprehensive Test of Basic Skills, 4th

---

[1]The study also involves one cohort of students who began the Teach Baltimore program after the first grade during the summer of 1999. Analyses of the multiyear outcomes for these students are currently in process. In comparison to the kindergarten cohorts, the treatment effects for these students are more difficult to conceptualize and to measure, in that these students were more frequent participants in the mandatory summer school program offered by the Baltimore City Public School System.

Edition (CTBS/4), was administered to all treatment and control students from both cohorts.

Soon afterward, the Teach Baltimore program was offered to 1999 and 2000 cohort students from June 21, 2001, to August 9, 2001. After the program, we used existing BCPSS databases to access student background data and other information. In late August, before the first week of the regular school year, the evaluation team obtained updated student rosters from all participating schools. Using information obtained from the schools and from the original application forms, the evaluation team identified transfer students and attempted to locate them at their new schools. Subsequently, all students (both those who transferred and those who remained in their original schools) took the CTBS/4 reading test at their current schools.

Previous publications have investigated the internal and external validity of the experiment. These analyses, which were documented by Borman, Rachuba, Hewes, Boulay, & Kaplan (2001), concluded that randomization was successful and found no serious threats to the study's internal validity. Regarding external validity, we found that applicants consistently had higher regular school-year attendance rates than did nonapplicants, which may suggest that students and parents who applied for the summer program were more motivated, or otherwise more able, to take advantage of schooling opportunities than were nonapplicants. These outcomes clearly established that the study was without any major technical or methodological flaws, and that we had established a good foundation from which to estimate treatment effects.

Sample

The total sample includes 475 students from 10 high-poverty, urban schools. This sample is composed of two year-specific kindergarten cohorts: a group of 217 students who joined the study during the spring of 1999, and 258 children who joined the study in spring 2000. The number of applicants and the number of available spaces in the program varied by site and by year. Therefore, selection probabilities were unequal across sites and across years. The number of applicants, the selection probabilities for treatment, and the resulting treatment and control sample sizes for 1999 and 2000 are summarized in Table 10.1. To adjust for the unequal selection probabilities across sites and across years, we computed analytical weights for each treatment case that were equal to the inverse of the selection probability at the site and, when applicable, grade. Control cases were weighted by the inverse of 1 minus the selection probability.

The baseline demographic and background data for the 1999 and 2000 cohorts and for both treatment and control samples are shown in Table

TABLE 10.1
Summary of Sampling Frame for 1999 and 2000
Kindergarten Summer Academy Applicants

Site and School	1999 Kindergarten Cohort			2000 Kindergarten Cohort		
	Applied	Selected for Treatment	Selection Probability	Applied	Selected for Treatment	Selection Probability
Site No. 1	37	29	.79	63	35	.55
Dallas Nicholas	19	15		30	17	
Guilford	18	14		33	18	
Site No. 2	79	51	.65	98	59	.60
Johnston Square	26	17		19	11	
Bernard Harris	23	15		36	22	
Madison Square	30	19		43	26	
Site No. 3	29	18	.63	58	31	.53
Steuart Hill	17	11		24	13	
Franklin Square	12	7		34	18	
Site No. 4	29	17	.59	39	20	.51
Barclay						
Site No. 5	43	30	.70			
Kelson	30	21				
Pinderhughes	13	9				
Total	217	145	.68	258	145	.56

10.2. The students from both cohorts came from high-poverty schools and were predominantly minority and economically disadvantaged. The samples were greater than 90% African American, and over 80% of control and treatment students were eligible for the federal free or reduced-price lunch program. All students had relatively high attendance rates during the regular school year, and the parents of treatment and control students typically had completed just over 12 years of formal schooling.

For each cohort, data completion rates decreased somewhat over time. A key contributor to this phenomenon was the increasing number of mobile students at each testing point and the increasing difficulty in locating students who had transferred. In spite of these obstacles, we were still able to test 75% or more of both cohorts for the fall 2001 testing, which was the sixth test point for the 1999 cohort and the fourth test point for the 2000 cohort. In addition, our year-to-year data completion rates have consistently remained between approximately 75% and 95%. During most years, data completion rates have exceeded 80%.

Measures

During the spring, the evaluation team administered Level 10, Form B of the CTBS/4 reading test to all treatment and control students at one of the 10 schools listed in Table 10.1, or at the new school to which they had transferred. The 1999 kindergarten students, most of whom were in third grade, received the CTBS/4 Level 13, Form B, and the 2000 kindergarten students, who were typically in second grade, received the CTBS/4 Level 12, Form B. The evaluation staff readministered the same test level to each cohort during the fall. During this testing, we administered the alternate form, Form A, so as to minimize potential spurious gains due to relatively closely spaced pretests and posttests.

These tests represented the third and fourth tests administered to the 2000 cohort. For the 1999 cohort, the spring and fall tests were, respectively, the fifth and sixth tests that they had been administered. Over the course of the full 3 years of evaluation, treatment and control children will take norm-referenced reading achievement tests seven times: at the beginning and end of each of the three summers, and at the end of fourth grade. These testing periods capture both school-year and summer learning.

The CTBS/4, published by CTB Macmillan/McGraw–Hill, is a widely used and highly regarded achievement test. The items for the CTBS/4 reflect the educational objectives that are commonly found in state and district curriculum guides and in major textbooks, basal series, and instructional programs. Prior analyses of national norming sample data indicate high item and scale reliabilities, absence of ceiling and floor effects, absence of obvious cultural biases, and a low error of measurement. The

TABLE 10.2
Background Data for 1999 and 2000 Kindergarten Cohort Students

| | Race | | | | Gender | | | School-Year Attendance Rate | | Free-Lunch Eligibility | | Parent's Years of Education | |
	n	African American	White	Other	N	Male	Female	n	M (SD)	n	Percentage	n	M (SD)
1999 Cohort													
Treatment	144	96.5	3.5	0.0	145	51.7	48.3	144	0.94 (0.06)	145	82.8	141	12.66 (1.48)
Control	70	100	0.0	0.0	72	52.8	47.2	70	0.94 (0.06)	72	86.1	67	12.83 (1.62)
2000 Cohort													
Treatment	145	94.5	3.4	2.1	145	51.7	48.3	145	0.94 (0.06)	145	84.1	142	12.55 (1.94)
Control	112	93.8	3.6	2.7	112	45.5	54.5	112	0.94 (0.06)	111	91.0	110	12.23 (1.85)

CTBS/4 is vertically equated, and it provides vertical scale scores that are appropriate for analysis of longitudinal achievement growth. In this analysis, we analyzed scale-score outcomes for the Total Reading test. In analyses of final outcome data, however, we analyze the two subtests that make up the Total Reading score: (a) Reading Vocabulary, and (b) Reading Comprehension.

In addition to test scores, we collected demographic data on the students based on information abstracted from the Baltimore City Schools' Pupil Information File (PIF). Data abstracted from the district-compiled PIF include the following: gender, race and ethnicity, free-lunch eligibility status, and 1999 to 2000 school-year attendance rate. Also, we obtained from the Teach Baltimore application forms treatment and control parents' reports of their years of schooling.

Analytical Methods

First, we outline the steps involved in retaining treatment students in the Teach Baltimore program and examine data to determine how successful those efforts have been. Second, we perform comparisons between treatment and control students' longitudinal posttest outcomes. These estimates of the program effect are derived from simple "intention-to-treat" analyses. Regardless of the treatment students' actual Teach Baltimore participation status, this analysis compared all students assigned to the treatment condition to all those assigned to the control condition.

All analyses were conducted using the developed analytical weights. The original sample weights were adjusted to take into account attrition from the sample. We performed a logistic regression analysis to predict the probability of students' response or nonresponse to each achievement test, and we used those predicted probabilities to adjust the baseline weights for the intention-to-treat analyses reported here. Also, applying White's (1980) method, we used robust covariance matrices and standard errors for all model estimates and statistical tests of significance. Typical statistical methods assume that observations are obtained from a simple or probability sample, but due to our initial sampling and randomization of students from within the five site-level clusters, White's method was appropriate.

RESULTS

A key to the success of the 3-year summer school initiative is, of course, effective multiyear retention of the students in the program. In conjunction with the intensive student tracking necessary for pretesting and posttesting, staff from the Teach Baltimore program and from the evaluation team worked together to develop a comprehensive retention plan. The following steps were taken to ensure maximum retention of treatment students in the program:

- During the spring of 2001, evaluation assistants contacted the schools to identify the names and new schools of all students who had transferred. This was essential for both testing and future retention.
- We contacted transfer schools to determine if transfer students had remained in their last reported school. If a student had transferred again, we contacted his or her new school to confirm the student's attendance. This also was essential for both testing and future retention.
- During March and April of 2001, coordinators were hired at each school to assist with the spring and fall testing and to aid in the retention of returning Summer Academy students. Coordinators assisted with the logistics of student testing and assured that students and parents were notified of the return of the upcoming Summer Academy.
- In the spring of 2001, we distributed "welcome back" notices to parents through their children's homeroom teacher to remind them that they were guaranteed a space in the Summer Academy and to encourage them to RSVP. We mailed letters for the parents of transfer students directly to the parents' homes.
- During April and May of 2001, evaluation assistants recorded which parents had confirmed their child's return and made phone calls to all other parents who had not yet responded.
- During late May and early June, as we located and tested transfer students at their new schools, the test proctors brought Summer Academy reminder letters along to the testing for the children to take home.
- During their June 2001 training session, the Teach Baltimore college student instructors prepared handwritten postcards to all Summer Academy students, introducing themselves, providing program dates, and encouraging attendance.
- Program assistants contacted parents of transfer students who had raised concerns about transportation to the Summer Academy sites. Teach Baltimore staff arranged two shuttle vans to transport approximately 10 transfer students to the program sites.
- Summer coordinators and instructors continued to call Summer Academy no-shows for several weeks into the program. If a student was a no-show, we made every attempt to document reasons behind his or her absence so that the program staff might address these issues in ensuing years.

Program retention rates were also affected by the BCPSS's decision in March 2000 to institute mandatory summer school for all second- and fourth-grade students who scored below a cutoff level on the district test. For the summer of 2001, mandatory summer school was extended to first- and third-grade students as well. The two kindergarten cohorts included in this analysis were, therefore, primarily affected by only the most recent summer 2001 BCPSS program. During the summer of 2001, the 1999 kindergarten students had completed second grade and the 2000 kindergarten cohort had completed first grade.

At the end of the 1999 to 2000 and 2000 to 2001 school years, BCPSS sent out a memo and list of all affected children to principals at each of the 10 main schools served by the Teach Baltimore Summer Academy. The memo stated that Teach Baltimore was recognized by BCPSS as an acceptable alternative, and informed principals that they should allow parents to choose between the city program and the Teach Baltimore Summer Academy. Thanks to repeated calls by instructors and a letter home to parents, many students stayed with the program, but there were inevitable losses of some students. At site number 5, in particular, the principal placed many Teach Baltimore students in the BCPSS program.

Teach Baltimore Summer Academy Attendance Rates

Table 10.3 presents the number and percentage of treatment students who attended the Teach Baltimore Summer Academy during each of the summers the program was offered and also indicates the total number of summers (one, two, or all three) that students attended. For both cohorts, the percentage of students who attended was largest during the first summer the program was offered. For the summer of 1999, 80% of the kindergarten students attended Teach Baltimore. The percentage of students who at-

TABLE 10.3
Number and Percentage of Treatment Students Who
Attended the Teach Baltimore Summer Academy

	1999 Kindergarten Cohort (n = 145)		2000 Kindergarten Cohort (n = 145)	
	n	Percentage	n	Percentage
Attended Summer 1999	116	80.0		
Attended Summer 2000	107	73.8	124	85.5
Attended Summer 2001	67	46.2	90	62.1
Attended one summer only	23	15.9	56	38.6
Attended two summers only	51	35.2	79	54.5
Attended all three summers	55	37.9		

tended during the summer of 2000 dropped to 74%, and for the third summer of the program (2001), 46% of the 1999 kindergarteners attended the program. Of the 1999 cohort students, 16% attended one summer only, 35% attended two summers only, and 38% attended all three summers. For the 2000 cohort, 86% of treatment students attended during the first summer the program was offered to them (2000), and 62% attended during the summer of 2001.

Analyses of Longitudinal Intention-to-Treat Effects for the 2000 and 1999 Cohorts

Table 10.4 summarizes the achievement outcomes for the 2000 cohort across four time points: spring 2000, fall 2000, spring 2001, and fall 2001. The Teach Baltimore treatment effects displayed in the table are adjusted for the following covariates: gender, race or ethnicity (i.e., African American or not), free lunch participation, school transfer status, participation in the BCPSS mandatory summer school program, average 2-year regular school year attendance rate, the Teach Baltimore site at which the child was randomized, and the spring 2000 pretest. As stated previously, all results are weighted.

Focusing on the 2000 cohort, the spring 2000 results did not show a 1-year program effect, $d = -0.03$. Instead, program students and control students experienced an achievement loss. In other words, the program did not counteract the summer slide effect. Although both groups showed achievement growth during the ensuing school year, the spring 2001 cohort continued to show no program effect, $d = -0.05$. After the second summer of intervention during 2001, the treatment effect had improved, $d = 0.02$, but remained very slight. This pattern of effects supports our theory of the cumulative effects of a multiyear summer intervention, but the overall effects of summer school must further increase to be of statistical and practical significance.

Table 10.4 also summarizes the achievement outcomes for the 1999 cohort across six time points: spring 1999, fall 1999, spring 2000, fall 2000, spring 2001, and fall 2001. The program effects displayed in the table are adjusted for the following covariates: gender, race or ethnicity (i.e., African American or not), free lunch participation, school transfer status, the 3-year regular school year attendance rate, the original Teach Baltimore site at which the student was randomized, participation in the BCPSS mandatory summer school program, and the spring 1999 pretest.

The results for the 1999 kindergarten cohort are similar to our hypothesized cumulative effects of a multiyear summer school program. That is, the treatment students showed essentially no initial benefit after 1 year of summer school, $d = 0.01$. Since that time, however, the program effect has

TABLE 10.4
Summary of Treatment Effects on Reading Outcomes
for the 1999 and 2000 Kindergarten Cohorts

	Spring 1999 Scale Score	Fall 1999 Scale Score	Spring 2000 Scale Score	Fall 2000 Scale Score	Spring 2001 Scale Score	Fall 2001 Scale Score
1999 Cohort						
Treatment	426.50	434.13	535.47	527.27	591.67	598.60
	(64.45)	(70.86)	(61.87)	(67.90)	(71.61)	(62.23)
	$n = 130$	$n = 123$	$n = 126$	$n = 112$	$n = 112$	$n = 103$
Control	448.06	445.96	536.23	526.65	602.37	596.78
	(72.43)	(56.51)	(74.90)	(78.64)	(76.51)	(59.40)
	$n = 67$	$n = 56$	$n = 57$	$n = 50$	$n = 54$	$n = 49$
Covariate-Adjusted Treatment Effect						
β (SE)		0.36	17.57	15.83	2.39	14.38*
		(6.74)	(16.97)	(10.91)	(12.89)	(6.18)
Effect Size		0.01	0.25	0.22	0.03	0.24
2000 Cohort						
Treatment			441.07	415.58	551.04	567.40
			(72.18)	(73.10)	(73.13)	(73.62)
			$n = 140$	$n = 119$	$n = 122$	$n = 111$
Control			445.06	423.69	557.95	568.46
			(75.22)	(65.77)	(61.16)	(62.18)
			$n = 110$	$n = 93$	$n = 97$	$n = 91$
Covariate-Adjusted Treatment Effect						
β (SE)				−1.97	−3.39	1.26
				(5.34)	(9.69)	(6.65)
Effect Size				−0.03	−0.05	0.02

*$p < .05$.

remained relatively strong. Indeed, after the 3rd year of the program, summer 2001, the treatment effect grew to $d = 0.24$ and reached statistical significance.

DISCUSSION

The large and persistent achievement gaps between minority poor students and White middle-class students are enduring national problems. As a result of recent research on seasonal learning differences, it has become an increasingly well-established fact that what happens during the summer may have tremendous implications for understanding and addressing these achievement gaps that separate poor and minority students from their middle-class peers (Borman, 2001). The combination of this finding and the outcomes of our ongoing longitudinal study may have important implications for educational equality. If, as the work of Alexander et al. (2001) suggested, summer learning differences, compounded year after year, are the primary cause of widening achievement gaps, could a series of yearly summer school programs for disadvantaged students prevent the gap from widening?

Cooper et al. (2000) summarized the 1-year effects of summer vacation and summer school on middle-socioeconomic status (SES) and disadvantaged students' learning. Expanding on this model, Fig. 10.1, which is adapted from Borman (2000), depicts the hypothetical reading achievements of middle-SES and disadvantaged students across three summers and 4 school years. Reflecting the findings of Alexander and Entwisle (1996), the figure shows the cumulative widening of the achievement gap between middle-income and economically disadvantaged students who did not attend summer programs.

Alternatively, expanding on Cooper and colleagues' (Cooper et al., 2000) findings for the one-year effect of summer school, the figure also indicates that disadvantaged students who are afforded summer programs year after year are able to keep pace with the achievements of middle-SES students. As Borman (2002/2003) argued, achieving equality will require additional interventions—both preschool programs to help bridge the gap separating advantaged and disadvantaged students when they begin their formal schooling, and research-proven interventions designed to accelerate the school-year growth of disadvantaged students. If the multi-year effects of summer school are cumulative and are similar to the 1-year effects found by Cooper and colleagues, summer school may be the primary intervention through which educators prevent the widening of the achievement gap.

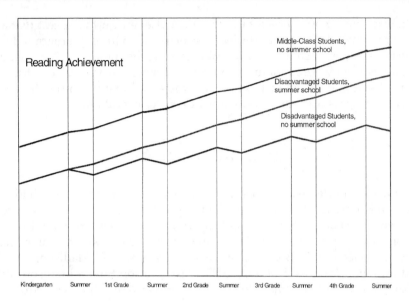

FIG. 10.1.   Expected reading achievement growth trajectories.

This report offers an incomplete perspective on our efforts to study this longitudinal phenomenon. The progress of the 1999 and 2000 kindergarten cohorts provides some evidence of the cumulative impact of, respectively, 2 and 3 years of summer interventions. The statistically significant intention-to-treat effect size of 0.24 for the 1999 kindergarten group is considerably stronger than the effect size of 0.11 found by Borman and D'Agostino (1996) in their meta-analysis of compensatory education programs offered during the regular school year. The final results for these groups will, obviously, provide important information regarding longitudinal achievement trends and the potential cumulative impact of multiple summer interventions.

The study is also a commentary on the difficulties in assuring multiyear attendance in a voluntary summer program and illustrates the complexities in carrying out randomized field trials in the "messy" world of schools. When the evaluation began during the summer of 1999, the city of Baltimore had no widely available summer school programs for students. The implementation of the program, although probably good for all of the city's students, complicated the delivery and evaluation of the Teach Baltimore Summer Academy. The Summer Academy's marked attendance declines during the summer of 2001 were, in large part, attributable to students' participation in the city's mandatory program rather than the Summer Academy. The city summer school attendance data are currently being examined more closely, but these data also appear to suggest that as much as 50% of the control students participated in the city program during the summer of 2001. Thus, in reality, during the summer of 2001, many students who were randomized into the Summer Academy actually received summer school instruction elsewhere and many control students were not necessarily in a no-treatment control condition.

ACKNOWLEDGMENTS

The work reported herein was supported by a grant from the Smith Richardson Foundation, Children and Families at Risk Program. The data presented, the statements made, and the views expressed are solely the responsibility of the authors. Direct all correspondences concerning this article to Geoffrey D. Borman, University of Wisconsin—Madison, 1161D Educational Sciences Building, 1025 West Johnson Street, Madison, WI 53706. Electronic mail may be sent to gborman@education.wisc.edu.

REFERENCES

Alexander, K. L., & Entwisle, D. R. (1996). Schools and children at risk. In A. Booth & J. F. Dunn (Eds.), *Family-school links: How do they affect educational outcomes?* (pp. 67–89). Mahwah, NJ: Lawrence Erlbaum Associates, Inc.

Alexander, K. L., Entwisle, D. R., & Olson, L. S. (2001). Schools, achievement and inequality: A seasonal perspective. *Educational Evaluation and Policy Analysis, 23,* 171–191.

Ascher, C. (1988). Summer school, extended school year, and year-round schooling for disadvantaged students. *ERIC Clearinghouse on Urban Education Digest, 42,* 1–2.

Austin, G. R., Rogers, B. G., & Walbesser, H. H. (1972). The effectiveness of summer compensatory education: A review of the research. *Review of Educational Research, 42,* 171–181.

Borman, G. D. (2000). The effects of summer school: Questions answered, questions raised. *Monographs of the Society for Research in Child Development, 65*(1, Serial No. 260).

Borman, G. D. (2001). Summers are for learning. *Principal, 80,* 26–29.

Borman, G. D. (2002/2003). How can Title I improve achievement? *Educational Leadership, 60*(4), 49–53.

Borman, G. D., & D'Agostino, J. V. (1996). Title I and student achievement: A meta-analysis of federal evaluation results. *Educational Evaluation and Policy Analysis, 18,* 309–326.

Borman, G., Rachuba, L., Hewes, G., Boulay, M., & Kaplan, J. (2001). Can a summer intervention program using trained volunteer teachers narrow the achievement gap? First-year results from a multi-year study. *ERS Spectrum, 19,* 19–30.

Cooper, H., Charlton, K., Valentine, J. C., & Muhlenbruck, L. (2000). Making the most of summer school: A meta-analytic and narrative review. *Monographs of the Society for Research in Child Development, 65*(1, Serial No. 260).

Cooper, H., Nye, B., Charlton, K., Lindsay, J., & Greathouse, S. (1996). The effects of summer vacation on achievement test scores: A narrative and meta-analytic review. *Review of Educational Research, 66,* 227–268.

Entwisle, D. R., Alexander, K. L., & Olson, L. S. (1997). *Children, schools, and inequality*. Boulder, CO: Westview.

Entwisle, D. R., Alexander, K. L., & Olson, L. S. (2001). Keep the faucet flowing: Summer learning and home environment. *American Educator, 25*(3), 10–15, 47.

Heyns, B. (1978). *Summer learning and the effects of schooling*. New York: Academic.

Phillips, M., Crouse, J., & Ralph, J. (1998). Does the Black–White test score gap widen after children enter school? In C. Jencks & M. Phillips (Eds.), *The Black–White test score gap* (pp. 229–272). Washington, DC: Brookings Institute.

Wasik, B. A. (1997).*Volunteer tutoring programs: A review of research on achievement outcomes* (CRESPAR Rep. No. 14). Baltimore: Johns Hopkins University, Center for Research on the Education of Students Placed at Risk.

White, H. (1980). A heteroskedasticity-consistent covariance matrix estimator and a direct test for heteroskedasticity. *Econometrica, 48*, 817–830.

Worsnop, R. L. (1996). Year-round schools: Do they improve academic performance? *CQ Researcher, 6*, 433–456.

11

How Families, Children, and Teachers Contribute to Summer Learning and Loss

Meredith Phillips and Tiffani Chin
University of California, Los Angeles

A number of studies over the past century have yielded two consistent findings about summer loss (Cooper, Nye, Charlton, Lindsay, & Greathouse, 1996). First, students generally gain academic skills at a slower pace over the summer than during the school year. Second, summer loss, at least in some subject areas, may be especially large for less advantaged children. Several scholars have argued that the cumulative effects of this differential summer drop-off are large enough to account for most of the achievement gap that emerges between middle-class and lower-class children during the school years (e.g., Entwisle & Alexander, 1992; Entwisle, Alexander, & Olson, 1997; Heyns, 1987).

Despite this consensus about the extent of summer loss and its association with economic disadvantage, previous research provides little evidence on its causes. Barbara Heyns's 1972 study of sixth-grade children in Atlanta, GA, provides the best evidence to date on the family activities associated with summer loss (Heyns, 1978). Heyns asked children's parents a number of questions about their summer activities and found that time devoted to reading was strongly and consistently associated with vocabulary gains over the summer. Library use over the summer was also correlated with vocabulary gains, as were visiting relatives or friends overnight and owning a bike. Heyns speculated that these last two activities were proxies for parental values that encouraged independence and initiative.

More recent data on family activities and summer loss come from Doris Entwisle's and Karl Alexander's (1992, 1994) Beginning School Study (BSS), which began following a cohort of first graders in 1982. Like Heyns, Entwisle et al. (1997) found that using the public library and taking a trip over the summer were associated with summer gains. These authors also argued that other resources that are more easily purchased by middle-class families might be related to summer gains (e.g., reading materials in the home, computers, music and art lessons, and trips to museums).

This chapter uses national data from the early 1990s to try to replicate these earlier findings and answer additional questions about how children, families, and teachers may affect children's summer learning (see also Chin & Phillips, 2001, for qualitative evidence on these questions). Although previous studies have discussed the contribution of children's ethnic background, social class, and gender to their summer learning, none have emphasized the contribution of children's academic or social skills to their subsequent summer gains. Previous research also has not examined the effects of family composition and parenting practices (other than reading and library use) on children's summer learning.

Previous studies have also ignored the question of whether teachers' school-year practices are related to students' summer learning. Without empirical evidence, a number of hypotheses about the benefits of different teaching styles for summer gains are equally persuasive. Perhaps teachers who emphasize basic phonics and math skills best equip their first-grade graduates to continue reading and learning over the summer. Or perhaps the best teachers instill in their students a love and appreciation for literature that encourages children to devour new books over the summer. Or perhaps the best teachers involve parents in their children's schoolwork, connecting them with the school-year curriculum so that they can then build on it at home during the summer.

Using national data on first graders from the summer of 1992, we try to adjudicate among these possibilities. We first describe the extent of summer loss in our sample and its association with gender, ethnicity, and social class. We then examine whether first graders' academic skills and social skills are related to how much they learn over the summer following first grade. Next, we investigate how parents' beliefs and values, cultural capital, and parents' and children's literacy practices influence children's summer learning. We then turn to an analysis of whether first-grade teachers' education, experience, or teaching practices influence summer gains. We conclude with a summary of our results and implications for enhancing summer learning.

METHODOLOGY

Data and Sample

The data we use in this chapter come from "Prospects: The Congressionally Mandated Study of Educational Growth and Opportunity" (U.S. Department of Education, 1994). "Prospects" is a nationally representative sample of first graders who attended public schools in the fall of 1991. Although the majority of the Prospects sample cannot be used to study summer learning, because Prospects did not test everyone in both fall and spring, Prospects did test a small subsample of students in the fall and spring of first grade, and in the fall of second grade. We focus on this subsample throughout the chapter.

Our analytic sample includes the 1,141 first graders who have valid Comprehensive Tests of Basic Skills (CTBS) scores for reading comprehension, reading vocabulary, math computation,[1] and math concepts and applications for all three time points, as well as basic demographic information. Although this longitudinal summer sample contains students from 32 school districts across the United States, it is not a random sample of the original sample. Table 11.1 shows that the summer sample is generally more advantaged than the nationally representative, cross-sectional sample of first graders. The summer sample contains more Whites, fewer children from urban areas, and fewer children whose mothers dropped out of high school. Relative to the cross-sectional sample, the summer sample also contains more children from the Midwest and South and fewer children from the Northeast and West. In addition, the summer sample scored about a fifth of a standard deviation higher on the spring CTBS tests than did the cross-sectional sample.

Analysis

Because previous studies have shown that children learn and forget different amounts in different subject areas, we followed the recommendation of Cooper et al. (1996) to analyze results separately for reading comprehension, vocabulary, math concepts, and math computation.[2] For our multivariate analyses, we standardized students' CTBS scale scores on all four tests in both the spring and fall and then differenced them. Standardized scores allow us to compare the various independent variables in

---

[1]The math computation section was not administered to first graders in the fall of first grade, so there are no fall-of-first-grade scores for this exam. We also dropped from the sample two children whose spring scores on one subtest seemed highly unlikely, given their scores on the same subtest in both falls and their scores on the other subtests in the spring. We used the original scale scores for all analyses because the adjusted scale scores for the fall of second grade are incorrect.

[2]Few students scored at the ceiling or floor of the tests in the spring or fall. Fewer than 1% of students obtained the lowest possible score on any of the tests in the spring of first grade and fewer than 2% obtained the highest possible score on any of the spring tests. In the fall of second grade, fewer than 1% of students scored at the floor on any of the tests, but a larger number of students obtained the highest possible score: 6% on math computation, 4% on reading vocabulary, 3% on reading comprehension, and 2% on math concepts and applications.

TABLE 11.1
Descriptive Comparison of First-Grade Cross-Sectional
Sample and Longitudinal Summer Sample

	Cross-Sectional Sample			Longitudinal Summer Sample		
	Mean	SD	N	Mean	SD	N
Male	0.52	0.50	10776	0.53	0.50	1141
Asian American	0.03	0.17	9933	0.01	0.11	1141
African American	0.14	0.34	9933	0.09	0.29	1141
Latino	0.14	0.34	9933	0.10	0.31	1141
Other ethnicity	0.02	0.15	9933	0.02	0.15	1141
White	0.67	0.47	9933	0.77	0.42	1141
Suburban	0.38	0.49	10820	0.49	0.50	1141
Rural	0.36	0.48	10820	0.44	0.50	1141
Urban	0.26	0.44	10820	0.07	0.26	1141
Primary caregiver is high school dropout	0.15	0.36	9329	0.09	0.29	1105
Primary caregiver is high school graduate	0.32	0.46	9329	0.28	0.45	1105
Primary caregiver attended college	0.37	0.48	9329	0.45	0.50	1105
Primary caregiver is college graduate	0.17	0.37	9329	0.17	0.38	1105
Income > $35,000/yr	0.38	0.48	9086	0.46	0.04	1059
Income < $15,000/yr	0.29	0.45	9086	0.21	0.04	1059
Northeast	0.17	0.37	10820	0.08	0.27	1141
Midwest	0.18	0.39	10820	0.25	0.43	1141
South	0.41	0.49	10820	0.53	0.50	1141
West	0.24	0.43	10820	0.14	0.34	1141
Spring 1st grade Reading Comprehension scale score	554.17	77.03	8004	568.38	67.97	1141
Spring 1st grade Reading Vocabulary scale score	564.42	61.94	8011	573.98	59.67	1141
Spring 1st grade Math Concepts and Applications scale score	556.68	72.57	7800	569.32	69.27	1141
Spring 1st grade Math Computation scale score	475.81	84.14	7808	497.45	74.29	1141

Note. The cross-sectional sample includes all first-grade students in the core sample and is weighted with the 1991 core weight. The longitudinal summer sample includes all students who have valid scores on all subtests from the fall of 1991, spring of 1992, and fall of 1992, data on gender, race or ethnicity, urbanity, region, and a weight for the spring of second grade. Statistics for the summer sample are weighted with the spring 1993 core weight.

terms of their effects on standard deviation changes in the dependent variables. All of our estimates are weighted and all of the standard errors are adjusted for nonindependence within districts (because districts were the primary sampling units in Prospects). Finally, because the length of the interval between spring and fall testing varied substantially across classrooms (the standard deviation was 16 days), all of our equations control for the length of the testing interval.

RESULTS

Descriptive Differences in Summer Gains

Table 11.2 shows that the average first grader gained significantly on all subtests over the summer. Because the average testing interval in Prospects was 169 days, however, an unknown, but probably large, portion of these gains may be attributable to the school year rather than the summer.[3] Table 11.2 also shows that students' gains differ by ethnicity and social class. First graders in Prospects learned fewer vocabulary words over the summer if they were African American, if their mothers had dropped out of high school, or if they came from relatively poor families.[4] African American first graders also gained less in math concepts and applications than did Latino first graders. However, children who came from poor families gained more in math concepts and applications over the summer than those who came from better-off families, and children whose mothers had graduated from high school but did not attend college gained the most in math concepts and applications relative to other children.

Table 11.3 examines whether these ethnic and social class differences persist in a multivariate model.[5] After controlling for social class, the Black–White difference in vocabulary gains disappears, but the difference in math concepts becomes statistically significant. Holding ethnicity and other indicators of family background constant, children whose mothers dropped out of high school still gain less in vocabulary, and children whose mothers graduated from high school but did not attend college still gain the most in math concepts. Holding educational attainment constant, children from higher income families gain less in math computation than do other children. In addition, holding other family background measures constant, children who live in single-parent families gain more in math

---

[3]Assuming that the average summer is approximately 70 days (or 10 weeks), that leaves 99 days (over 14 weeks) of instruction included in the average student's "summer." This long testing interval makes it impossible to assess the "pure" effects of summer vacation on students' scores.

[4]Although we refer to the educational attainment variable as "mother's education," it actually reflects the educational attainment of whomever filled out the primary caregiver survey (85% of respondents were the children's biological mothers).

[5]We used family background data from parent surveys in the spring of first grade when available. When these data were missing, however, we replaced the missing values with data from the second- and third-grade parent surveys when available. The native English variable comes from the parent survey and reflects whether the primary caregiver's native language is English. We coded children as having "both parents in home" if the respondent on the parent survey noted that his or her spouse or partner lived in the home. Because we have so few Asian ($N = 13$) and "other" ($N = 12$) children in our sample, we do not discuss results for these ethnic groups in the text.

TABLE 11.2

Summer Gains, by Gender, Ethnicity, Mother's Education, and Family Income

	Reading Comprehension				Vocabulary				Math Computation				Math Concepts and Applications			
	Mean	SE	SD	SIG?	Mean	SE	SD	SIG?	Mean	SE	SD	SIG?	Mean	SE	SD	SIG?
Total sample	29.81	3.12	55.70		26.36	2.69	39.84		14.16	5.19	61.86		25.68	2.46	54.49	
Gender																
Female	25.11	3.70	53.19	**	25.47	2.99	36.86		10.98	5.54	66.11		25.22	3.08	55.53	
Male	33.95	3.63	57.56		27.15	3.19	42.31		16.96	5.56	57.76		26.09	3.60	53.60	
Ethnicity																
White	31.01	4.12	54.20		27.63	3.12	39.37	**(w. v. b.)	14.16	5.00	61.11		24.89	2.59	54.58	*(b. v. l.)
African American	20.44	3.90	55.67		17.27	2.39	37.22		12.45	4.82	56.26		20.33	4.58	57.08	
Latino	27.60	5.36	65.41		20.42	2.70	38.48		21.21	8.85	67.95		34.82	4.50	57.55	
Mother's education																
High school dropout	25.82	4.13	43.90		5.92	6.68	46.67	**(d. v. h.)	18.43	4.98	63.05		18.42	8.76	59.02	
High school graduate	28.17	4.84	56.80		28.62	2.46	36.06		16.60	5.05	59.31		38.77	6.04	54.05	*(h. v. s. c.)
Some college	29.59	5.00	52.58		26.14	2.78	40.11	**(d. v. s. c.)	13.07	6.07	65.14		23.61	2.21	52.75	*(s. c. v. c.)
College graduate	33.89	8.05	67.66		34.24	6.37	38.52	**(d. v. c.)	11.90	10.35	57.44		13.30	4.57	55.67	**(h. v. c.)
Family income																
<$15,000	30.06	3.63	54.13		16.26	5.71	41.35	**(lo. v. hi.)	26.18	7.72	69.22		33.32	5.26	55.12	
$15,000 to $35,000	27.31	4.88	55.87		23.31	2.66	39.19		16.88	6.60	56.26		23.54	4.34	45.97	
>$35,000	28.35	4.29	59.07		33.43	2.99	37.59	***(mid. v. hi.)	6.00	9.04	57.77		21.72	1.61	54.59	*(lo. v. hi.)

Note. "SIG?" indicates if differences between groups are statistically significant. * = $p < .05$; ** = $p < .01$; *** = $p < .001$. We note which groups differ significantly in parentheses. For ethnicity, w = White, b = African American, l = Latino. For mother's education, d = dropout, h = high school graduate, s.c. = some college, c = college graduate. For family income, lo = <$15,000, mid = $15,000 to $35,000, hi = >$35,000. The standard errors and statistical tests are corrected for nonindependence within school districts. Mother's education and family income come from the first-grade parent survey unless the data were missing for that year. When that was the case, we used parent survey data from the second or third grade, if available.

TABLE 11.3
Effects of Family Background on Summer Gains

	Reading Comprehension	Reading Vocabulary	Math Computation	Math Concepts and Applications
Male	0.14**	0.03	0.16*	−0.01
	(0.04)	(0.03)	(0.08)	(0.10)
Asian American	0.46 +	−0.13	0.48	0.07
	(0.27)	(0.12)	(0.33)	(0.22)
African American	−0.02	−0.01	−0.04	−0.17*
	(0.07)	(0.07)	(0.10)	(0.07)
Latino	0.05	−0.04	0.04	0.18
	(0.09)	(0.07)	(0.12)	(0.12)
Other ethnicity	−0.11	0.51*	−0.57***	0.13*
	(0.24)	(0.23)	(0.11)	(0.05)
R. is high school dropout	−0.02	−0.28**	−0.08	−0.34
	(0.04)	(0.09)	(0.09)	(0.24)
R. has some college	−0.01	−0.11	−0.02	−0.18*
	(0.12)	(0.07)	(0.04)	(0.09)
R. is a college graduate	−0.04	−0.11	−0.08	−0.23*
	(0.15)	(0.07)	(0.11)	(0.11)
Family income <$15,000	0.12*	−0.10	0.14	0.04
	(0.06)	(0.09)	(0.15)	(0.09)
Family income >$35,000	−0.04	0.09 +	−0.17*	0.02
	(0.05)	(0.05)	(0.07)	(0.07)
Household size	−0.06 +	−0.02	−0.01	0.04 +
	(0.03)	(0.03)	(0.04)	(0.02)
Both parents in home	0.15 +	−0.05	0.08	−0.30*
	(0.08)	(0.07)	(0.10)	(0.14)
R. works full time	−0.03	0.03	0.15**	0.16*
	(0.08)	(0.08)	(0.05)	(0.07)
Native English	0.02	−0.05	−0.33*	0.34
	(0.17)	(0.08)	(0.13)	(0.22)
Rural	0.24*	0.05	0.00	−0.02
	(0.09)	(0.08)	(0.13)	(0.10)
Suburban	0.12 +	−0.01	−0.13	0.02
	(0.06)	(0.06)	(0.12)	(0.06)
Midwest	0.08	0.06	−0.04	−0.23**
	(0.08)	(0.08)	(0.09)	(0.08)
Northeast	0.06	0.16**	0.03	−0.05
	(0.07)	(0.06)	(0.09)	(0.05)
West	0.15	0.17*	0.14	−0.15
	(0.10)	(0.08)	(0.13)	(0.09)
R-Squared	0.07	0.08	0.10	0.08

Note. $N = 1,141.$ + = $p < .1$; * = $p < .05$; ** = $p < .01$; *** = $p < .001$. Dependent variables are standardized gains. Numbers are unstandardized coefficients. Standard errors are in parentheses. Equations include missing data dummies for all variables on which students have missing data. All equations control for the interval between spring and fall testing. Equations are weighted using the 1993 core weight, and all the standard errors are corrected for nonindependence within school districts.

concepts than other children. And children whose primary caregivers work full time gain more on both math subtests than do other children. Although these results may seem counterintuitive, children who live with only one parent, or whose primary caregiver works full time, may experience more autonomy over the summer, which seems to be positively associated with summer learning (Chin & Phillips, 2001; Heyns, 1978).

Children's Skills and Summer Gains

Although children's ethnicity, social class, and family structure are associated with summer gains, indicators of children's skills and home environments likely explain much more of the gap in summer learning. Column 1 of Table 11.4 examines the contribution of children's academic and nonacademic skills to summer learning. We measured children's academic skills with their scores on each of the CTBS subtests in the spring of first grade and with a scale that reflects teachers' ratings of children's verbal and math achievement in the spring of first grade.

The teachers in Prospects also rated each child on a range of social skills. We made four scales to represent four characteristics that we thought might matter for summer learning. We suspected that children who were motivated and worked hard in first grade might be more motivated to learn things over the summer. We also hypothesized that children who were good at paying attention would be more likely to concentrate on summer tasks for longer periods of time.

Our "motivated" and "pays attention" scales were correlated .80, however, so we combined them into a scale that we refer to as the "good student" scale.[6] Teachers also rated children on how much they seemed to enjoy school and on how creative they were. We suspected that, independent of how motivated and mature students are, students who really enjoy school or who are very creative may create especially good learning environments for themselves over the summer.

Because our dependent variables are gain scores, students' scores in the spring on the same test are negatively correlated with their gains.[7] The

---

[6]This scale averages several questions in which first-grade teachers rate each student's "maturity level," "attention span," "motivation to learn," and ability to "pay attention in class" on a *high, medium,* or *low* scale and whether students "work hard at school," "care about doing well in school," and "can concentrate for at least half an hour" on a *very much, somewhat,* or *not at all* scale. This scale has a reliability of .93.

[7]Note that the simple gain equation becomes a "residualized" gain equation once we add students' spring scores. The equation is now mathematically equivalent to regressing students' fall-of-second-grade scores on their spring-of-first-grade scores. The only difference is that the spring score on the same subtest as the dependent variable enters with a negative sign because the errors are negatively correlated. If we had regressed fall scores on spring scores, it would enter with the same coefficient but with a positive sign.

TABLE 11:4

Effects of Family Background, Children's Skills, Home Environment, and Family Practices on Summer Gains

	Reading Comprehension		Reading Vocabulary		Math Computation		Math Concepts and Applications	
	1	2	1	2	1	2	1	2
Male	-0.06	-0.01	0.03	0.09*	0.19**	0.14*	0.09 +	0.12*
	(0.07)	(0.06)	(0.03)	(0.04)	(0.07)	(0.06)	(0.05)	(0.05)
Asian American	0.43	0.41	0.19	0.15	0.64*	0.64*	0.00	-0.24
	(0.28)	(0.28)	(0.21)	(0.20)	(0.28)	(0.29)	(0.22)	(0.16)
African American	-0.13 +	-0.15*	-0.04	-0.03	0.03	-0.04	-0.23**	-0.25**
	(0.07)	(0.07)	(0.05)	(0.05)	(0.10)	(0.09)	(0.08)	(0.08)
Latino	-0.02	-0.02	-0.01	0.01	0.16	0.15	-0.02	0.02
	(0.10)	(0.12)	(0.07)	(0.07)	(0.15)	(0.09)	(0.07)	(0.08)
Other ethnicity	0.01	-0.13	0.30	0.19	-0.21**	-0.05	-0.16 +	-0.12
	(0.19)	(0.10)	(0.27)	(0.20)	(0.06)	(0.11)	(0.09)	(0.10)
R. is high school dropout	-0.11	-0.05	-0.19**	-0.12 +	-0.16**	-0.16**	-0.11	-0.10
	(0.08)	(0.05)	(0.06)	(0.07)	(0.05)	(0.06)	(0.10)	(0.09)
R. has some college	0.02	0.01	-0.09	-0.09	-0.05	-0.13	-0.05	-0.08*
	(0.15)	(0.16)	(0.08)	(0.07)	(0.06)	(0.09)	(0.05)	(0.04)
R. is a college graduate	0.05	0.05	-0.06	-0.07	0.10	-0.06	0.04	-0.06
	(0.15)	(0.19)	(0.05)	(0.05)	(0.10)	(0.08)	(0.08)	(0.07)
Family income <$15,000	0.11	0.08	-0.06	-0.05	0.02	0.03	-0.13*	-0.05
	(0.07)	(0.06)	(0.06)	(0.06)	(0.07)	(0.10)	(0.06)	(0.06)
Family income >$35,000	0.03	0.07	0.14*	0.16*	-0.04	-0.04	0.05	0.01
	(0.06)	(0.06)	(0.06)	(0.05)	(0.06)	(0.05)	(0.06)	(0.06)
Both parents in home	0.22**	0.23**	0.02	0.02	0.00	0.02	-0.24**	-0.21**
	(0.07)	(0.08)	(0.05)	(0.05)	(0.05)	(0.07)	(0.10)	(0.07)
Household size	-0.08**	-0.09*	-0.05 +	-0.05 +	0.01	0.01	0.03	0.03
	(0.03)	(0.04)	(0.03)	(0.03)	(0.02)	(0.02)	(0.03)	(0.02)

(Continued)

TABLE 11.4
(Continued)

	Reading Comprehension		Reading Vocabulary		Math Computation		Math Concepts and Applications	
	1	2	1	2	1	2	1	2
R. works full time	-0.03	-0.05	-0.04	-0.01	0.12**	0.13*	0.09 +	0.10
	(0.07)	(0.08)	(0.05)	(0.04)	(0.04)	(0.05)	(0.05)	(0.07)
Native English	0.03	0.02	0.10	0.08	-0.23 +	-0.17 +	0.16 +	0.25*
	(0.09)	(0.11)	(0.11)	(0.14)	(0.12)	(0.10)	(0.09)	(0.11)
Suburban	0.18**	0.18**	0.08	0.08	0.21*	0.18*	0.06	0.09
	(0.06)	(0.06)	(0.05)	(0.06)	(0.08)	(0.08)	(0.06)	(0.09)
Rural	0.14	0.15 +	0.08	0.08	0.27*	0.25*	0.05	0.08
	(0.08)	(0.09)	(0.08)	(0.09)	(0.10)	(0.10)	(0.11)	(0.15)
Northeast	-0.01	-0.03	0.11 +	0.07	-0.02	0.02	-0.07	-0.03
	(0.04)	(0.04)	(0.06)	(0.06)	(0.05)	(0.05)	(0.08)	(0.08)
Midwest	-0.15*	-0.18**	-0.02	-0.04	-0.14	-0.13	-0.06	-0.08
	(0.07)	(0.06)	(0.06)	(0.06)	(0.10)	(0.10)	(0.09)	(0.09)
West	-0.07	-0.10	0.07	0.03	0.05	0.06	0.07	0.03
	(0.07)	(0.07)	(0.07)	(0.07)	(0.09)	(0.08)	(0.12)	(0.11)
Spring 1st grade math computation (standardized)	0.01	0.01	0.03	0.03	-0.73***	-0.74***	0.15***	0.11**
	(0.05)	(0.06)	(0.03)	(0.02)	(0.03)	(0.03)	(0.03)	(0.04)
Spring 1st grade math concepts and applications (standardized)	0.10**	0.10*	0.00	-0.01	0.17**	0.19***	-0.71***	-0.69***
	(0.03)	(0.04)	(0.05)	(0.04)	(0.06)	(0.04)	(0.05)	(0.04)
Spring 1st grade reading comprehension (standardized)	-.67***	-0.67***	0.33***	0.32***	-0.06 +	-0.04	0.08	0.11 +
	(0.06)	(0.07)	(0.05)	(0.05)	(0.03)	(0.03)	(0.05)	(0.06)
Spring 1st grade reading vocabulary (standardized)	0.23***	0.22**	-0.58***	-0.59***	0.24**	0.24**	0.12	0.10
	(0.07)	(0.07)	(0.05)	(0.05)	(0.07)	(0.06)	(0.07)	(0.06)
Teacher rating; reading and math skills (standardized)	0.05	0.05	0.06	0.03	0.14 +	0.14*	0.22**	0.20**
	(0.08)	(0.07)	(0.04)	(0.03)	(0.07)	(0.06)	(0.07)	(0.06)

	(1)	(2)	(3)	(4)	(5)	(6)	(7)
Teacher rating: good student (standardized)	0.08	0.01	0.03	0.10*	0.07*	0.10*	0.10*
	(0.05)	(0.04)	(0.04)	(0.04)	(0.03)	(0.04)	(0.04)
Teacher rating: very creative (1/0)	-0.06	0.08*	0.07 +	-0.08	-0.09	-0.13	-0.14
	(0.08)	(0.03)	(0.03)	(0.08)	(0.07)	(0.08)	(0.09)
Teacher rating: enjoys school (1/0)	-0.08	-0.04	-0.03	-0.05	-0.01	-0.11	-0.10
	(0.10)	(0.07)	(0.06)	(0.05)	(0.05)	(0.09)	(0.08)
Parents' expectations for children's educational attainment (years)	-0.01		0.00		0.06**		0.07***
	(0.02)		(0.02)		(0.02)		(0.02)
Few rules for child (1/0)	-0.14		0.02		-0.26 +		0.01
	(0.14)		(0.07)		(0.13)		(0.15)
Many rules for child (1/0)	0.03		-0.09*		-0.02		-0.03
	(0.07)		(0.04)		(0.04)		(0.05)
Go to museums (1/0)	-0.08 +		-0.08		-0.04		-0.14*
	(0.05)		(0.08)		(0.04)		(0.07)
Child takes art, music, or dance lessons (1/0)	-0.07		0.03		-0.12*		0.08
	(0.08)		(0.09)		(0.05)		(0.13)
Child takes sports lessons (1/0)	-0.08		-0.04		0.03		-0.01
	(0.07)		(0.07)		(0.07)		(0.10)
Child went to summer school (1/10)	0.05		-0.27*		0.19		0.11
	(0.08)		(0.13)		(0.21)		(0.15)
Have home computer (1/0)	-0.04		-0.06 +		0.17*		0.04
	(0.06)		(0.04)		(0.07)		(0.05)
Home reading materials	-0.01		0.02		-0.01		-0.01
	(0.03)		(0.03)		(0.04)		(0.05)
Child reads >.5 hrs per day (1/0)	0.18*		0.09 +		-0.02		0.05
	(0.07)		(0.05)		(0.05)		(0.04)
Parents read with child at least 2 times per week (1/0)	0.25*		0.02		0.11		0.05
	(0.11)		(0.06)		(0.09)		(0.08)
Visit the library (1/0)	0.15		0.20*		-0.04		-0.02
	(0.11)		(0.07)		(0.05)		(0.13)

(Continued)

265

TABLE 11.4
(Continued)

	Reading Comprehension		Reading Vocabulary		Math Computation		Math Concepts and Applications	
	1	2	1	2	1	2	1	2
Time child watches TV (hours per day)		0.00 (0.03)		0.00 (0.03)		0.02 (0.03)		-0.01 (0.03)
Parents watch TV with child daily (1/0)		-0.09 (0.06)		-0.04 (0.05)		-0.05 (0.05)		-0.25*** (0.06)
Time talking with adults (hours per day)		0.00 (0.02)		0.00 (0.02)		-0.02 (0.02)		-0.02 (0.02)
Parent information regarding progress >6 times per year (1/0)		-0.08 (0.07)		-0.04 (0.04)		0.08 (0.06)		-0.09 + (0.05)
Times parents observed in class (0–3)		-0.02 (0.02)		0.03 + (0.01)		0.07* (0.03)		0.07 + (0.04)
R-squared	0.29	0.33	0.36	0.40	0.47	0.51	0.39	0.44

Note. $N = 1,141$. + = $p < .1$; * = $p < .05$; ** = $p < .01$; *** = $p < .001$. Dependent variables are standardized gains; coefficients are unstandardized (unless otherwise noted). Standard errors are in parentheses. All equations include missing data dummies for all variables with missing data and control for the interval between spring and fall testing. All equations are weighted using the 1993 core weight, and all the standard errors are corrected for nonindependence within school districts. "Few rules" is a dummy variable for students who have one to three of seven possible parental rules. "Many rules" is a dummy variable for students who have all seven rules. Home reading materials is a sum of three dummy variables (50+ books in home, daily newspaper, monthly magazine subscription). See text for more details.

positive correlation of children's scores on the other subtests with their summer gains suggests, however, that children who have stronger academic skills in the spring of first grade tend to gain more over the summer, other things being equal. Teachers' ratings of children's academic achievement also help explain some of the variance in children's math gains, over and above the variance explained by spring test scores. In addition, children with better social skills seem to gain more over the summer, other things being equal. Holding family background, children's spring scores, and teachers' ratings of academic skills constant, children who are more motivated and mature gain a little more in math computation, math concepts, and possibly reading comprehension, over the summer. And children who are very creative gain a little more in vocabulary over the summer.

Home Environment and Summer Gains

An important drawback of Prospects is that, for the most part, its surveys did not ask parents or children about their summer activities.[8] Therefore, we are forced to rely on parents' reports about activities in the spring of first grade and use them as proxies for activities the following summer. Although children's summer activities differ in many obvious ways from their school-year activities (camps, vacations, etc.), we suspect that children's relative participation in activities does not change all that much between the school year and summer. For example, we suspect that first graders who read more than 30 minutes a day during the school year also read more during the summer. Likewise, we suspect that parents who enroll children in lessons during the school year are also more likely to enroll them in lessons during the summer. And children who visit the library during the school year are probably more likely to visit the library during the summer. Thus, although it would be preferable to have parents' and children's concurrent, or even retrospective, reports about summer activities (see Chin & Phillips, 2001), we believe that measures from the spring of first grade are reasonably good proxies for similar activities over the summer.

Column 2 of Table 11.4 examines whether parents' expectations, practices, and children's activities are associated with summer gains, holding constant family background and children's social and academic skills in the spring of first grade. First, we investigated whether parents' general attitudes and practices affect summer learning. We suspected that parents with higher educational expectations for their children might work harder to

---

[8]In the spring of second grade, parents responded to a question about whether their child attended summer school after first grade.

prevent "brain drain" over the summer. In our summer sample, most parents expect their first graders to graduate from high school and then attend a vocational school or a 2- or 4-year college. Yet, about 11% expect their first grader to complete high school only, and another 15% expect their first grader to attend graduate school after college. These differences in parents' expectations seem to matter for first graders' summer math gains, holding family background and children's academic skills constant. For each additional year of school that parents expect their first graders to complete, first graders gain about .06 standard deviations over the summer in both math computation and math concepts.[9] This finding suggests that parents who have higher expectations may work harder to create math practice and learning situations for their children during summer vacation.

Drawing on Baumrind's (1975) theory of authoritative parenting, we also suspected that children might gain more skills over the summer if their parents were neither permissive (had very few rules for their first grader) nor authoritarian (had all seven of the rules asked about on the parent survey) (see also Steinberg, 1996).[10] Although children may learn fewer vocabulary words over the summer when their parents have the maximum number of rules and may learn less math when their parents have very few rules for them, these results do not hold for the other subtests.

We also tested the hypothesis that cultural capital influences children's summer gains by using a measure of whether parents take their child to art, science, or history museums. Holding family background, children's skills, and other family practices constant, however, going to museums is, if anything, negatively associated with children's gains over the summer. Whether first graders take art, music, or dance lessons may also be a proxy for cultural capital or families' cultural values, but, other things being equal, lessons are negatively associated with math computation gains over the summer and unrelated to gains on the other subtests. Because Entwisle et al. (1997) found that organized sports may improve math scores, especially for boys, we also tried to examine this hypothesis using the Prospects data. Our best proxy for organized sports participation over the summer is whether first graders took sports lessons during the school year. However, sports lessons are not associated with summer gains, and although the association may be stronger for boys for some subtests, none of the interactions between sports participation and gender is marginally statistically significant (results available from the authors).

---

[9]We coded the parent expectations variable in terms of estimated years of schooling. Because the question provided ambiguous response categories (e.g., whether parents expect their first grader to "graduate from a 2- or 4-year college"), however, our coding is only approximate.

[10]Prospects asked parents if they used seven types of rules concerning homework, chores, level of school performance, friends, curfew, and amount and type of TV child can watch.

We also hypothesized that parents who were most concerned about maintaining or boosting their children's skills over the summer might enroll their children in summer school. However, only 3% of the children in the summer sample attended summer school, and Prospects did not ask about the types of summer schools they attended. Other things being equal, however, the children who did attend summer school lost about a quarter of a standard deviation in vocabulary over the summer, relative to those who did not. Although the coefficients on summer school are positive for both math tests, neither of these effects is statistically different from zero.

Parents in Prospects described several aspects of their home environment that we thought might be related to children's summer gains. Parents reported on whether they had more than 50 books, received a daily newspaper, or had a monthly magazine subscription; we summed these practices to create a measure of the reading materials in the home. Holding constant other aspects of family background, having these reading materials is not related to children's summer gains.

Researchers have also speculated that middle-class children gain more over the summer because their parents can afford learning tools like a home computer. Holding constant family background and other aspects of the home environment, first graders who have a home computer gain over .15 standard deviations more on the math computation test over the summer than other first graders. Although it is possible that children improve their math skills by playing math-related games on the computer, we cannot test this hypothesis because the Prospects survey did not ask whether or how the children used their home computer.

The one consistent result in the summer learning literature is that reading is related to summer gains on verbal tests (see Chin & Phillips, 2001; Entwisle et al., 1997; Heyns, 1978). In Prospects, parents reported both on how often their child read and how often they read with their child. Holding constant family background, children's spring test scores in all subjects, teachers' ratings of children's academic and social skills, and the other measures of family practices shown in Table 11.4, children who read more than a half-hour a day gain about .18 standard deviations more in reading comprehension over the summer relative to children who read less. In addition, children gain almost a quarter of a standard deviation in reading comprehension if their parents read to them at least two times a week. Because reading is associated with gains in reading comprehension but not in math, these results provide strong evidence that reading on one's own and being read to improve children's reading comprehension skills.

Like Heyns (1978), we also found that children who read more or who visit the library improve their vocabulary skills over the summer. Visits to the library probably improve vocabulary skills because they provide a ready supply of new books, with a wide range of new vocabulary words, for parents to read to their children or for children to read to themselves. Although we also suspected that the amount of time children spend interacting with adults might be related to their vocabulary gains (because adults have wider vocabularies than children), time interacting with adults is not related to children's gains, other things being equal.

Finally, because watching TV may take time away from more educational activities, such as reading, Table 11.4 examines the association between time spent watching TV and summer gains. Other things being equal, the number of hours children spend watching TV is not related to how much they gain or lose over the summer on any of the subtests. However, Prospects also asked parents how often they watch TV with their child, which may be a proxy for whether parents provide varied activities and academic-related practice and experiences to their children during their time together over the summer. Independent of how much TV children themselves watch, children whose parents watch TV with them daily lose about a quarter of a standard deviation in math concepts and applications over the summer.

Home Environment and Family Background

Like other scholars (e.g., Entwisle et al., 1997), we assumed that the association between family background and summer gains would be attributable to many of the family practices included in Table 11.4. Table 11.4 shows, however, that many of the associations between basic demographics and summer gains increase, rather than decrease, when we control for children's skills and family practices.[11] Some of these remaining demographic "effects" may be very important for understanding the growth of academic inequality during the school years. For example, when we compare first-grade boys and girls with the same social and academic skills, social class, family structure, and family practices, the boys learn more math skills over the summer than do the girls. This widening gender gap in math skills may be an early cause of gender differences in math skills among older children and indicates that boys' summer environments fa-

---

[11]Table 11.4 also shows that a few of the associations of family background with summer gains disappear when we control for children's skills. These results tell us that some of the associations of family background with gains have nothing to do with the "effects" of family background on children's summer experiences, but rather serve as proxies for how much children with different skill levels gain over the summer. In particular, the apparent negative "effect" of a child's mother having a college education on children's gains in math concepts shrinks considerably once we add children's skills to the model. A similar result occurs for the association between gender and reading comprehension; boys gain more in reading comprehension over the summer but mostly because boys have poorer reading skills than girls at the end of first grade.

cilitate the development of math skills in ways that the Prospects data do not capture.

Summer vacation may also contribute to a growing racial gap in academic skills. When we compare African American and White first graders who have the same social and academic skills, social class, family structure, and family practices, the White first graders gain about a sixth of a standard deviation more than their African American counterparts in reading comprehension over the summer. These White first graders also gain nearly a quarter of a standard deviation more than their African American counterparts in math concepts and applications. These results suggest not only that summers contribute to the widening of the Black–White gap over the school years (see Phillips, Crouse, & Ralph, 1998), but also that we need to find out exactly what differs about the summers of African American and White first graders who seem similar in many other ways.

The most unusual family background results in Table 11.4 relate to growing up in a two-parent family and having a primary caregiver who works full time. Growing up in a two-parent family is positively associated with summer gains in reading comprehension but negatively associated with gains in math concepts and applications. Although we might suspect that living in a two-parent family would be beneficial for reading comprehension because parents would have more time to read to their children and interact with them, the two-parent family advantage for reading comprehension persists even after controlling for these variables. It is even more difficult to invent an explanation for why children who live with two parents gain less in math concepts over the summer. Perhaps, other things being equal, children who have fewer adults in the household spend more time taking care of themselves, which may improve their problem-solving skills. A similar explanation may help account for the positive association between mothers' full-time work and children's summer gains in math computation. However, we need better data on how children spend their time over the summer to begin to test these post hoc hypotheses.

Family practices do seem to mediate some of the effects of family background on children's summer learning, however. For example, Table 11.4 shows that children whose mothers dropped out of high school gain less in both vocabulary and math computation than children whose mothers are high school graduates. Although the dropout effect on math computation gains does not shrink when we add family practices to the equation, the effect on vocabulary shrinks by about a third. Most of the reduction in the coefficient is attributable to the fact that parents who are high school dropouts are less likely to report taking their child to the library. Table 11.4 also shows that children in lower income families gain less in math concepts and applications over the summer. This association shrinks by over half after controlling for family practices. Parents' expectations, whether parents watch TV daily with their child, and the number of times parents observed in their child's classroom, seem to account for the association between income and math concepts gains.

Home–School Links and Summer Gains

In addition to expecting that family practices such as reading would be related to summer gains, we also hypothesized that children might gain more over the summer if their parents were better informed about how well their children were mastering schoolwork and what they were learning in class. Parents can learn about their child's progress by receiving information from teachers. They can also learn about their child's curriculum (and how the teacher demonstrates and drills academic concepts) by observing in the classroom. Other things being equal, each additional time that parents observe in their first grader's classroom seems to have some positive effect on children's math gains over the summer (and perhaps a small positive effect on vocabulary gains). Whether parents receive frequent information about their child's progress at school is not, however, positively associated with their child's summer gains (see Table 11.4).

Teachers' Practices and Summer Gains

In addition to keeping parents informed about their child's progress, teachers may provide school-year activities that encourage children to practice academic skills over the summer (Chin & Phillips, 2001). Because first-grade teachers in Prospects responded to a survey about their practices in the spring, these data provide a unique opportunity to examine whether teachers' characteristics and practices influence children's summer gains. Table 11.5 shows how teachers' education, experience, and a few basic practices are associated with children's summer gains. Because "better" parents often select "better" schools and teachers for their children, the equations in Table 11.5 control for children's academic and social skills and for all the family background and home environment variables in Column 2 of Table 11.4.[12]

Although we expected that certified and better-educated teachers might be more skilled at providing classroom experiences that encourage children to continue learning over the summer, we did not find that to be the case. We did, however, find that new teachers (those who have taught

---

[12]Although the equations in Table 11.5 control for all the variables shown in Column 2 of Table 11.4, we exclude these coefficients to conserve space.

TABLE 11.5
Effects of Teacher Characteristics and Practices on Summer Gains

	Reading Comprehension	Reading Vocabulary	Math Computation	Math Concepts and Applications
No or temporary certification (1/0)	0.186 +	−0.047	0.132	0.119
	(0.11)	(0.06)	(0.12)	(0.11)
More than BA (1/0)	0.021	0.002	−0.027	−0.130
	(0.07)	(0.06)	(0.09)	(0.12)
New teacher (1/0)	−0.102	0.017	−0.218	−0.325**
	(0.07)	(0.08)	(0.16)	(0.12)
Uses primarily phonics (1/0)	−0.097 +	0.016	−0.004	−0.079
	(0.06)	(0.05)	(0.09)	(0.07)
Uses primarily whole language (1/0)	−0.074	−0.092	0.125	−0.040
	(0.07)	(0.08)	(0.10)	(0.06)
Uses manipulatives at least weekly (1/0)	−0.021	0.029	0.061	0.003
	(0.11)	(0.05)	(0.12)	(0.10)
Assigns reading projects (standardized)	0.052 +	0.021	0.070*	0.082 +
	(0.03)	(0.02)	(0.03)	(0.04)
R-squared	0.34	0.41	0.52	0.46

Note. $N = 1{,}141$. $+ = p < .01$; $* = p < .05$; $** = p < .01$; $*** = p < 001$. All equations control for all of the variables in Column 2 of Table 11.4 and include dummies for missing data. Dependent variables are standardized gains; coefficients are unstandardized (unless otherwise noted). Standard errors are in parentheses. All equations are weighted using the 1993 core weight, and all the standard errors are corrected for nonindependence within school districts. "New" teachers have 3 or fewer years of experience. Use of phonics and whole language are based on teachers' reports of their "primary approach to teaching reading." The excluded category is teachers who report using neither (mostly an "eclectic" approach). The manipulatives variable comes from teachers' reports of how often they use "rulers, shapes, and blocks." Assigns reading projects is a scale of teachers' reports of how often they have students do projects about what they read, write reports, do oral presentations, and publish their writing. See text for more details.

for 3 years or less) may not have developed the necessary skills to promote learning in math concepts and applications over the summer.

The Prospects survey asked teachers what approach they primarily used to teach reading during first grade—phonics, whole language, or an "eclectic" approach. Table 11.5 hints that an "eclectic" approach may be better than primarily phonics or whole language for reading comprehension gains over the summer, although differences among these approaches are not statistically significant. Teachers also described their math teaching practices on the Prospects survey. Although we thought that teachers who used manipulatives (e.g., rulers, blocks, and shapes) more often might make it easier for children to acquire math concepts skills over the summer, we did not find any evidence that teaching with manipulatives improves children's summer math gains.

Finally, we included a scale of teachers' reports of how often they encouraged children to extend what they had read by doing projects, writing reports, doing oral presentations, and publishing their writing.[13] We
thought that encouraging children to link their academic activities to projects might both inform parents about their child's curriculum and encourage children to do creative learning activities in the summer. Because the
Prospects survey asked teachers only about reading-related projects, we
consider the "projects" scale to be a proxy for similar project-related math
activities. Our results provide some weak evidence that, other things being equal, project-centered learning may enhance children's summer
gains in reading and math.

Because the Prospects teacher survey included only a few questions
about teachers' practices that might be related to summer gains, we ran
additional models that included teacher fixed effects (not shown). These
equations allowed us to compare the percentage of variance explained by
the model in Table 11.5 with a model that included all differences among
teachers, even those not measured in the Prospects survey. This comparison gives us a sense of whether including more survey questions about
teachers' practices might yield additional information about how teachers' school-year practices spill over into summer learning. For the reading
comprehension and vocabulary models, we found no evidence that better
measures of teachers' school-year reading practices would enhance our
understanding of how to improve children's verbal gains over the summer. For math concepts and math computation, the fixed effects models
increased the explained variance (adjusted R-squared) of the model in Table 11.5 by 2% and 3%, respectively. These results imply that better measures of teachers' school-year *math* practices may account for a little more
of the variance in children's summer math gains than we were able to explain in Table 11.5.

CONCLUSIONS

Although this chapter replicates some results from the summer learning
literature, it also shows that our current understanding about who learns
more over summer vacation, and why, may be too simple. First, at least
for some outcomes, whether children from disadvantaged families gain or

[13]The projects scale is composed of several questions from the English language arts
teacher survey. Teachers reported how often they had students "do projects related to reading," "write factual reports," "give oral presentations," and "publish their own writing."
Teachers answered these questions on a scale that allowed them to choose among the following categories: *almost every day, 1–2 times/week, 1–2 times/month, 1–2 times/year,* or *never.* This
scale had a reliability of .70.

lose over summer vacation depends on how we measure summer loss. When we measure summer loss in absolute terms, by simply subtracting students' scores in the spring from their scores the following fall, disadvantaged children gain less than advantaged children in vocabulary but gain more in math computation and math concepts and applications. Likewise, when we measure gains in absolute terms, African American first graders gain less than White first graders in vocabulary but do not gain less in other subjects.

When we analyze the data by comparing children who had the same academic and social skills in the spring, however, we find that children from disadvantaged families experience larger summer losses than more advantaged children do in most subject areas. Moreover, when we compare African American and White children who have the same academic and social skills in the spring, the African American children gain less than the White children in reading comprehension and math concepts and applications but not in vocabulary or math computation. Thus, our analysis indicates that descriptive portraits of who gains the most or the least depend on how we measure summer gains.[14]

Second, previous work offers conflicting findings on whether race is associated with summer loss independent of social class. Although Heyns (1978) argued that African Americans gained less than Whites over the summer, Entwisle et al. (1997) found no race differences in summer gains after controlling for social class. Cooper et al. (1996) also found that race was not associated with summer loss after controlling for social class. The Prospects data yield a somewhat different conclusion. Holding traditional measures of social class and family structure constant, we find that African American first graders lose ground relative to Whites in math concepts and applications over the summer. And, among children who also have the same academic and social skills at the end of first grade, African American first graders lose ground relative to Whites in reading comprehension, as well. Moreover, these racial differences in summer learning do not disappear when we control for differences in parents' expectations, reading prac-

---

[14]Absolute gains apparently wash out family background effects to some extent, because students with the lowest scores on any particular subtest gain the most on that test over the summer. Most, but not all, of this association seems to be due to regression toward the mean. When we examine correlations among students' gains, their spring scores on the other subtests, and their teachers' ratings of their math and reading skills, we find that students who scored lower on the vocabulary test, or received lower reading ratings from their teachers, gained a little more in reading comprehension over the summer. Students who received lower reading ratings from their teachers in the spring also gained more in reading vocabulary over the summer. Students who scored lower on math computation in the spring gained slightly less in math concepts and applications over the summer. However, neither teachers' math ratings nor students' math concepts and applications scores in the spring were associated with math computation gains over the summer.

tices, and the like. According to Prospects, African American first graders who are equally well-prepared academically at the end of first grade fall behind their White counterparts over the summer for reasons other than socioeconomic disadvantage or measured parenting practices.

Third, previous studies have assumed that differences between lower-class and middle-class parents' values and practices would help explain why disadvantaged children lose ground over the summer. Although our results do show that some socioeconomic status (SES) differences are mediated by parental practices, such as going to the library, and by attitudes, such as having higher expectations for children's eventual educational attainment, many SES differences persist despite our controls. These results imply that if future studies want to account for the differential summer drop-off of children from different racial and social class backgrounds, they will need to document children's summer activities and social interactions much more extensively than previous surveys have done.

Although most children (regardless of their social class, ethnic background, gender, or academic skills) do few academic activities over the summer (Chin & Phillips, 2001), even a little academic practice seems to improve children's skills. Both teachers and parents play a role in encouraging learning over the summer. In our analysis, teachers who assign projects that build on reading, writing, and research skills seem to have a small but lasting effect on children's learning over the summer, independent of family background and parenting practices. Students whose teachers assign more projects over the school year seem to gain more over the summer in all subjects, which suggests that these teachers give students better tools to integrate their academic knowledge and experiences into activities (perhaps drawing, building models, putting on plays, etc.) that are not strictly academic. Assigning, presenting, and working on these projects may also be a way for teachers to keep parents informed about what their children are doing in class and what types of "fun" academics parents can do with their children over the summer.

Teachers' ability to show children and parents how to continue learning over the summer may be crucial because families' beliefs and practices influence summer learning. When children read more, are read to by their parents more, and go to the library more, they improve their verbal skills over the summer.

Although almost any interaction that small children have with adults will likely introduce them to new vocabulary words, and almost any book they read will provide practice in reading comprehension, math may require more explicit practice. What students and their parents can do to practice math over the summer remains elusive to both parents and researchers, however. Educational surveys do not typically ask about children's use of flashcards and math workbooks. And the math content of everyday practices such as counting change, comparison shopping, measuring, counting and grouping toys, distributing a limited number of cookies to friends, or deciding how many pizzas to order for a party, seems nearly impossible to measure with survey data.

Our results imply, however, that these subtle practices may improve children's math scores over summer vacation. Although Prospects did not measure these concrete family practices, several variables seem to be proxies for parents who work to create a math-related learning environment for their child. Children learn more math over the summer when their parents have higher expectations for them, do not watch TV with them daily, and observe in their classrooms. Parents who have higher expectations may be more likely to practice math activities with their children, whereas parents who spend much of their time with their children in front of the television may be less likely to expend the effort required to incorporate math into their children's everyday activities. Parents who observe in the classroom may gain an understanding of how first-grade teachers teach addition and subtraction (e.g., by counting, working with manipulatives, and practicing math facts by rote) and the confidence to encourage children to use these skills over the summer.

Our results also suggest that independence and autonomy may benefit children's summer learning (for similar results, see Entwisle & Alexander, 1994; Entwisle et al., 1997; Heyns, 1978). We found that children gain more in math when their mothers work full time. Although the mechanism behind this effect is still unknown, children who have less supervision may improve their problem-solving skills, which, in turn, may improve their performance on math tests. We also found that children from single-parent families seem to gain more in math over the summer. This may be because they experience more autonomy, more opportunities for problem solving, or more varied environments (e.g., home, day care, etc.). On the other hand, children who live with two parents seem to improve their reading comprehension skills over the summer. Additional parental time may provide more opportunities for children to talk with adults and to ask questions about what they have read. These contradictory effects imply that both single and dual parents need to strike a balance between working with their children to promote reading, learning, and questioning and giving their children sufficient autonomy to figure things out for themselves. Summer, when life is somewhat slower paced, may be the perfect time to mix guided learning and independent exploration.

In sum, these results do not offer any quick fixes or magic bullets for improving the summer learning of young children. However, they do point to some general strategies that might help teachers and parents create summers that are more conducive to summer learning and practice. First, although no one teaching technique seems to be the key to summer learning, using a range of materials and approaches, and providing children with ways to apply what they read and learn to other activities, seem to help children maintain their skills over the summer. Second, reading with children, encouraging them to read on their own, and providing access to a wide range of new books, improve children's performance on reading comprehension and vocabulary tests. Finally, because observing in the classroom seems to give parents some information about concrete ways to help children improve their math skills, teachers should encourage parents to observe in their classrooms, even if just once or twice. Teachers should also try to send home information to parents—not just about their child's progress but about what the class is covering and ways that parents can help children practice these skills at home. Social scientists should also lend a hand by studying how children's family and neighborhood environments stimulate young children to develop their academic skills when they are not in school.

REFERENCES

Baumrind, D. (1975). The contributions of the family to the development of competence in children. *Schizophrenia Bulletin, 14,* 12–37.
Chin, T., & Phillips, M. (2001, August). *Cartoon Network, razor scooters, and Harry Potter: How educational are children's summer activities?* Paper presented at the meeting of the American Sociological Association, Anaheim, CA.
Cooper, H., Nye, B., Charlton, K., Lindsay, J., & Greathouse, S. (1996). The effects of summer vacation on achievement test scores: A narrative and meta-analytic review. *Review of Educational Research, 66,* 227–268.
Entwisle, D., & Alexander, K. (1992). Summer setback: Race, poverty, school composition, and mathematics achievement in the first two years of school. *American Sociological Review, 57,* 72–84.
Entwisle, D., & Alexander, K. (1994). Winter setback: The racial composition of schools and learning to read. *American Sociological Review, 59,* 446–460.
Entwisle, D., Alexander, K., & Olson, L. (1997). *Children, schools, and inequality.* Boulder, CO: Westview.
Heyns, B. (1978). *Summer learning and the effects of schooling.* New York: Academic.
Heyns, B. (1987). Schooling and cognitive development: Is there a season for learning? *Child Development, 58,* 1151–1160.
Phillips, M., Crouse, J., & Ralph, J. (1998). Does the Black–White test score gap widen after children enter school? In C. Jencks & M. Phillips (Eds.), *The Black–White test score gap* (pp. 229–272). Washington, DC: Brookings Institute.
Steinberg, L. (1996). *Beyond the classroom: Why school reform has failed and what parents need to do.* New York: Touchstone.
U.S. Department of Education. (1994). [Prospects: The congressionally mandated study of educational growth and opportunity]. Unpublished raw data.

12

Why Wait for Summer? Quicker Intervention, Better Results

Charles Ballinger
National Association for Year-Round Education

> *[There] is the pretense that because yesterday's calendar was good enough for us it should be good enough for our children—despite major changes in the larger society.* (p. 8)
>
> *Our usage of time virtually assures the failure of many students.*
> —from *Prisoners of Time*, National Education Commission on Time and Learning (1994, p. 15)

For more than a century, North American schools have used a school-year calendar which includes an interruption of formal instruction for 3 months at a time. In the early years of this arrangement, there were clear purposes for the interruption. Helping hands, even young hands, were needed during the summer on farms and ranches to process cash crops or tend the animals to increase the family's income and to provide for the family's welfare. This agriculturally-based, economically-driven calendar served its purposes well: rural family survival depended on a productive summer of work, whereas wealthier urban families could provide their children with suitable activities that befitted their standing, such as dispatching their children to foreign cities or specialized socialization programs.

Today, this well-established pattern of school scheduling—traditionalists call it the traditional school schedule—has a solid, although continually weakening, hold on society, parents, educators, and the business community alike. Although some school districts have attempted to camouflage the pattern by stretching the year a little beyond 9 months, the basic school year still includes an incredibly long summer vacation. Indeed, one large urban school district in the United States actually scheduled a 12.5-week summer vacation for the summer of 2000.

Although the original intent of the traditional calendar was very clear, the need for an extended summer vacation has all but vanished for today's students. Few children today are needed to supplement family income and guarantee survival by working on farms and ranches. Affluent families are able to go on vacation any season of the year. Helping hands may still be available, but they have little to do in summer. Moreover, a long summer vacation has become an increasingly doubtful tradition in an era where parents work outside the home throughout the summer months, requiring their children to fend for themselves for an extended period of time or requiring an expenditure of money for child care. Of what value is it to society and the nation to have several million minor children largely unoccupied, unsupervised, and, if older, unemployed for up to 3 months at a time? That is a surefire prescription for social trouble for many of these youth.

To counter possible unfortunate social dynamics for idle youth, and, more important, to have a program of presumed educational value, summer school is offered in many, probably most, North American communities. The numbers of students involved is not great, however. In those communities where summer school is available, student registration typically ranges from 5% to 30% of a school's total enrollment. Nonschool summer learning activities also have minimal enrollment. One official at the American Camping Association has indicated to me that no more than 15% of America's children attend summer camp programs. The 15% who do participate may only attend 1-day or 1-week camps or programs.

These low percentages suggest that although summer school and camp experiences may be supportive in a positive way to a small number of students, a clear majority experience a lengthy vacation from formal, planned instruction. Educational research confirms that the ensuing summer learning loss is not educationally desirable for most students (see New York State Department of Education, 1978; Cooper, Nye, Charlton, Lindsay, & Greathouse, 1996; Entwisle & Alexander, 1992; Entwisle & Alexander, 1995; Heyns, 1987; Huttenlocher, Levine, & Vevea, 1998). The result of this loss is a learning minus for North American students.

Summer school, a staple of American education for decades, has probably been studied less than any other regular aspect of the education enterprise. Accordingly, an examination of summer learning is on target and long overdue. Because other contributors to this volume have rightfully delved extensively into the issues surrounding both summer learning loss and summer school, I wish to move beyond those issues to ask, "Why 'summer' school at all"?

As the introductory quotes from *Prisoners of Time* suggest (National Education Commission on Time and Learning, 1994), any review of summer learning loss begs for an examination of the administrative arrangement (i.e., the school year) that causes the need for summer school in the first place. Saddled with the agriculturally-based, economically-derived calendar of yesteryear—and aided and abetted by colleges of education in North America—kindergarten through 12th-grade schools have perpetuated a system that is, in fact, detrimental to the primary purpose of school, which is the realization of maximum learning and growth potential of each student. After conducting hearings across the United States, members of the National Education Commission on Time and Learning (1994) became convinced that there is a basic design flaw in the use of school time and urged an evaluation of both the school day and year. That is precisely my intention in this chapter.

To begin the review, one might ask the following questions: What justification can be offered for a system in which a learning blockage that surfaces in late October cannot be treated until the 3rd week of June? What sense is there in a system which ends a formal learning program in late May or early June and resumes it 3 months later? What sense is there in a system that has a first semester which usually ends 3 weeks after a 2-week holiday period? What educational rationale is there for a system which ends the first semester on a Thursday or Friday and begins a second semester 3 or 4 days later, without adequate time for teachers to consider the results of the first semester and plan the goals of the second semester?

Although it is relatively easy to ask probing questions about the existing school year and to demonstrate the lack of logic inherent in the "traditional" school year, it has proven far more difficult to modify it because a whole societal culture has developed around the established long summer vacation. While it may be little more than an afterthought or add-on, summer school has become accepted as an adaptation to the existing administrative arrangement of schooling—an awkward attempt to bridge the space between two formal learning periods. Summer school has been criticized by its harshest critics as a Band-Aid on a patch of cancerous skin, and its kinder critics have compared it to drinking a soda after the fizz is gone.

What I propose in place of the established school calendar is an instructional time model that has scheduled pauses—intersessions, in the lexicon of those who advocate year-round education—in the curriculum sequence to allow more immediate intervention when a student struggles with a learning blockage or to provide enrichment experiences in preparation for a succeeding instructional unit. Why wait until summer to provide remediation? Why provide only "summer" enrichment? Why can't educators also envision an "autumn" school, a "winter" school, or a "spring" school for intervention and enrichment? These scheduled pauses (breaks—vacations—intersessions) in modified calendars can be available each of the four seasons.

The summer learning loss detailed in existing educational research is confirmed by experience as well. Teachers have acknowledged for decades the reality of the loss by reviewing the previous year's curriculum for a period of 4 to 8 weeks each autumn, while muttering to all within hearing range that the students' teachers in previous grades must not have covered all of last year's curriculum, and if they did cover the material, they did so inadequately.

When research, practical experience, and a national education commission are in agreement in determining that the traditional school year calendar is flawed, it seems reasonable to assume that educators and policy leaders at all levels would work diligently to alter the system, negating the need for seminars on reducing summer learning loss and improving summer school. Instead, seminars would bring together scholars and practitioners to discuss methods of rapid diagnosis and to consider intervention for recurring learning problems. They would explore the possibilities of intersession programs each season of the year for more immediate intervention—leading to better, more sustained results. Although the assumption may be reasonable, it bears no relation to reality. There has been a less-than-urgent attempt to change the calendar for improved, sustained learning.

Intersessions (meaning "between sessions") may be one of the strongest, if not "the" strongest, reasons for modifying the school year into a balanced year-round, or nearly continuous, instructional program. Usually designed to be from 3 to 6 weeks in length, intersessions can be thought of administratively as summer school rescheduled two to four times a year, and instructionally as intervention and enrichment within the school year.

Intersession classes can be as functional or as creative as those who organize them allow them to be. Clearly, one can make a strong argument for using this time productively as a focused response to learning blockages that may have recently occurred in the school lives of individual students, or as a time to prepare students for new learning experiences to come. One-on-one intervention in October may relieve a student's anguish and embarrassment of not understanding geometric principles. A review in late March or early May of course content previously covered may advance student comprehension for upcoming advanced placement tests or final examinations. Waiting for summer to do intervention may be too late for realistic remediation, after a student has succumbed to 5 or more months of confusion, anxiety, and finally, withdrawal.

Intersession is not to be thought of solely as intervention and remediation, however. This time space can also be used for enrichment and preparation, which may prevent the need for later intervention. Acknowledging that pupils take from a lesson in proportion to what they bring to it, educators can design programs to enrich students' experiential and vocabulary backgrounds as preparation for an ensuing learning unit. Such preparation can as easily be conducted in September, December, and April, as in July and August.

School districts which have purposely modified the school calendar and vigorously pursued the possibilities of intersessions are reporting exciting results. Danville (VA) City Schools have very purposely shaped their intersession program as part of an integrated whole in the school's instructional program and are seeing significant results (Danville Public Schools, 2000). Further, Danville is reporting a promising circumstance that warrants further study: an extraordinary reduction in teacher referrals of students to be assessed for special education classes. This circumstance is surely because of intersession interventions and enrichment, and in-school, rather than home–neighborhood, behavior modeling.

Balancing the school-year calendar between scheduled periods of learning and periods of vacation has a distinct logic to it. With clearly defined blocks of learning time, students usually receive a more focused unit of work. Teachers understand that the unit must be completed within 9, 12, or 18 weeks. As such, the units of work are organized in a different fashion than would be true for teachers who plan a year of classes as essentially one or two units of work. On completion of the unit(s), the scheduled pause (i.e., the intersession or vacation) allows time for diagnosis, prescription, and intervention if a learning blockage has occurred; it also allows time for thoughtful preparation for the beginning of the next learning unit. If intervention is available in October, January, or April (as well as in June and July), and if enrichment classes in preparation for the next instructional unit are also available, the chances for failure and retention of a student are significantly reduced. Reducing student failure should be the goal of both educational researchers and school districts; propping up a flawed "summer school" system will not achieve that goal.

The current political climate, and education's persistent critics, often drive educational policymakers to call for a cessation of social promotion, which in turn triggers the prospect of higher retention rates under the present system. The bulk of educational research cautions against retention, in that retention may not improve learning in the long run and indeed may cause other unpleasant and undesirable circumstances. Given a sociopolitical climate rejecting social promotion, and a thoughtful resistance among many educators to retention, there is clear logic and purpose to organizing schools with learning blocks of 9 or 12 weeks, followed by a vacation (intersession) of 3 or 4 weeks. An even more personalized, continuous instructional program with vacations scheduled, or allowed, as needed by a school's families, would be the optimum schedule.

By providing flexible, but continuous, instructional time each year, schools will have moved into a scenario long envisioned by educational theorists: a continuous, modified, year-round, instructional program. A form of balanced calendar is now available to over 2,300,000 students in the United States (National Association for Year-Round Education, 2003). With these numbers, the modified calendar movement is one of the largest restructuring efforts in North America, easily outpacing other important restructuring movements such as charter schools, Success for All, Accelerated Schools, and the Coalition for Essential Schools.

Although year-round, balanced-calendar schools comprise one of the largest restructuring movements, the movement has not been the subject of as much university research as one might expect. Summary reports of studies of modified-calendar schools are generally favorable to the schools that have implemented balanced, year-round schedules (Kneese, 2000; Winters, 1995). Individual studies likewise suggest positive results, sometimes significantly (Fass-Holmes & Gates, 1994; Grotjohn & Banks, 1993; Haenn, 1995; Kneese, 1996). Admittedly, review, analysis, and comparison of the results of modifying school calendars can seem elusive to some researchers because there are so many variables within the calendar modification movement, including the following: school vacation periods that range from 2 to 8 weeks (8 weeks is the outer limit allowed for inclusion in the directories of the National Association for Year-Round Education), schools that offer intersession classes and others that do not, schools that offer only a reorganized calendar of 180 instructional days and others that offer 180 basic instructional days plus another 20 to 50 intersession days, schools that extend the school year beyond 200 or more instructional days annually, and schools incorporating two strands of calendar arrangements called single-track and multitrack. Longitudinal studies are complicated by modified calendar pilot programs at the elementary level only, or, on occasion, at the high school level only. To all of these calendar variables would be added the usual research variables. Nevertheless, further research in the field of calendar modification, intersessions, and year-round education is greatly needed.

In its report, *Prisoners of Time,* the National Education Commission on Time and Learning (1994) explicitly warned that schools' usage of time virtually assures the failure of many students. Notwithstanding the possibilities summer school may have to lessen student summer learning loss, it is important to remember that the system that necessitates a summer school needs an overhaul to allow immediate intervention and focused enrichment all seasons of the year to avoid the student failure forecast by the National Education Commission on Time and Learning (1994).

REFERENCES

Cooper, H., Nye, B., Charlton, K., Lindsay, J., & Greathouse, S. (1996). The effects of summer vacation achievement test scores. *Review of Educational Research, 66,* 227–268.

Danville Public Schools. (2000, February). *Quality learning in intersessions: Putting forward our best efforts.* Paper presented at the annual conference of the National Association for Year-Round Education, San Diego, CA.

Entwisle, D. R., & Alexander, K. L. (1992). Summer setback: Race, poverty, school composition, and mathematics achievement in the first two years of school. *American Sociological Review, 57,* 72–84.

Entwisle, D. R., & Alexander, K. L. (1995). A parent's economic shadow: Family structure versus family resources as influences on early school achievement. *Journal of Marriage and the Family, 57,* 399–409.

Fass-Holmes, B., & Gates, K. (1994). *Report on single-track year-round education in San Diego Unified School District.* San Diego, CA: San Diego City Schools, Planning, Assessment and Accountability Division.

Grotjohn, D. K., & Banks, K. (1993). *An evaluation synthesis: Year-round schools and achievement.* Raleigh, NC: Wake County Public School System.

Haenn, J. R. (1995, April). *Evaluating the promise of single-track year-round schools.* Paper presented at the annual meeting of the American Educational Research Association, San Francisco.

Heyns, B. (1987). Schooling and cognitive development: Is there a season for learning? *Child Development, 58,* 1151–1160.

Huttenlocher, J., Levine, S., & Vevea, J. (1998). Environmental input and cognitive growth: A study using time-period comparisons. *Child Development, 69*(4), 1012–1029.

Kneese, C. C. (1996). *The impact of year-round education on student differences in learning. A program evaluation for Alameda Unified School District, California.* Alameda, CA: Alameda Unified School District.

Kneese, C. C. (2000). *Year-round learning: A synthesis relating to student achievement.* San Diego, CA: National Association for Year-Round Education.

National Association for Year-Round Education. (2003). *Twenty-ninth reference directory of year-round education programs for the 2002–2003 school year.* San Diego CA: Author.

National Education Commission on Time and Learning. (1994). *Prisoners of time.* Washington, DC: Author.

New York State Department of Education. (1978). *Learning, retention and forgetting. Technical report no. 5, a study of school calendars conducted for the Board of Regents, state of New York.* Albany, NY: Author.

Winters, W. L. (1995). *A review of recent studies relating to the achievement of students enrolled in year-round education programs.* San Diego, CA: National Association for Year-Round Education.

Author Index

A

Achilles, C. M., 89, 101
Adams, M. J., 10, 22
Akiba, M., 54, 62, 66
Alexander, K. L., 26, 33, 36, 37, 39, 46, 47, 49, 50, 122, 161, 165, 181, 232, 233, 234, 250, 252, 253, 255, 268, 269, 270, 275, 277, 278, 280, 285
Allensworth, E., 74, 102
Alsalam, N., 186, 198
Aronson, J., 77, 102
Aronstamm Young, B., 186, 198
Arroyo, C., 209, 227
Ascher, C., 239, 252
Austin, G. R., 6, 22, 234, 235, 239, 252

B

Bacon, J., 75, 102
Bae, Y., 186, 198
Baker, D. P., 54, 56, 61, 62, 64, 66, 68
Baker, T., 200, 228
Banks, K., 284, 285
Bankston, C., 199, 228
Barnett, A., 19, 22

Barnett, W. S., 46, 50
Baumrind, D., 268, 278
Beaton, A. E., 57, 66, 67
Berkner, L., 199, 228
Berliner, D. C., 57, 67, 121, 161
Bernstein, J., 199, 228
Biddle, B. J., 121, 161
Blair, C., 46, 51
Blakely, C., 14, 22
Bomster, M., 49, 50
Borg, W. R., 57, 67
Borman, G. D., 165, 166, 179, 181, 234, 241, 250, 251, 252
Boulay, M., 241, 252
Bowles, S., 2
Bowie, L., 25, 50
Bray, M., 61, 67
Bryk, A. S., 36, 50, 74, 89, 102
Buckman, L. A., 210, 228

C

Cadigan, D., 46, 50
Caldwell, J., 126, 161
Campbell, F. A., 46, 51
Carter, L. F., 122, 161

Charlton, K., 4, 10, 19, 27, 46, 50, 75, 84, 85, 88, 101, 112, 115, 119, 122, 123, 125, 145, 154, 161, 165, 166, 169, 171, 172, 175, 176, 177, 178, 181, 217, 222, 228, 233, 234, 235, 238, 250, 252, 255, 257, 275, 278, 280, 285
Chase, C., 196, 198
Chavez, L., 199, 228
Chen, Z., 209, 228
Chin, T., 256, 262, 267, 269, 272, 276, 278
Choy, S., 186, 198
Cladas, S., 199, 228
Clark, K., 159, 161
Cogan, L. S., 54, 56, 68
Cohen, J. S., 53, 68
Coleman, J. S., 49, 50
Coleman, R.W., 16, 22
Conant, J. B., 7, 22
Congdon, R. T., Jr., 36, 50
Cooper, G., 5, 22
Cooper, H., 4, 10, 27, 46, 50, 75, 84, 85, 88, 101, 112, 115, 119, 122, 123, 125, 145, 154, 161, 165, 166, 169, 171, 172, 175, 176, 177, 178, 181, 217, 222, 228, 233, 234, 235, 238, 250, 252, 255, 257, 275, 278, 280, 285
Croninger, R. G., 57, 67
Cross, D. R., 125, 161
Crosswhite, F. J., 56, 67
Crouse, J., 26, 51, 234, 253, 271, 278

D

D'Agnostino, J. V., 251, 252
Darling-Hammond, L., 165, 181
Davis, E. L., 57, 68
de Silva, W. A., 61, 67
Denton, J., 14, 22
Denton, K., 26, 51
Dornbusch, S., 209, 228
Dossey, J. A., 56, 67
Dougherty, J. W., 6, 22

E

Easton, J. Q., 74, 75, 102
Eccles, J., 219, 228
Embretson, S. E., 142, 161

Entwisle, D. R., 26, 33, 36, 46, 47, 49, 50, 122, 161, 165, 181, 219, 228, 232, 233, 234, 250, 252, 253, 255, 268, 269, 270, 275, 277, 278, 280, 285
Epps, E. G., 26, 51
Epstein, J. L., 46, 50

F

Farley, R., 20, 22
Fass-Holmes, B., 284, 285
Featherman, D. L., 29, 50
Feldman, S., 209, 210, 211, 228
Finn, J. D., 57, 68, 89, 101
Fish, J., 46, 50
Fisher, C. W., 57, 67
Foondun, A. R., 61, 67
Fordham, S., 77, 101
Frase, M., 217, 228
Freehorn, C. L., 16, 22
Fullan, M., 165, 181

G

Gamoran, A., 54, 56, 67, 199, 228
Gándara, P., 46, 50
Gates, K., 284, 285
George, C., 61, 67
Germino-Hausken, E., 26, 51
Gintis, H., 2
Glasgow, K., 209, 228
Gonzalez, E. J., 57, 66, 67
Gordon. A., 55, 67
Greathouse, S., 4, 10, 22, 27, 50, 122, 161, 165, 172, 181, 222, 228, 233, 234, 252, 255, 257, 275, 278, 280, 285
Grotjohn, D. K., 284, 285

H

Haenn, J. R., 284, 285
Hambleton, R. K., 142, 161
Harrington-Lueker, D., 112, 119
Hasbrouck, J. E., 141, 161
Hauser, C., 223, 228
Hazelton, J. E., 14, 22
Hedges, L. V., 89, 102
Henke, R. R., 46, 51

Hess, G. A., 78, 101
Hess, R. D., 26, 50
Hewes, G., 241, 252
Heyns, B., 9, 22, 27, 47, 51, 53, 56, 67, 122, 161, 233, 234, 253, 255, 262, 269, 275, 277, 278, 280, 285
Hofferth, S. L., 46, 51
Holloway, S. D., 26, 50
Holsinger, D. B., 57, 67
Hopfenberg, W., 196, 198
Horsey, C., 49
Houang, R. T., 54, 56, 68
House, E. R., 74, 101
Hussein, M. G. A., 61, 67
Huttenlocher, J., 280, 285
Huyvaert, S. H., 53, 57, 67

J

Jacob, B., 74, 102
Jakwerth, P. M., 54, 68
Johns, J. L., 128, 161
Johnson, D. W., 210, 228
Johnston, R. C., 73, 101
Johnson, R. T., 210, 228

K

Kabbani, N., 49, 50
Kanner, A. D., 210, 228
Kaplan, G. R., 48, 51
Kaplan, J., 241, 252
Karweit, N., 14, 22, 36, 51
Kaufman, P., 217, 228
Kelly, D. L., 57, 66, 67
Kemple, J., 186, 198
Kifer, E., 56, 67
Kingsbury, G., 223, 228
Klein, S., 217, 228
Knapp, M., 196, 198
Kneese, C. C., 284, 285
Konstantopoulus, S., 89, 102
Krallman, D. A., 57, 68
Kwan-Terry, A., 61, 67

L

Laird, J. A., 209, 210, 211, 228

Larsen, R. W., 57, 67
Lee, S., 122, 161
Lee, V. E., 57, 67
Lem, P., 54, 68
Leslie, L., 126, 161
LeTendre, G. K., 54, 61, 62, 66, 67
Levin, H., 196, 198
Levine, D., 56, 68
Levine, S., 281
Levy, F., 200
Lindsay, J., 4, 27, 123, 166, 223, 234, 256
Loveless, T., 48, 51

M

MacIver, D. J., 76, 77, 101
Main, S. R., 76, 77, 101
Martin, M. O., 57, 66, 67
Mathews, J., 73, 101
McKnight, C. C., 54, 56, 67, 68
Means, B., 196, 198
Meisels, S. J., 123, 161
Meyer, J. W., 55, 62, 67
Michel, R., 199, 228
Mickelson, R., 77, 101
Miedel, W. T., 47, 51
Mishel, L., 199, 228
Mitchell, D. E., 16, 22
Mitchell, R. E., 16, 22
Mont-Reynaud, R., 209, 228
Mosteller, F., 10, 22
Muhlenbruck, L., 27, 46, 50, 75, 84, 85, 88, 101, 112, 115, 119, 123, 125, 145, 154, 161, 165, 166, 169, 171, 175, 176, 177, 178, 181, 217, 228, 235, 238, 250, 252

Mullis, I. V. S., 57, 66, 67
Myers, D., 183, 198

N

Nagaoka, J., 75, 102
Nagel, J., 55, 67
Nelson, S., 57, 68
Nicholls, J., 210, 228
Nye, B., 4, 10, 22, 27, 50, 89, 102, 165, 172, 181, 222, 228, 233, 234, 252, 255, 257, 275, 278, 280, 285

O

Oakes, J., 54, 68
Oberg, S. L., 53, 68
Ogbu, J., 77, 101
Olson, L. S., 26, 33, 36, 47, 50, 122, 162, 232, 233, 234, 250, 252, 253
Orellana, M. F., 16, 23

P

Pallas, A. M., 46, 50
Paris, S. G., 125, 161
Pearson, P. D., 159, 161
Phillips, M., 26, 51, 234, 253, 256, 262, 267, 269, 271, 272, 276, 278
Pill, G., 54, 68
Poe, J., 53, 68
Purvis, A., 56, 68

R

Rachuba, L. T., 241, 252
Raizen, S. A., 54, 56, 68
Ralph, J., 51, 57, 68, 234, 253, 271, 278
Ramey, C. T., 46, 51
Ramirez, F. O., 62, 67
Raudenbush, S. W., 36, 50
Reise, S. P., 142, 161
Resnick, L., 196, 198
Reuman, D. A., 76, 77, 101
Reynolds, A. J., 47, 51
Ricciuti, A., 36, 51
Richards, P. S., 210, 228
Richmond, M. J., 4, 23
Riordan, C. H., 56, 68
Ritter, P., 209, 228
Roderick, M., 74, 75, 78, 102
Rogers, B. G., 6, 22, 234, 235, 239, 252
Rohlen, T., 61, 68

S

Salmon, M. J., 57, 68
Schiefele, O., 219, 228
Schmidt, W. H., 54, 56, 68
Schneider, B. L., 36, 51
Schrim, A., 183, 198

Schweinhart, L. J., 46, 51
Scott-Jones, D., 26, 51
Shauman, K. A., 46, 51
Shields, C. M., 53, 68
Singham, M., 196, 198
Sirotnik, K. A., 54, 68
Slattery, P., 57, 68
Slaughter, D. T., 26, 51
Smith, B., 56, 57, 68, 86, 89, 102
Smith, J. B., 57, 67, 89, 102
Smith, T. A., 57, 66, 67
Snipes, J., 186, 198
Soysal, Y. N., 62, 67
Stanovich, K. E., 122, 161
Steele, C. M., 77, 102, 196, 198
Steinberg, L., 209, 228, 268, 278
Stephens, J. M., 36, 51
Stevens, G., 29, 50
Stevenson, D. L., 61, 64, 68
Stevenson, H. W., 56, 57, 68, 122, 161
Stigler, J. W., 56, 68
Stipek, D., 76, 102
Stover, D., 53, 55, 68
Suarez-Orozco, C., 77, 102
Suarez-Orozco, M., 77, 102
Swafford, J. O., 56, 67
Swaminathan, H., 142, 161
Sweller, J., 5, 22

T

Taylor, B. M., 159, 161
Tedesco, L. A., 57, 68
Temple, J. A., 47, 51
Thompson, B., 36, 51
Thorne, B., 16, 23
Tindal, G., 141, 161
Topel, R., 199, 228
Travers, K. J., 56, 67
Triesman, P., 196, 198
Troyer, L., 209, 228
Tsukada, M., 61, 68
Tyack, D., 55, 67

V

Vaishnav, A., 104, 119
Valentine, J. C., 27, 46, 50, 75, 84, 85, 88, 101, 112, 115, 119, 123, 125, 145, 154,

161, 165, 166, 169, 171, 175, 176, 177, 178, 181, 217, 228, 235, 238, 250, 252
Veenman, S., 54, 68
Velez, W., 199, 228
Vevea, J., 280, 285

W

Walberg, H. J., 57, 69
Walbesser, H. H., 6, 22, 234, 235, 239, 252
Walpole, S., 159, 161
Wasik, B. A., 235, 253
Wayne, F. C., 57, 69
Weikart, D. P., 46, 51
Weinstein, M., 54, 56, 67

Wentzel, K. R., 210, 229
West, J., 26, 51
White, H., 245, 253
Wigfield, F., 219, 228
Wilson, J., 199, 229
Winkelmolen, B., 54, 68
Winters, W. L., 284, 285
Wiseman, A. W., 62, 66
Worsnop, R. L., 6, 23, 234, 253

Y–Z

Yair, G., 57, 64, 69
Zigler, F., 209, 227

Subject Index

A

Achievement gains, 11, 26, 36, 38, 43, 45, 48, 74, 79, 85, 89, 97, 235
Achievement gap, 2, 26–27, 32, 46, 49, 64, 82, 122, 124, 154, 166, 198, 234, 237, 250, 252, 255
Albuquerque Public Schools, 10, 22
America Reads Initiative, 235, 237
AmeriCorps, 237, 238, 240
At-risk students, 103, 105–107, 123, 164, 188–190, 192–193, 195, 197

B

Baltimore City Public Schools (BCPS), 26, 28, 33, 235–238, 240–241, 247–248
Basic Reading Inventory (BRI), 128, 131, 133–135, 141–143, 150, 152–155
Beginning School Study (BSS), 2, 27–28, 30–32, 46–48, 234, 255
Boston Public Schools (BPS), 103–111, 117, 119

C

Calendars, school, 2–4, 6, 13, 15–22, 53, 57–58, 122, 231, 279, 282, 284, 285
California Achievement Test (CAT), 28–45
Chicago Longitudinal Study, 47, 51
Chicago Public Schools (CPS), 7, 22, 73–75, 78, 86, 88, 90, 101
Comprehensive Test of Basic Skills, (CTBS), 240–241, 243, 245, 257, 262
Curriculum, 26, 47, 72, 75–76, 88–89, 98, 99–100, 104–106, 109, 112–115, 117–119, 125, 156–158, 164, 167, 180–181, 201, 223, 239, 243, 256, 272, 274, 281–282

D–F

Demographics, 28, 78, 81, 84, 91, 96, 98–101, 188, 212, 227, 242, 246, 258
Early Childhood Longitudinal Study, 26
Elementary and Secondary Education Act (ESEA), 7
Faucet theory, 231, 233
Federal Work Study program, 235, 237, 240

G–H

Gates-MacGinitie Reading Test (GMRT),
    131, 134, 136, 145–147, 149, 150–151,
    154
Hierarchical Linear Modeling (HLM),
    36–37, 40, 44, 50, 79, 81, 90–91, 93,
    95, 149–150, 154
High-stakes testing, 73, 76–77, 86, 98–100

I

Independent reading, 137–139, 156
Individuals with Disabilities Education
    Act (IDEA), 7
International education comparisons, 2,
    53–66
Intersessions, 18, 20–21, 281–285
Iowa Test of Basic Skills (ITBS), 74–76, 79,
    82, 84–89, 91, 93, 95–96, 99
Item Response Theory (IRT), 142–145, 150,
    153–155

M

Maryland School Performance Assessment
    Program (MSPAP), 237
Massachusetts Comprehensive Assessment
    System (MCAS), 104–105, 119
Massachusetts Education Reform Act, 104
Mathematics, 5, 7, 10, 12, 20, 25–26, 30, 33,
    44, 48, 57–59, 62–63, 65, 74–75, 79,
    83–85, 88–90, 95–97, 103–108, 110,
    115, 117, 122–123, 179, 186, 200,
    202–203, 211, 222–224, 226–227, 232,
    234, 236, 256–257, 259, 262, 267–278
Matthew effect, 122
Michigan Department of Education, 124,
    126, 130, 158
Michigan Educational Assessment Pro-
    gram (MEAP), 131, 142
Michigan Literacy Progress Profile
    (MLPP), 126–127, 130–131, 133–134,
    150–151, 156, 158
Motivation, student, 76–77, 88–89, 95–97,
    100

N

Nation at Risk, 59
National Assessment of Educational Prog-
    ress (NAEP), 142
National Education Commission on Time
    and Learning, 14, 23, 57, 67, 232,
    281, 284–285

P–Q

Parents, 9, 12, 16–21, 29, 40, 47–48, 62, 72,
    96, 108, 116, 118, 121, 125, 127–128,
    132, 136, 153, 158–159, 169, 179, 197,
    199–200, 211, 238, 241, 243, 245–247,
    255–256, 259, 267–272, 274–280
Prisoners of Time, 68, 279, 281, 284
Prospects study, 232, 256–259, 262,
    267–278
Qualitative Reading Inventory (QRI), 126,
    155

R

Reading, 5–7, 10–12, 15, 20, 25, 30, 44,
    47–49, 56, 72, 74–75, 79, 83–86,
    88–90, 95–98, 100, 103–107, 109–110,
    117, 122–128, 130–145, 149–157, 160,
    166, 168–170, 172–174, 178–179,
    202–203, 205, 208, 211, 222–224,
    226–227, 232–234, 236–239, 241, 243,
    250–251, 255–257, 267, 269–278
Reading Recovery, 130, 150, 155
Remedial programs & approaches, 5–11,
    17, 62, 64–65, 73, 75, 85, 88, 99, 112,
    114, 123–124, 154, 192–193, 196, 211,
    235
Retention, 54, 56, 64, 71–72, 76–77, 80, 82,
    89–90, 95, 100, 110–111, 118, 123,
    195, 211, 232, 234–235, 240, 245–246,
    248, 284
Running Start summer program, 13

S

Scholastic Reading Inventory, 106–107, 109
Science, 57–59, 65, 105, 186, 211, 236, 268
Stanford Diagnostic Reading Test-IV
    (SDRT-IV), 170–175
Shadow education, 61–67

Socioeconomic status (SES), 26, 29–36, 38, 40–45, 48, 126, 170–171, 250, 276

Student characteristics, 80, 97, 98, 176, 187

Students' Opinions About Reading (SOAR), 128, 132–133, 136, 152–153

Success for All, 150, 284

Summer Bridge program (Chicago), 7, 71–72, 73–100, 181

Summer gains, 28, 33–36, 42, 43–44, 74, 79, 83, 88, 90, 100–101, 150, 154–156, 256, 262, 267–272, 274–275

Summer learning loss, 1–2, 4–6, 10, 54–56, 65, 98, 122, 143, 146, 150–151, 160, 165–166, 231–232, 235, 237, 255–256, 275, 280–282, 284

Summer school, 1, 3, 6–14, 20, 27, 47–48, 71–75, 78–79, 81, 87, 89, 97, 101, 104, 108–112, 114–119, 122–129, 131, 138, 140–142, 144, 146–147, 150–161, 164–167, 170, 176–180, 201, 232–233, 235–236, 241, 246, 248–249, 251–253, 268, 270, 281–285

"Summer slide", 34, 222, 226–227, 233–234, 240, 248

Summer vacation, 4–5, 8, 15, 17, 53, 123, 232, 250, 259, 268, 274–275, 277, 280–281

Summerbridge program, 164, 199–208, 211–225, 226–228

Sustaining Effects Study, 122, 257

T

Teach Baltimore Summer Academy, 231–241, 245–248, 251–252

Teachers, 8–13, 15–17, 19, 48, 57, 72, 75–77, 79, 86, 88–89, 96, 99, 106, 108–109, 112–115, 117–119, 121, 124–125, 127–128, 130, 133, 136–137, 139–141, 149–150, 155–160, 167–169, 194, 200–203, 211, 213, 217–219, 223, 227, 232, 238–240, 256, 262, 267, 269, 272–278, 281–283

Test scores, 4–5, 22, 25, 37, 45, 47, 49, 71–74, 77–78, 80, 82, 85–90, 98–100, 104, 118, 154, 161, 172, 181, 228, 232–233, 245, 252, 267, 269, 278, 285

Third International Mathematics and Science Study (TIMSS), 2, 57–59, 62, 67–68

Time Trackers, 180

TimeWarp programs, 166–173, 179–180

Transition Services Program (Boston), 71–72, 103–119

U–V

Upward Bound, 164, 183–198

Voyager Expanded Learning program, 163–181

Y

Year-round education, 15, 34–35, 45–46, 49, 66, 123, 201, 232, 281–282, 284